ADVANC

"In their 2016 report The Future of Jobs, the World Economic Forum highlighted that cognitive skills are becoming the skill most required by employers by 2020. A book which highlights how you can develop these vital skills in a clear and informative way is well timed. Within MBA programmes personality and aptitude have been de rigour for many years and it is well known why this is critical in order to help develop personal and professional performance. Keiron Sparrowhawk's contribution to an extension of this to the understanding of Executive Functioning is warmly welcomed as a means to simply and clearly build this complex and important area into MBA programmes of the future. "
Dr Kellie Vincent, Principal Lecturer – MBA Director, Westminster Business School

"This thoughtful integration of cognitive expertise with illustrative managerial case studies provides a unique opportunity to deepen one's self-awareness as well as to assimilate practical and effective strategies to improve executive performance and strengthen leadership abilities. A must read for those facing the personal challenge of growing their business."
Dr Linda Allan, Academic Director, Bioscience Enterprise programme, University of Cambridge

EXECUTIVE FUNCTION

COGNITIVE FITNESS
FOR BUSINESS

KEIRON SPARROWHAWK

LONDON   MONTERREY
MADRID   SHANGHAI
MEXICO CITY BOGOTA
NEW YORK   BUENOS AIRES
BARCELONA   SAN FRANCISCO

Published by
LID Publishing Ltd.
One Adam Street, London. WC2N 6LE

31 West 34th Street, 8th Floor, Suite 8004,
New York, NY 10001, US

info@lidpublishing.com
www.lidpublishing.com

A member of:

BPR
Business Publishers Roundtable

www.businesspublishersroundtable.com

Printed in Great Britain by TJ International
ISBN: 978-1-910649-75-6

Cover and page design: Caroline Li

Dedicated to my Dad,
Henry Sparrowhawk
(1922 – 1992).

TABLE OF CONTENTS

ACKNOWLEDGEMENTS

I would like to thank Sue Libretto and Martina Ratto for their help with the scientific research.

Dr. Stephen G. Payne of Leadership Strategies has been a senior leadership coach for over 22 years. I thank him for coaching me and for his work in the creation of the leader styles and the Leader-Think concepts and material used in this book.

Karina Robinson is a business advisor and searches for senior leaders to run companies and organisations. Her insights were invaluable.

John Harrison and Raj Kumar have spent their entire lives working on the scientific and medical aspects of cognitive health. I thank them for enabling me to grasp some of their knowledge. Jurriaan van Rijswijk has worked on over 500 applied games. Without his inspiration I would still be searching for the answer to so many of the questions posed in this book.

I thank Sara Taheri and the team at LID for their advice and guidance.

Most of all I thank my family. My love, pride and appreciation for them grows with every passing day.

Please note, I have received much help and support, but any errors are entirely my fault.

INTRODUCTION

"I think the big difference between management and leadership is the leader can persuade people to do the impossible."

Sir Michael Moritz, Sequoia Capital

What is cognitive fitness?

It's the ability to plan and organize, to think of the consequences of your actions before undertaking them. It's the ability to calculate and problem solve; recall previous events that can help the current situation; the ability to focus and switch tasks with speed, smoothness, and accuracy. It's all the cerebral thinking that leads to you living your life to the full and reaching your goals. Along with physical health, it is the most important aspect of your being. It underpins your use of language, movement, and functional expression. Personality, emotions, and values are based on the state of your cognitive fitness.

This then begs several questions…

Are you doing the best you can in all walks of life; at work, at home, and within your communities? Do you know how you can improve your performance, increase your ability and lead a better life?

Are you looking after and improving your cognitive fitness, ensuring it is healthy and fit? Are you doing all you can to improve the cognitive fitness of the people in your workplace, in your family, and your community?

Are you using your cognitive fitness to the best of its ability, to serve society and the world at large?

There are a lot of questions and, to be honest, there could be so many more. Your cognition is a gift. How it develops depends on how you treat it. If you keep it healthy, treat it well, nourish and exercise it, your cognition should serve you well throughout your life. If you fail to look after it, mistreat and neglect it, you might find it will leave you wanting.

Indeed, your good and bad life experiences (all your life experiences) have helped shape your cognition. It is pot-luck when it comes to the genes you have, but you do have some choice when it comes to the environment in which you live, and further choice depending on the lifestyle you adopt. It is clear, you do have choices, and you can't say everything about the state of your cognitive fitness was based on luck. Where you have choices, you should do your best to make the right ones. Ultimately, you do have a choice over what lifestyle you lead and that has a big impact on your cognitive fitness.

If you want to be a good leader and manager, you can do so through improving your cognition and, particularly, your executive function. Executive function is a set of cognitive processes responsible for your ability to plan and organize, to think creatively, and, critically, to think of the consequences of actions before you take them. It is an over-arching area of cognition that has some control over other cognitive domains and enables you to think beyond the here and now. This is a cognitive function that humans have developed way beyond other species.

Improving your executive function may not be easy, but it's possible and the rewards are worth it. Therefore, you have a choice. If you choose to improve your leadership skills through your executive function and other cognitive domains, you must realize from the start that it isn't going to be an easy journey. In fact, it will be a never ending journey of gaining a better cognitive fitness for as long as you live. In addition, by taking on this challenge you take on the responsibility to use your improved cognition to make this world a better place. No pressure, then! So, what is stopping you?

The working of your brain, as measured through cognitive function, is the single most important aspect of your being. Whereas physical health and fitness are important, cognitive health and fitness are critical. Cognitive fitness determines the ability to lead and manage, not just simply to cope with your working and daily life. A fully functioning, efficient, and effective cognition allows you to operate and excel at the maximum capacity and reach an optimum performance in the same way an elite athlete performs at the highest level. An improved cognitive fitness allows you to become sharp, accurate, confident, precise, attentive, and a source of wisdom. It enables you to be a bundle of energy that others can feed off. Improving cognitive fitness will enable you to have a fuller understanding of the power of your leadership and management thinking and a means to improve these skills.

You will look great, sound great, act, and be great. You will help others look great, sound great, act, and be great. You will be able to accomplish all of this at work with your colleagues, with your friends, within your family, and across your community.

Major advances in neuroscience over the last 30 years have built on two hundred years of psychological and cognitive research as to how the human brain works and how you function cognitively. We still know more about the far reaches of the universe, the dark side of the moon, and the depths of the oceans, while we are just beginning to uncover discoveries that will change the way we think about the brain.

This book will provide a comprehensive overview of the key cognitive domains and how they impact on your ability to operate at your best. You will understand the importance of each domain in order to maximize your cognitive fitness and to be your best. You will also know what to watch out for when your cognitive fitness may not be as robust as it could be. As is the case with physical fitness, cognitive fitness goes through ups and downs. Some declines are due to simple, acute poor health, like colds and flu. More serious, chronic problems may be associated with your genetic profile and you may be predisposed to mental health problems. Environmental factors, such as where you live and work, also have an impact, and, of course, much depends on your lifestyle. Regardless of these factors, you can always do something to improve your cognition, whatever your age, gender, class, culture, or health status.

This book will help to improve cognitive fitness; and as a leader with improved cognition, you have a greater responsibility and can influence the total cognitive fitness of your organizations, the community in which you live, your family, and friends.

Within the book are 50 training habits to improve cognition. You can adopt these habits so that they are with you for the rest of your life. They can be personalized to suit needs and circumstances, so that you can choose those which are critical and work best for you. There are a wide range of cognitive fitness solutions, from simple changes in your daily behaviours to more complex endeavours, which will meet your personal needs. Just like brushing your teeth last thing at night, these habits will become a part of your daily routine.

However, this will require determination and hard work since you will be orchestrating your own change. If you think this sounds too difficult and you haven't yet bought the book, then please put it back on the shelf. It's not for you. It's for those who want to make a positive difference to themselves, their work, community, and family.

The next chapters give a thorough overview of the five key cognitive function domains. These are: executive function, working memory, episodic memory, attention, and processing speed. Two hundred years of neuropsychological research has been amalgamated to understand these five key cognitive domains. Some of the science background has been included in this book to help you understand each of the five key domains. It isn't required that you read all of the scientific descriptions, but it will help if you do.

More recently, technology has allowed you to transform and apply this research and utilize it to the benefit of your cognitive fitness. By considering the domains in more detail you can gain the capability to undertake a self-assessment of the five domains. You can analyse them and see how they can be improved in a personalized way.

There is no better way to know yourself than by knowing the strength of your cognitive fitness across the five domains. You will know where your strengths lie, when, and where to apply them. Equally, you will know where your weaknesses lie, where you need to seek help, delegate, and encourage others to take the lead.

Alongside this you can see the gaps in your organizations and readily fill them. You can develop internal succession, built on strength. Again, through online tools, you can know yourself better as leaders. This is a gift that every executive should give themselves.

Cognitive fitness encompasses the processes that enable you to focus, understand, and respond with speed and accuracy; to store, retrieve, and remember information; to plan, process, and solve problems. All mental activities are governed by your cognitive function.

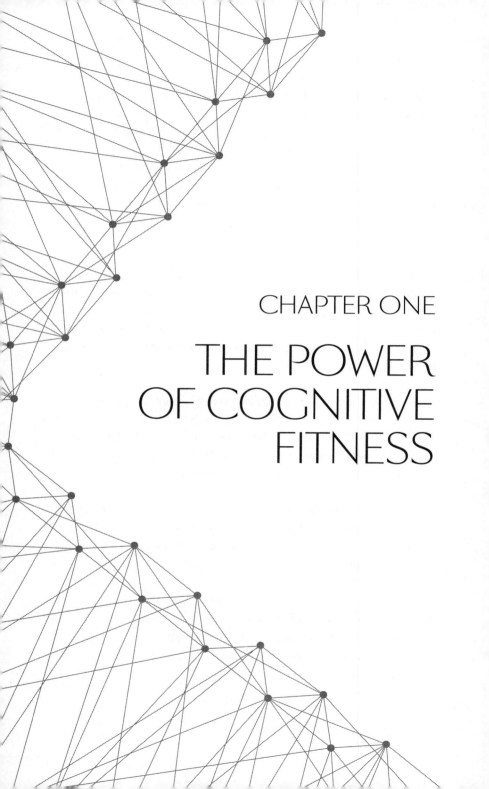

CHAPTER ONE

THE POWER OF COGNITIVE FITNESS

INTRODUCTION
Where does leadership come from?

Its foundations are buried deep in your cognitive core. Having some knowledge of that cognitive core foundation will help you understand the power of leadership and management thinking. That knowledge will even allow you to improve that thinking.

Read on.

WHAT'S MY COGNITION GOT TO DO WITH IT?

There is a growing need amongst executives to extend the quality as well as the quantity, of their lives. You are living longer and, therefore, want to ensure that you build and protect your health and functionality throughout your life. You want to be the best you can be at work, in your community, to your family and friends. You want to give and get as much satisfaction throughout your entire life. You want to live a long, healthy life. You want to leave a lasting legacy by which you will be remembered. It's never too late to start to achieve this and even if you believe that you are cognitively fit, there is always more that you can do.

With advancements in technology the ability to understand the function of the brain has improved greatly. There is still a lot to be discovered, but there is now important fundamental knowledge that allows an assessment of the cognitive functioning of the human brain and, consequently, how to improve its function.

Over the last 200 years, scientists have attempted to divide cognition into meaningful areas of research. This work is ongoing, but cognition can be seen as the grouping of five key domains, one of which is "executive function", the title of this book. All five domains are important and make an impact on the ability to lead and manage, but executive function is the most significant when it comes to leadership.

It is also important to note that the five domains are not totally distinct. They overlap, support, and, in the case of executive function, also play a central role in controlling the characteristics of the other cognitive domains. The idea of a "homunculus", a mythical being that lives in your brain and pulls the levers, has been around for a long time.[1] Executive function is the kingpin among the five core cognitive domains, making decisions on how you fully utilize your cognition across all of them. We are only beginning to realize how it does this.

Imagine the brain is a computer and the executive function is the hard-code in the central processing unit (CPU). In most computers, the hard-code is fixed, limiting what a computer can do. The working memory part of the computer can compute, but it's directed by the CPU. Every time the computer solves a problem, it does so by running through as many iterations as it can, in the time it has, with the memory it has, until it comes up with an answer. For example, if you asked a traditional computer to find the highest prime number (the current record is ((2 to the power of 74,207,281) minus 1) discovered in 2016),[2] it would run through the solution from scratch. The algorithms it uses are fixed. Newer computers are able to reset the hard coded area, to let it "learn", and by doing so, "grow". This is very risky, because the computer doesn't know if there are any implications for allowing its hard-coding to be manipulated like this. Potentially, the new-coding could be allowing something new to be integrated into the computer's hard-code that could, in time, cause a major malfunction.

We now believe that this is what our brains do all the time. The executive function, the primary cognitive domain, is like the CPU. From the moment your brain is formed in the womb, the manipulation of its executive function coding begins. Essentially, your brain records experiences from all the other domains; those that establish how we solve problems and make decisions, recall events and knowledge, focus and process all these with speed and accuracy.

Throughout evolution humans have used experiences from the other domains to allow their brains to evolve and develop. The fascinating thing is that this evolutionary process continues in real time during our lives. The elevation of your executive function is real time evolution. That's why it seems as though our minds are driven by the imaginary being, the homunculus. That 'imaginary being' is the brain upgrading through this process of self-deployed elevation (SDE). It's an amazing risk to take because just as a bad code in the CPU will cause a major malfunction in a computer, entering bad code into the executive function will cause a major malfunction in us.

Great leadership comes from those whose minds allow the greatest level of SDE. Leaders with exceptional genius will guide you to previously thought impossible levels of your ability. However, not all strong leadership is good. SDE contributes to your executive function and in doing so defines what it means for you to be human. Along with our human strengths and resilience are our human faults and frailties.

Back down to earth, let's look in detail at the five cognitive fitness domains in the following sections.

GENERAL COGNITIVE FITNESS

Five domains make up the main part of your cognitive function. As with physical health, a weakness in one part could, in the wrong circumstance, bring the others down. For example, if you are a runner and damage your left knee, you might see a physiotherapist. The physiotherapist will ensure your entire body is well, but will spend most of their time directing therapy on your left knee. They won't say, "forget the left knee and make the right one strong so you can hop everywhere". Instead, they fix the weakness. It's the same with cognition. As well as seeing in which domains you are the strongest, it's also important to know which of your domains are weaker. Ideally, you would want to see a good balance of strength across all five domains.

It is, therefore, important to assess the full functioning of your cognitive fitness across all key domains. You probably have a reasonable idea of your blood pressure, heart rate, blood glucose, and cholesterol as markers of your physical fitness. When it comes to cognitive function you need to have similar knowledge of the functioning of your cognition across each of the five domains.

Your cognitive contribution is the sum of what your cognitive fitness is to your organization, community, and family, as well as to yourself. In turn, organizations, communities, and families can also be cognitively strong and weak across all five domains because we all contribute strengths and weaknesses to them. It is entirely possible for a company to be "sick", i.e. not operating at its best. Indeed, the collective cognition of an entire nation could be in a poor state, or "stuck in a rut". For now, let's focus on your individual cognitive fitness and return to wider views later on in the book.

To fully understand your own leadership and management strengths you have to systematically "assess" your cognitive function. Once you know your strengths you can make the most of them. Equally, by knowing your weaknesses you can improve them through the adoption of habits and training to improve specific cognitive domains. You can also use this knowledge to decide how to put teams together; who is best to hire to fill a specific role and who needs help to overcome shortcomings. This knowledge enables you to delegate and share work with colleagues effectively to make the most of their strengths and yours.

Initially, we will walk through a series of examples, illustrations, and case studies that will enable you to comprehensively assess your cognition. Only on completing this assessment will you be able to choose the order and the intensity of the 50 habits, described in the following chapters, for you to achieve a better cognitive fitness. The habits you choose and the order in which you attempt to acquire them will be unique to you. Eventually, you can attempt all 50 habits, but some habits will take on a greater priority than others.

ESTABLISHING THE DOMAINS

The principal neuropsychological method of establishing the independence of the five domains has been to employ a 'dissociative' methodology. This approach is based on historical case studies of individuals who exhibited selective cognitive deficits; for example, that were incurred after brain injury. That is, following the occurrence of brain injury, the patient presented major deficits in one of the five key domains. However, the domains are not completely separate constructs. They overlap just as heart rate will impact blood pressure, and vice-versa. But, dissociative methodology presents the best means by which we can study each cognitive fitness domain in relative isolation.

An example from the research is the case of a patient treated in the 1950s. This patient was identified by the initials, "HM" (Scoville & Milner, 1957). HM had epilepsy and had suffered from it for many years. He underwent neurosurgery to remove parts of his brain; the medial temporal lobes bilaterally, including the hippocampus, and nearby structures. The purpose of the surgery was to reduce the frequency of the epilepsy which, if it continued, could kill him. The surgery had the intended effect, but also caused severe anterograde amnesia. This meant that HM was not able to commit new information to his semantic memory (general knowledge that we have accumulated throughout our lives). However, the operation did not impact his working memory (his ability to comprehend and solve problems), or his semantic memory for concepts and events which were acquired up until about ten years prior to the operation. Thus HM had a specific and selective deficit for new memories, a dissociation of new episodic memories.

In the case of HM, researchers had a patient who had cognitive function in all domains, except that of acquiring new memories of an episode in his life. Thus the ability to acquire new memories, episodic memory, was completely absent from this patient. The other domains have been identified through researching patients with a complete deficit in each domain.

In addition to patient case studies, other sources of information to prove the legitimacy of independent cognitive domains have included experimental psychology and psychopharmacological studies. In these experiments and studies various parts of the brain have been removed, over stimulated or inhibited, by electrophysiological or pharmacological means.

THE SCIENCE BIT

The word cognition is derived from the Latin *cognitiō*, a variant of *cognōscere*, meaning "to get to know" (from *com* [with] and *(g) nōscere* [to learn]).

Cognition is "the mental action or process of acquiring knowledge and understanding through thought, experience, and the senses".[3]

Generally, "cognition" refers to all mental activities involved in receiving information, understanding it, storing it, retrieving it, and using it. Thus, cognition includes sensory and perceptual processes such as sight, sound, smell, taste, and tactile sensations, enabling receipt of information from your surroundings. The physical faculties in these respects are, therefore, very important contributors to overall cognitive fitness. Cognitive processing of information embraces memory, perception, thinking, reasoning, problem solving, decision making, language, motivation, and concept formation. A healthy intact brain is thus an advantage!

We also need to use this information to make decisions about actions, problem solving, and in communication. This comes from experience.

In most people cognitive fitness improves with age and plateaus at around 24 years of age. Studies show that the domains strengthen and weaken at different rates as we grow up and then age.

In psychology, "cognition" usually refers to information processing of a person's psychological functions; cognitive psychology is the study of the mental processes that underlie behaviour.[4]

In the term "social cognition", cognition refers to attitudes, attribution, and group dynamics. Social cognition is the study of what information people pay attention to, how they analyse it, reach judgments on the information, how these judgments influence their behaviour, and what bits of information they remember.[5]

In leadership and management, you should be aware of the social aspects of cognition, particularly with regard to people's attitudes and beliefs. There is a need to be mindful of the group dynamics within your organization and the group dynamics of those your organization interacts with.

Cognition may be viewed as a collection of processes and systems that are independent in terms of each other, and of the individual's emotions and desires, and the context of action.[6] This view underlies many cognitive functioning tests, and cognitive training and retraining programs that target specific cognitive processes with specific cognitive exercises.

Traditional cognitive retraining focuses on neuropsychological impairment, with the aim of restoring cognitive functions (e.g. organization, memory, reasoning, problem solving). Retraining often uses residual cognitive skills to help the impaired ability, and is in a clinical setting.[7] An interrelated set of mental processes that guides actions and problem solving in the "real world".[8] This more functional and integrated view underlies cognitive intervention programs that target cognitive processes within the context of educational and everyday activities. It supports cognitive intervention plans that are particularly effective in producing functional outcomes for a variety of populations with a disability.

Context-sensitive cognitive intervention and support translates the neuropsychological impairment of an individual into negative impact upon the individuals functioning in the real world. The intervention occurs in the individual's natural environment (e.g. at home or school) and uses environmental adaptations and supports to enable participation in real-world activities.[9]

Deficits, impairments, or reductions in cognition[10] may result in the inability to undertake a range of processes critical to leadership and management. These include:

- paying attention;
- rapidly processing information;
- remembering and recalling information;
- rapidly responding to information;
- thinking critically, planning, organizing, and solving problems;
- initiating speech.

Natural ageing is associated with an increasing likelihood of developing, among other things, memory loss. Such age-associated memory impairment is characterized by self-perceived memory loss and a decline in objective memory performance compared with younger adults. Approximately 40% of people aged 65 or older have age-associated memory impairment, and of these, about 1% will progress to dementia each year.[11] A more severe form of memory loss is that characterized by important memory deficits that do not display functional impairments. About 10% of people aged 65 years or older have these levels of cognitive impairment, and of these, nearly 15% of them develop Alzheimer's disease each year.[12]

WHAT COMPRISES COGNITIVE FITNESS?
The ability to live your life to the full is dependent on the mental processes known as cognition. Cognitive fitness is based on the use of the knowledge and the experience that you have to develop

strategies, focus your attention, modify your actions in order to achieve specific outcomes, and the ability to learn new things. Working simultaneously towards a desired goal, there are many individual components of cognitive functioning (see Table 1).

Table 1: Components of cognition are generally thought to include the following (those with * comprise the five core cognitive domains)

Attention*	Cognitive process of selectively concentrating the mind on one aspect
Executive function*	Processes involving planning and initiating appropriate actions, while selecting the relevant sensory information
Judgment	Discriminating between two or more states or conditions, making logical, rational decisions and conclusions
Long-term memory	Ability of the brain to retain, recall and use knowledge gained from past experiences
Episodic memory*	Remembering past experiences
Working memory*	Recall subject matter to the mind and retain in the memory while undertaking new analyses
Processing speed*	Output modalities (e.g. speech and movement) and their control and coordination

[Adapted from: the Center for Disease Control and Prevention and the Alzheimer's Association, 2007]

In terms of measuring cognitive fitness and applying cognitive training, some domains of cognition are more important than others. Areas of particular interest include: processing speed, episodic memory, executive function, and working memory (see Figure 1).

Figure 1: Key domains of cognitive function and cognitive training

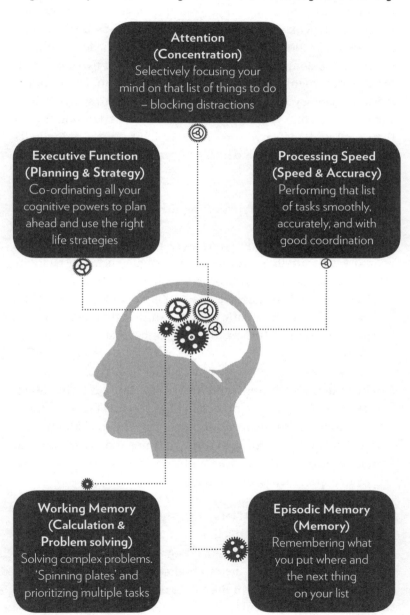

MEASURING COGNITION

Cognitive tests (also known as neuropsychological, psychometric, psychological, and neurocognitive tests) are used to measure a person's cognition. Cognitive tests can be classified according to the cognitive domain that they aim to assess. The five most commonly cited cognitive domains are working memory, attention, episodic memory, executive function, and processing speed. Tests can be designed to evaluate several domains of cognition (rather than one) and enable you to create a picture of an individual's cognitive fitness, through which you can interpret their ability to lead and manage.

There are generally two types of cognitive tests:

1. Hand-written cognitive tests were the first to be developed and were initially used to measure intelligence and facilitate the diagnosis of brain disorders such as Alzheimer's disease. They are used to measure the extent of and recovery from brain disease or traumatic injury. Hand-written tests required specialist administration; they are difficult to apply and are time consuming.

2. Computerized testing with electronic test administration, data capture, and data processing has recently enabled standardization of test delivery and scoring. This has allowed for more accurate recording of reaction times and has minimized human error and bias. Generally, computerized tests do not require specialist administration.

KEY DOMAINS OF COGNITION RELEVANT TO COGNITIVE TRAINING

By way of introduction to specific domains, let's review the functions of the four lobes of the cerebral cortex. Figure 2 shows the location of the four lobes of the cerebral cortex and cerebellum.

Figure 2: Location of the lobes of the cerebral cortex

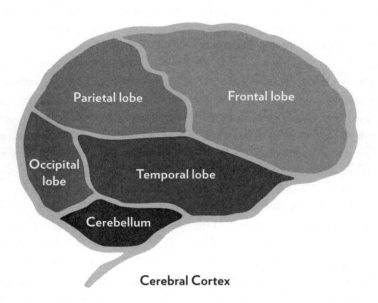

The frontal lobe is located at the front of the brain and is associated with reasoning, motor skills, higher level cognition, and expressive language. The motor cortex at the back of the frontal lobe receives and processes information from the other cortical lobes to affect body movements. Damage to the frontal lobe can cause changes in attention, socialization, and sexual habits.

The parietal lobe, in the middle ventral part of the brain, is associated with processing tactile sensory information, such as pressure, touch, and pain. The somatosensory cortex, located within this lobe, is required for processing input from the body's senses. Parietal lobe damage can lead to problems with verbal memory, eye control, and language.

The temporal lobe – The temporal lobe is at the base of the brain. It houses the primary auditory cortex (important for interpreting sounds and language), and the hippocampus (associated with memory formation, especially working memory). Problems with memory, speech perception, and language can be detected when the temporal lobe is damaged.

The occipital lobe – The occipital lobe at the back of the brain is associated with interpreting visual stimuli and information. The primary visual cortex located in this lobe receives and interprets information from the retinas of the eyes. Occipital lobe damage can cause problems with vision, including object and word recognition, and colour identification.

LINKS BETWEEN LEARNING AND MEMORY

Learning enables an individual to retain acquired information, affective states, and impressions. Learning is the initial process of remembering, and adding to memory.[13] How the information is processed in the brain will determine how you perceive an object, the relationships between shape, colour, sound, etc. Also, isolated pieces of information are less well remembered than those you can associate with existing memories. Thus, it is easier to memorize new information if there are many associations to things you already know. The association of new memories to older ones increases wisdom and explains why you get wiser as you age.

A number of factors are believed to affect memory function:[14]

- alertness, attentiveness, and concentration;
- interest, motivation, and need;
- emotional state;
- context in which information is memorized.

You have some control over some of these factors but they are also influenced by the environment in which you live and work, as well as your lifestyle and genetic predisposition.

NEUROPLASTICITY AND THE EXECUTIVE

Up until the 1980s-90s it was believed that the brain reached a certain level of development and then it was inevitable that it declined. We now know that this couldn't be further from the truth. As is the case with physical fitness, cognitive fitness can be improved at any stage of your life. In the same way that you can undertake physical exercise at any age, you can also do the same with cognitive exercises to improve the way your mind works. What does this mean for you?

Don't get stuck in the mind-set that your cognitive fitness is fixed or bound to deteriorate. Whatever your situation you can improve your cognitive fitness.

This is because of "neuroplasticity" and, in particular, its impact on executive function.

WHAT IS NEUROPLASTICITY?

Neuroplasticity, otherwise known as brain plasticity or cortical remapping, refers to the capacity of the nervous system, essentially the brain, to change or adapt its structure and function over a lifetime.[15][16] This means that the brain is not static or in permanent decline, but that it is able to develop and regenerate like any other organ or tissue in the body. Not only that, but your cognitive fitness can be improved by external stimulation.

Neuroplasticity is intrinsic to the nervous system responding to the changing environment.[17] It is a consequence of many factors including sensory input, motor action, association, and awareness.[18] Neuroplasticity occurs as a result of normal brain development based on the acquisition of knowledge and learning, experience and memory, and injuries or illnesses that impact your brain. The brain is able to modify its own structure and function as we discussed above when considering the homunculus.

Neuroplasticity will impact the development of the brain through structural and functional mechanisms. It will do this structurally, whereby the physical structure of the brain is altered as a result of experience and learning. The concept of neuroplasticity underlies theories of memory and learning. Memory formation requires long-term storage of information in the brain, and the plasticity of synapses is thought to play an essential role in information storage.[19]

Neuroplasticity also helps the brain's functionality, whereby brain activity associated with a given function can be moved to a different location as a consequence of normal experience or when recovering from brain injury or disease. In general, the brains of younger people can reorganize more effectively and quickly than those of older adults, but reorganization and new functionality is possible at any age. The concept of reorganization after brain damage as a function of developmental restructuring is known as the "Kennard principle".[20]

There are several dynamic processes that occur in the adult brain indicating that it undergoes changes.[21] These include the formation of nerve cells (neurogeneration) and extension dendrites, which help communication across the brain by allowing connections to be made.

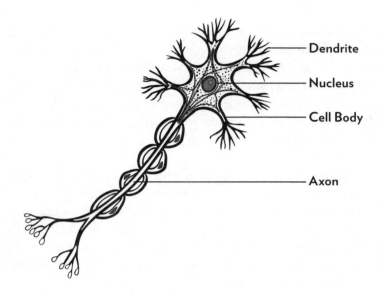

Dendrite

Nucleus

Cell Body

Axon

The health of nerve cells affects brain functionality through the following three processes:

- Apoptosis (programmed cell death)
  o Apoptosis is required for neuroplasticity, synaptic turn-over, and for removing dysfunctional neurons and their support network (glia), enabling adaptive re-modelling of nerve cell networks in the ageing process.
- Inflammation (acute phase of injury)
  o Acute inflammation is responsible for the removal of dead and dying tissues and their products (glial cells play an important role).
- Generation of free radicals (oxidative stress)
  o Free radicals released during inflammation provide a protective mechanism by destroying foreign invaders in the brain.

These processes are beneficial to cognitive functioning as they help to maintain healthy nerve cell networks, but their malfunctioning may lead to cell loss (neurodegeneration) and cognitive decline.

Neuroplasticity occurs at all ages,[22] [23] contributing to normal brain development, regeneration and renewal, and life-long cognitive fitness. If you don't look after your brain, the lack of positive neuroplasticity can lead to brain degeneration, cognitive decline, psychological, and neurodegenerative disorders. Poor levels of cognitive fitness are associated with a range of poor education and health outcomes.

Poor cognitive fitness is associated with few or no qualifications; a higher likelihood not to obtain paid work; a higher predisposition to psychiatric disorders (e.g. depression, anxiety), addictions (e.g. drugs, alcohol, the internet); a much higher likelihood of involvement in the criminal justice system; and with earlier and more prolonged neurodegenerative disorders, such as Alzheimer's and Parkinson's disease.

Neuroplasticity, in its positive state, is retained throughout life, allowing modification of function and structure by the addition or deletion of neuronal connections (synaptic connections) and by promoting the formation of nerve tissue (neurogenesis).

Neuroplasticity occurs from birth until death, in two forms.[24] In the first form there are long-term adaptations in brain structure and related changes in cognitive fitness and behaviour that occur as a result of the growing and ageing process. These may be considered as your "life-long developmental process", which is thought to be the basis of the life-time changes in your cognitive fitness and associated behaviour. The second form of neuroplasticity are mechanisms that modify the brain structure and function on a daily basis. The healthy brain is continuously changing every day as a result of changing environments and experiences and the acquisition of new knowledge and thought processes.

Life-long adaptations are mapped out by your genes, but they are themselves modified by events in your lives. It is the cumulative effect of your environment, events, and experiences that determines much of who you are. You are not able to change your genes, but you can alter your work and living environments, and that of your colleagues and family. You can ensure that you have new experiences and learn new skills. You can, through assessing your cognitive fitness, choose those experiences and skills that are more beneficial to your cognitive fitness over those that are not. You can also change your lifestyle, building a healthier you.

BRAIN DEVELOPMENT

To understand neuroplasticity, it's useful to first review how your brain develops and how this development can be modified by your life experience and lifestyle. Brain development can be divided into seven specific stages:[25]

1. **Cell birth**

   Cells destined to produce the nervous system begin to form approximately three weeks after the fertilization of an egg in humans. By five months of the fertilization, most of the nerve cell formation (neurogenesis) will be complete.[26] New neurones are produced in the mammalian brain throughout the life span. There is general agreement that there are two regions where stem cells continuously give rise to neurogenesis. These are in the hippocampus and the lateral ventricles.[27] More controversial is that neurogenesis occurs outside these areas in the cerebral cortex and cerebellum.[28] Interestingly, the same cell lines that develop into the brain also form the gut, the intestines. That is why the same transmitters that affect the brain also affect the gut and why there is a direct link between your brain and your gut.

2. **Cell migration**

   Once formed, the neurones begin to move or migrate to different areas in the brain. Growth and neuronal hormones are important in this process.

3. **Cell differentiation**

As neurones reach their destination, the interaction of your genes and the environment influences them towards differentiating into a particular cell type. Thus, they take on a specialized role in the different areas.

4. **Cell maturation**

Once embedded in their final destination, neurones mature by growing dendrites and extending axons.[29] Dendrites are branched projections that provide a surface area for synapses (junctions for connections – see neurone diagram on page 31) with other cells. Neurotransmitters are released from one cell to connect with adjacent cells across these synapses. Axons are long nerve fibres that extend to other nerves or targets for synapse formation, allowing transmitter release and thus neuronal communication to reach all areas of the central nervous system.

5. **Synaptogenesis**

The synapse is the gap between two neurones. Neurotransmitters (chemical messengers) are released from one neurone, across the synapse, to the connecting neurone. Synapse formation and neural connections in the brain will largely be guided by a variety of environmental cues and signals as the vast number could not possibly be genetically programmed.

6. **Cell death and synaptic pruning**

The brain overproduces neurones and neuronal connections during development because of the uncertainty in the number of neurones that will reach their destination and the healthiness of the connections that they form. The brain is able to remove unnecessary, unhealthy cells and connections by the processes of cell death and synaptic pruning. It does this mainly in a period following adolescence. The processes that impact pruning include your personal experiences (e.g.

levels of happiness and stress), and your hormone levels. The effect of this cell loss and synaptic pruning can be seen by changes in thickness of the brain cortex; the latter becomes measurably thinner following adolescence and can be correlated with behavioural development. This potentially explains the differences in development of behavioural skills in children versus adults.[30]

7. Myelogenesis
Finally, glial cells are produced to form myelin. Myelin is an insulator material, which forms a sheath around the neurone axon and functions to increase the propagation of impulses along the nerve fibre.[31] Myelin production continues throughout life, but begins in earnest in adolescence. Axons can function before myelination, although normal neuronal function in adults is attained only after myelination is complete (generally after the age of 18 years in some areas of the cortex).

Life experiences will affect neuroplasticity and brain development in different ways depending on the stage of brain development.[32] The characteristics of the brain that enable experiences to modify the organization of the brain cortex are due to cells called stem cells, which remain active throughout life. They can produce neural or glial progenitor cells that migrate to the cerebral cortex. These cells may remain inactive for long periods, but can be activated to produce either neurons and/or glial cells.[33] Their exact function is poorly understood, but they may be involved in neurogenesis and generating neurones destined for different brain regions. The generation can be influenced by many factors including your life experience, drugs, hormones, and injury and disease.[34]

In addition, dendrites show great plasticity (growth) in response to the experience of rapidly forming synapses,[35] which are necessary for learning and memory. Your specific life experiences result in both selective formation (adding) and loss (pruning) of synapses; thus, in the addition, as well as the deletion, of memories. Synaptic pruning occurs during brain development. Your brain continues to form synapses throughout your life.

DISRUPTION TO NEUROGENESIS

Impairment of neurogenesis in the hippocampus (dentate subgranular zone) is associated with hippocampal-dependent memory deficits.[36] Impairment of neurogenesis is found in a variety of disorders with impaired cognition as a characteristic. For example, impaired neurogenesis occurs early in the course of Alzheimer's disease, which may underlie the apparent disease-related memory impairments.[37] Additionally, in diseases such as Alzheimer's, impaired neurogenesis is the result of a reduction in the proliferation of neural progenitor cells and their neuronal differentiation. This leads to the production of a more simplified, less complex, sophisticated brain and lower cognitive fitness.

Research has shown that people with anxiety disorders often have impaired 'pattern separation'. This is the process where similar experiences are transformed into distinct memories and can lead to the overgeneralization of fear.[38] Studies have implicated neurogenesis in the adult hippocampus (which uses pattern separation to form new memories) in pattern separation, and have shown that reductions in neurogenesis may manifest as impairment in pattern separation and an over-generalization of memory; in other words, a distortion in memories. This is often seen in children and adults who suffer from post-traumatic stress disorder (PTSD).

Neurogenesis is also seen in genetic disorders. In disorders where there is a deletion in genes, such as Fragile X or Down's syndrome, there is evidence of severe impairment in neurogenesis in various areas of the anterior forebrain. The cerebellum has been found to contain fewer neuronal cells due to impairments in proliferation, suggesting that this underlies the cognitive abnormalities of these gene deletion related disorders.[39]

BIOCHEMICAL MECHANISMS IN NEUROPLASTICITY

Complex biochemical pathways are involved in the formation of new brain structures and vasculature (blood vessels) that bring nutrients and oxygen to the brain and take toxins and CO2 away from it. The growth factors, brain-derived neurotrophic factor (BDNF) and vascular endothelial growth factor (VEGF), both play important roles in neurogenesis.[40]

BDNF promotes the survival of new nerve progenitor cells and their incorporation into the neural structure. Its production is triggered by a local increase in neural activity.[41] DNF triggers an intracellular biochemical pathway that stimulates neural structures, such as dendritic spines and axon terminals, to expand.[42]

VEGF promotes the local proliferation of new nerve progenitor cells; the latter support neuronal cell health and growth. VEGF production is triggered by a lack of oxygen (hypoxia).[43] VEGF acts on the endothelial cells lining the blood vessel wall and stimulates them to divide and produce new blood vessels (angiogenesis).[44]

Both BDNF and VEGF increase with exercise.[45] BDNF is a key protein in promoting memory, growth, and survival of neurones. It is recognized as a molecule that is involved in neurological disorders (e.g. Alzheimer's disease and depression) and metabolic disorders (e.g. diabetes and obesity).[46][47]

VEGF plays a major role in the remodelling of the nervous system and the vascular system in regions of the brain that are ischemic, i.e. have a restricted blood supply, causing a shortage of oxygen and glucose required for cell metabolism.[48] VEGF, therefore, is critical following an ischemic stroke. Consequently, physical exercise plays a key role in the mechanisms associated with the development of your brain and cognitive fitness.

LIFE-LONG IMPACTS ON NEUROPLASTICITY

Changes in your brain occur through neuroplasticity due to features and experiences during your lifespan.[49][50]

Examples of features:

- Plasticity differs in different brain regions, meaning that the response by one brain area is different to that in another.
- Plastic changes are often focal (concentrated on one spot) and are not generally widespread across the brain.
- Plastic changes are time-dependent; they are not all permanent and may change greatly over time. Thus, not all changes from an experience incorporating a range of motor and sensory experiences may be retained, unless these experiences are repeated.

Examples of experiences:

- Habit formation, task learning, psychoactive drugs, reward, ageing, exercise, stress and diet.
- Experience-dependent brain changes gained over a lifetime interact with each other, such that one change will effect another. These can include the building of positive experiences that bring about constructive change, but also cumulative negative experiences bringing about destructive change.
- Neuroplasticity generally leads to improved motor and cognitive functions, although not all plasticity is beneficial and can interfere with behaviour. For example, drug-induced changes seen in response to psychomotor stimulants, pathological plasticity as seen in epilepsy, schizophrenia, and dementia can all be detrimental to cognition.
- Normal, injured, and diseased brains may respond differently to the same experience.
- Plastic changes are age dependent. A younger, developing brain is more responsive to experiences compared with an

adult or older brain, and the same experience can alter the brain differently at different ages. However, beneficial changes can occur at all ages, so never give up.

COGNITIVE FITNESS AND NEUROPLASTICITY

Clinical and other studies have shown that cognitive fitness can be improved and strengthened at any point in your life by performing tasks that are novel and complex. These include activities such as learning a new language or a musical instrument. Novel and complex tasks will stimulate your brain, especially the neuronal networks that are involved in the five key cognitive fitness domains.

Provoking good neuroplasticity allows you to build strong cognitive 'resilience'. A brain with good cognitive resilience is one that has formed many good cellular connections and has good cell density. A healthy brain and strong resilience have been shown to delay the onset of mentally deteriorating diseases such as Alzheimer's disease and psychiatric disorders, and to correlate with a better recovery following a stroke or traumatic brain injury. It doesn't guarantee that you will avoid neuropsychiatric disorders or diseases completely, but your chances of getting them are diminished, and if they do occur they will do so later in life.

There was a time when it was believed that the degeneration of the brain was inevitable after a certain stage, but now we increasingly know that improving and maintaining a healthy cognition gives you every chance of living your life to the full, and with a higher quality of life.

You may have heard people frequently describe good cognitive fitness as "staying sharp" or "being in the right frame of mind". Often it's the most successful individuals that you think of as "sharp minded". These individuals are most likely to have a healthy cognition and, therefore, a positive mental outlook; they are alert, have a good memory, and are socially involved within their workplace, community, and with those around them on a daily basis. These qualities go beyond the basic analytical skills measured by traditional intelligence scales such Intelligence Quotient (IQ), but involve the broad range of cognitive, organizational, environmental and social abilities attributed to intelligence, according to its current conceptions.[51]

If you continually aim to maintain or improve your cognitive fitness there is a good chance you will remain a high functioning individual throughout your life. Improving and maintaining a healthy cognition enables you to not only function better on a day-to-day basis, but it also leads to a purposeful and meaningful life outside of work as well. It allows you to function at the highest level for longer periods into advanced age with a better quality of life.

Your brain is kept cognitively healthy through the correct growth, renewal, and regeneration of neurones and the correct "wiring" between them. If the "wiring" gets mixed up, or the balance of neurotransmitter flow is mixed up, you can easily go into poor cognitive health, poor cognitive fitness.

Given how complicated your brain is, it's a wonder that you manage as well as you do. How often does a computer, which is a tiny fraction of the complexity of your brain, need rebooting?

In this regard, it's a wonder that any of us are truly 'sane'. Indeed, in truth, none of us are perfectly sane all the time. Your cognitive health is like your physical health. Do any of you truly believe that you are 100% physically healthy, all of the time? I doubt many of you do. When I ask this question to audiences, I always get some triathlon, super-fit people saying they are 100% fit. But if I ask them if there were any part of their physical performance that they could improve on, they soon agree they are not 100% fit. Something as simple as an ankle sprain or a cold will diminish your physical health, and it's the same with our cognitive health.

The trouble with mental health is that we have been conditioned to think of it in a binary sense. That is, we are either sane or insane, at either end of a spectrum. The truth is, like physical health, most people have good and bad days and reach levels of average physical and cognitive health. In addition, like physical health, cognitive health can improve or get worse at any one time. It is, therefore, important that it is measured regularly, to see what state it is in. It's important you look after it. For example, how many of you suffer cognitively following too many alcoholic drinks?

The Myth of Mental Health Measurement

We wrongly perceive mental health as binary – we are either sane or mentally ill. In fact, mental health is a sliding scale, from 100% to 0%, just like physical health

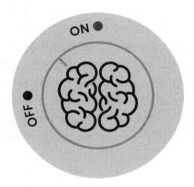

Physical Health
We realize it is a spectrum of many health states, from good, to average, to poor

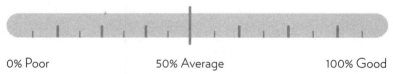

0% Poor   50% Average   100% Good

Cognitive Health
We assume there are only two health states – sane and mentally ill. In reality, the spectrum is as diverse as that for physical health

0% Mentally ill   100% Sane

Like the rest of us, you should be able to accept that you have episodes of good as well as poor cognitive fitness.

Take the trend among some university students. Some are taking drugs to enhance their chances in exams to overcome lapses in cognition. In a way, they are like the 'drug cheats' of athletics and in the same way they may regret using drugs because of the potential ill-effects on their overall health. In addition, if you hire such a student you are not getting the cognitive fitness you thought you were according to their exam results.

Something as common as a cold not only makes you feel physically poor, it also impacts on your cognition. Luckily, most things that impact your cognitive function do so temporarily, as they do your physical health. However, temporary blips in your cognitive fitness aside, it's when you face chronic problems that cognition can really suffer. Prolonged suffering may eventually express itself as mental illness. Depression, obsessive anxiety, and mania could be the result of chronic cognitive problems. Chronically poor cognitive function is a feature of all psychiatric disorders. Psychiatric disorders, such as bipolar disorder, depression, and schizophrenia are brought about by a "miss-wiring" of the brain's neurones, or they may also be caused by a chronic imbalance in neurotransmitters. This is where the careful transmitter balance that keeps you healthy and cognitively fit is out of equilibrium.

Neurodegenerative disorders, such as Alzheimer's disease, Parkinson's disease, and multiple sclerosis on the other hand, are brought about by a degeneration of the brain's neurones in specific areas of the brain. As the neurones break down, their connectivity across the brain breaks down too, thus affecting the natural, healthy balance of neurotransmitters.

By regularly assessing yourself you can look for signs of a downward trend in one or all of your cognitive domains and critically, you can do something to rectify these trends.

SCANNING THE BRAIN

Now you have the means to detect different states of cognitive fitness. You also know it's possible to improve your cognitive fitness because of neuroplasticity.

In the 1980s when I was studying the neurophysiological basis of behaviour at the City of London Polytechnic (now London Metropolitan University), we believed that the brain would get to a point of growth and then naturally decline, and that this decline was inevitable. Two main areas of research now show that this couldn't be further from the truth.

Firstly, brain scanning has shown how the brain can regrow, renew, and regenerate itself, at any time of life. By using magnetic resonance imaging (MRI), positron emission topography (PET), electroencephalography (EEG), and other scans, we can now observe the brain growing, developing, restructuring, and strengthening in adults and children. This positive growth was thought to be impossible once we had passed a certain age.

Secondly, major advances in neuroelectrophysiology have allowed us to measure the impact of the release of neurotransmitters on adjacent cells. Neuroelectrophysiology is the measurement of the impact of neurotransmitters on the change in electrical potentials (charge) across the inside and outside of a neurone. Overwhelmingly, the transmitters caused an instantaneous and rapid change in the potential in a post-synaptic neurone. This impact, the change in the electrical charge of the inside of the neurone to the outside, is due to the movement of ions, such as sodium ions, across the membrane. The duration of the change in electrical potential, allowing the movement of ions, was measured in microseconds. The change was so quick that it was difficult to see how it could bring about any long-lasting or permanent change in the post-synaptic neurone. However, in some cases, neuroscientists recorded longer term changes in the charge across the neurone, with a duration a thousand times longer than usual. The long-term excitatory changes were called long term potentiation (LTP).

LTP is, in effect, a persistent strengthening of synaptic transmission. The duration of the excitation is sufficient enough to bring about the production of a protein or other structure in the impacted (post-synaptic) neurone. Neuroscientists had, therefore, discovered how you make memories, how you learn, and how thought processes are developed and your cognitive fitness is established. Just like a computer that requires code to operate, your brain requires proteins and other structures to function, learn, and grow. Unlike a computer, all the coding isn't present from the outset and a brain is constantly updating itself.

Thus, LTP is now broadly considered to be one of the significant neurocellular mechanisms that underlies our cognition. Although LTP was first discovered through the work of Terje Lømo in 1966 in studies on the rabbit hippocampus, our understanding of it is still at a relatively rudimentary level, but it is accelerating.

I worked in the Wellcome Development and Research laboratories in the 1970s and 1980s alongside remarkable scientists who discovered new pharmaceuticals for disorders such as epilepsy and migraine. The drug discovered for epilepsy was lamotrigine, and the team was headed by a very special scientist, Alistair Millar. His type are no longer able to flourish in today's pharmaceutical industry, but that's another story. He was neither a medical practitioner nor had a PhD, but despite this he was a remarkable scientist and much respected by his colleagues. It was his determination and stamina that ensured lamotrigine was developed and today it's seen as one of the few major breakthroughs in neuroscience pharmacology over the last 30 years.

Epilepsy is characterized by an increase in excitatory activity in the brain. The seizures that are associated with epilepsy are the consequences of the over-excitation of the brain, an over-occurrence of LTP. Although we are still unsure of lamotrigine's exact mechanism of action, we know that it modulates sodium ion channels and can prevent the movement of sodium ions across the neuronal membrane that occurs during neurotransmitter release and LTP. The over-excitation of neurones observed in epilepsy through EEG is a similar process to that of LTP. Thus lamotrigine, through blocking sodium channels, also blocks some forms of LTP. Not surprisingly, therefore, lamotrigine, as well as reducing epileptic seizures can, as a side effect, also reduce LTP and thus have a detrimental impact on cognitive function.

LTP is a popular subject of research. We now have a better understanding of the consequence of LTP and are able to draw an underlying link between LTP and cognitive function as evidenced through MRI scanning, EEG, and behaviour. Many scientists are trying to develop methods, pharmacological or otherwise, to enhance LTP to improve learning and memory. It's not surprising, therefore, that LTP is a subject of clinical research in Alzheimer's disease and in a range of interventions to prevent disorders such as strokes, brain injury, bipolar disorder, and addictions. It is also not surprising that the drugs used by students to enhance LTP, to improve their cognition, can have side effects that can cause short epileptic seizures. When you play with your brain health with drugs you may have to pay for the consequences.

As discussed earlier, technology, through scans such as MRI and PET, have allowed us to look into the brain, see it perform, and measure its growth and development. The study of LTP through these neuro-electrophysiology techniques has shown how proteins and structures linked to the laying down of knowledge and memory can occur in the brain.

These discoveries have led to a greater understanding of neuro-plasticity, the ability of the brain to develop in normal growth and to repair itself after disease or injury. Neuroplasticity also occurs when the brain is stimulated, just as a muscle does when it's physically exercised. The brain can be stimulated to process data quicker, or to pay more attention and build stronger mem-ories depending on the type of stimulation it receives. Therefore, the type of brain training you may need can in fact be tailored according to what areas of cognitive fitness you require to develop.

I hope the science above hasn't been too much. For the purposes of this book it's necessary to convince you that your brain is able to perform amazing things and that you can take advantage of this ability.

The next chapter looks more closely at the five cognitive domains, starting with executive function. The chapter will analyse how the five domains underpin the cognitive power of your leadership and management thinking.

Case study

Fred Housego – the famous London black cab taxi driver

A good example of neuroplasticity is seen in the brains of London black cab, taxi drivers, before and after they learn all of the roads in London, something they call doing 'The Knowledge'. London roads were not designed on a grid system. Even though I live here I am more likely to get lost in London than in New York, Philadelphia, or any city built on a grid. There are thousands of possible routes between any sets of locations across London and black cab drivers have to learn these before they get a licence to hire, even in the days of 'sat-navigation'.

Scans have shown that as the taxi drivers go through the process of learning the roads, areas of their brain associated with cognition and memory (in this case the hippocampus) increase in volume. The process of learning the complex road system brings about a physical change in their brains, and gives them the opportunity to improve their overall cognition. They have a super-powered hippocampus that they can, if they wish, put to an even greater cognitive use.

Perhaps the most famous London taxi driver is a gentleman by the name of Fred Housego. Fred became a television and radio personality and presenter after winning the BBC television quiz *Mastermind* in 1980. The winners of Mastermind are usually associated with intellectual occupations or pastimes; professors, scientists, or engineers. Fred only had one qualification when he left school, but in doing The Knowledge it empowered his brain to obtain a higher cognitive fitness and function. This assisted his natural curiosity to amass a vast collection of facts and trivia which enabled him to win *Mastermind*. It physically changed his brain. It functionally improved his cognition with better neuronal pathways and connections. We now know that you can do the same, but you don't have to do The Knowledge to achieve this.

THE HUMAN AND FINANCIAL COST OF POOR COGNITIVE FITNESS

INTRODUCTION

As an executive, you want your cognition to be as fit as possible to perform better in everything you do. A healthy cognition is good to aspire towards because as well as a personal cost associated with a poor cognition, there is also a heavy clinical and social burden associated with poor cognitive fitness. Poor cognition can cost you, your company, society, and your family financially.

Productivity takes a big hit when fitness isn't in good shape. Your poor cognitive health could use large quantities of health and social care. One way or another, that bill is being picked up by every one of us.

As an employer, as a leader, you must consider these costs and what you can do about them. The responsibility for good cognitive health lies not just on health and social systems, but on individuals and employers too. As you understand more about cognitive health you can get a better view as to which employers and organizations help their people enhance and maintain their cognition throughout their working life and which don't. As a leader this is of great importance to you. You have a responsibility in your company or organization to ask what you are doing about the cognitive fitness of your working population.

THE COST OF POOR COGNITION

The problems associated with poor cognition are currently costing the UK around £70 billion a year. The cost of mental illness to UK businesses alone totals £26 billion annually and a recent Organization for Economic Cooperation and Development (OECD) report estimated that, at any one time, one in six individuals of working age suffer from a mental health problem. This means that every company is likely to be affected by poor cognition at any time. Companies of all sizes should recognize the need to take a proactive stance on cognitive fitness and on mental health. However, to date, responses tend to be generalist, *ad hoc*, and usually of a reactive nature, often too late to help individual employees. The costs and lack of responses are not restricted to the UK alone. They affect all developed and developing countries.

Many companies will feel enough pressure on their budgets already and may be deterred from looking into further health and wellness initiatives; they may lack additional funds to commit to cognitive health. However, not doing so could cost more in absenteeism and lower productivity. By going about this in the right way, companies can see their spending on cognitive fitness as an investment, not a cost.

Poor cognition at work is a significant problem, but often it isn't tackled directly because of the stigma associated with mental health. However, there are simple, cost-effective actions an employer can take that will have a big impact. We will look at these later.

THE GLOBAL COST OF POOR MENTAL HEALTH

The global cost of mental health care is greater than the cost of cancer. Unlike cancer, much of the economic burden of poor cognitive fitness is from the loss of income due to unemployment, productivity losses, social security costs, medical costs, and a range of indirect costs due to a chronic disability that begins early in life.[52]

The World Health Organization (WHO) reported the global cost of mental illness at $2.5 trillion ($1.6 trillion in indirect costs) in 2010, with a forecast of $6 trillion by 2030.[53] The report also stated that those with mental illness are at a higher risk of developing cardiovascular disease, respiratory disease, and diabetes. Therefore, the true costs of poor cognitive health are likely to be even higher.

NORTH AMERICA

Payments for health care, long-term care, and hospices are projected to increase from $203 billion in 2013 to $1.2 trillion in 2050.

EUROPE

In 2008, the total cost of illness of dementia (Alzheimer's disease and other dementias) in the 27 member countries of the European Union (EU27) was estimated to be €160 billion.[54][55]

The cost of illness of dementia is set to rise considerably. Costs are similar in Northern, Western and Southern Europe, although they are substantially lower in Eastern Europe where the prevalence of dementia is the highest.[56] It is estimated that the costs of dementia in Europe will increase by approximately 43% to over €250 billion between 2008 and 2030.[57]

UNITED KINGDOM

In the UK, there were an estimated 821,884 patients with diagnosed and undiagnosed dementia, representing 1.3% of the UK population.[58] In 2010, the cost of dementia to the UK economy was nearly £23 billion per year, which is more than cancer (approximately £12 billion per year) and heart disease (approximately £8 billion per year) combined.[59]

Informal care costs met by unpaid carers (£12.4 billion per year) and long-term institutional social care (£9 billion) make up the greatest proportion of the costs. Health care costs were

£1.2 billion, while the total cost of lost productivity in the UK was £29 million. Every patient with dementia costs the economy £27,647 per year.[60] The economic burden of poor cognitive health is increasing at such a rate that it is predicted to bring most economies to their knees during the next 25 years.

Two of the biggest problems organizations face are health insurance against poor mental health for employees ageing, and pensions. Pensions and health insurance are linked and will cause companies and society greater problems in years to come.

After having worked many years, older employees often have enough in their pension pots to retire early. They often choose to retire early because they are unhappy, stressed, or simply burnt out. However, early retirement in these circumstances is not beneficial for the employee or the employer. Those retiring have a skill set and abundance of wisdom that will be missed in the workforce and they will be difficult and costly to replace. In addition, by retiring early in a burnt-out state they will be an increasingly heavier burden on social and health care costs. With proper leadership, challenging opportunities, and the right training, this needn't be the case. They could be encouraged to improve their cognitive fitness and be further encouraged to work for a few more years, leaving with better cognition and saving their companies recruitment, productivity, and pension costs.

Early retirement across the globe may cause a crisis of gigantic proportions based on pension and social/health care alone. In fact, this is already a problem that is affecting all the developed and many of the developing countries.

What's the solution?

You could support older employees with help that keeps them cognitively fit so that they continue working for more years. With older employees working a few more years and leaving the organization in better health, they will be a lower burden on social and health care overall. This is a game changer.

Secondly, if you can encourage employers to use health insurance that provides access to good cognitive health as well as physical health, this would also be a game changer. Employees could take regular cognitive fitness tests and undertake regular cognitive training. Cognitive training and the adoption of healthy habits could also be "prescribed" through the insurance as appropriate based on an individual's cognitive needs.

Cognitive assessments "de-risk" the insuring of mental health and long-term care to insurance providers. By de-risking mental health, insurance companies will now be able to enter a market previously too risky for them. This is not just a simple game changer; it's a monumental game changer.

Leaders of organizations can help this by encouraging the use of mental health insurance schemes alongside their usual health and wellbeing programs and proactively encouraging their employees to take advantage of such packages. A properly executed cognitive fitness insurance scheme can be implemented against all risks of cognitive health because the outcome will see improvements in all health states, thus markedly reducing the costs associated with poor cognitive fitness.

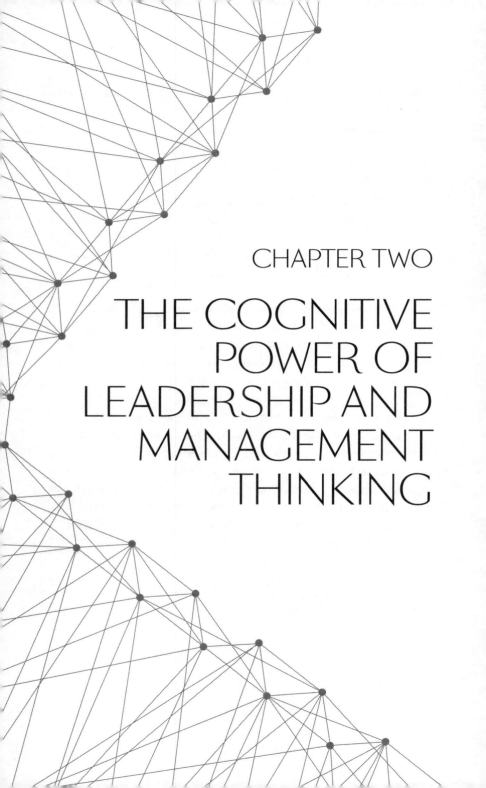

CHAPTER TWO

THE COGNITIVE POWER OF LEADERSHIP AND MANAGEMENT THINKING

Leadership and management skills are based on behaviour and, in turn, on cognitive fitness. You have seen how cognitive fitness can be enhanced or diminished through neuroplasticity regardless of your age or health state.

The next sections investigate the five key cognitive domains and how they form the foundation of your leadership and management thinking.

Before moving to the next stage it's a good idea to think what you consider to be your key leadership abilities. These have been listed in Table 2. Use Table 2 (over the page) to identify the five abilities that you regard as your strengths (one being the strongest and five the weakest). When you have completed the other assessments in this book you can come back to this table and compare your results.

Table 2: My top leadership and management strengths

Leadership and management strengths	My top strengths (from 1 to 5)
Strategy and planning	
Running team meetings	
Making good decisions	
Presenting plans and budgets	
Setting meeting agendas	
Responding to leadership crises	
Improving core processes	
Solving complex problems	
Providing feedback and coaching	
Creating practical solutions	
Directing team members' tasks	
Solving problems quickly	
Forecasting results	
Setting an example	
Retaining and growing people	

*This assessment and many of the leadership concepts in subsequent chapters are part of the LeaderThink development methodology created by Dr. Stephen G. Payne of Leadership Strategies.

EXECUTIVE FUNCTION
– THE PILOT

Executive function is involved in planning, organizing, time management, creativity, and thinking out of the box. It enables you to complete tasks that require forward thinking and has a controlling function over other cognitive domains to develop strategies and inhibit unwanted impulses.

Additionally, executive function plays an overarching role in meta-cognition. This is activities such as self-monitoring, self-control, and self-evaluation. Executive function can inhibit impulses that, on consideration, prove not to be in your best interests, nor in the best interests of your company, community, or family. This can sometimes cause its own tensions depending where your greatest loyalty lies.

Executive function enables you to consider the implication of your actions before you enact them. It enables you to manage your emotions and monitor your thoughts in order to work more efficiently and effectively.

If executive function is your core cognitive strength, then you are the "Pilot". You are in control of the direction of your company or organization. You know where you need to take your organization and plan thoroughly to do this. You are cool and calm in a crisis and have already thought of the contingencies you can put in place in case of a change in direction. You bring everyone with you on the journey and you praise everyone for their part in its success. You can take your company to new levels and through any challenge.

A strong and healthy executive function is critical for great leadership.

THE ROLE OF EXECUTIVE FUNCTION IN LEADERSHIP AND MANAGEMENT

The best leaders use their executive function to create strategies to make great companies. They have the ability to see ahead and interpret the changes in the environment they work in; they can visualize their company's requirements to be successful in those changing environments. They see it in action in their minds before implementing it, just like a high-jumper visualizing their body arching skywards just prior to a jump.

When you think of excellence in executive function, you think of people like Steve Jobs of Apple, Richard Branson of Virgin and Angela Ahrendts of Burberry. You think of sportspeople like Alex Ferguson of Manchester United, Steve Waugh of Australian cricket, Mike Brearley of English cricket; and great politicians such as Nelson Mandela and JF Kennedy.

Think of these greats and think of who leads your organization? Is it being led or is it simply floating in and out like a piece of flotsam with the tide? What is it that individual employees or members of a board of directors should look for when joining a company or looking to support or choose a leader? This is important because, not only do you want to be a great leader, you want to follow great leaders and have great leaders run your companies and organizations. You want to be among the best.

The best leaders will be strong in executive function. This is the strongest cognitive domain and, as with any good Pilot, executive function is always looking ahead and exerting control over other functions, over other cognitive domains.

Executive function is your ability to create a vision, to communicate with your staff and colleagues and convince them to join you on the "company journey". It's your ability to paint a picture to potential investors of the value of your company's current and future products and services.

As a leader with improved executive function you will excel in strategic thinking and goal planning because you will be able to think ahead. You will be able to avert a crisis because you will consider the implications of your activities and those around you. You will consider contingencies in your plans and think of numerous potential outcomes that could occur, both within and outside your area of control.

You will be a great leader, giving clear directions to your team members, obtaining the best from them. You will lead them through lean periods because you can paint a believable picture of what is beyond the current, immediate situation. You don't panic when you come across an uncommon task that requires a new and creative approach. You assess the situation and invent an innovative way to achieve the desired outcome. That's how you help your companies and businesses grow, even in lean times.

Steve Jobs famously said that he didn't read market research. Had he done so, then Apple would never have made the products and brought them to market in the way they did. Companies that rely too readily on market research do not have the ability to be creative, to take risks. They are more likely to be followers rather than leaders; following fashion rather than leading it. When you ask potential customers what they want, the majority of them will give a picture of something that already exists, but if you want something truly innovative you have to rely on your own creativity. Durable creativity is a consequence of strong executive function.

You use your executive function when it's required to bring about change in your organization. You may need to breathe new life into an organization that is stagnating, or continually keep it ahead of the curve by maintaining the change of direction in an already successful organization. You will continually challenge the strong members of your workforce, giving them opportunities to grow and improve. In doing so they are more likely to stay with you.

As well as people, any organization, region, or even a country, can have poor executive function and find itself stuck in a rut. An entire company can be depressed. In these cases, a leader with strong executive function is required to pull that organization, region, community, or country out of its collective rut. With great executive function and leadership you can lead them to the 'promised land'.

Your executive function gives you the ability to anticipate changes in the environment and respond before it's too late. You can see what happened to the companies that made carbon paper before photocopiers made their products redundant. You saw what happened to companies like Kodak, that relied on producing film for cameras before most of us went digital. You can see the future for your own company and anticipate what will be redundant in the next five years. You can see what you need to do now to replace it.

Look at the problems of some of our major industries. In the automotive industry every new car is simply a three by two metre box on wheels. The industry cannot justify the energy it uses to transport people in an energy poor world, so many lied about energy efficiency and pollution. Even with the advent of electric cars, we cannot justify the space they take up in our ever more congested cities. Or how about the pharmaceutical industry which brings new cancer drugs to market that extend survival by months, but take a lifetime to pay for? Or the financial services market which bases its existence on keeping one step ahead of regulators? Are any of these strategies sustainable? Are any of these industries using or allowing executive function?

To bring about change in the above industries and ones like them, someone has to lead with a new vision and reawaken the desire to change across their companies, including their board members, employees, and management, many of whom may be stuck in a rut. These industries need to select a team with strong executive function to bring this about and shake up the executive function in their workforces to prevent them being a drag on change. We will all benefit from positive changes in these organizations.

Executive function requires you to consider the implications of your actions. It enables you to manage people in a better way to ensure they do their best and that they can achieve the highest levels of job satisfaction in doing so. There may be times when you feel frustrated or irritated by the failings in a member of staff. You could shout at them and maybe even humiliate them in front of others (it happens), but what would the consequence be? Would that make them a better employee? Instead, it is better if you sit calmly with them and talk them through how they could do a better job. You could offer to help them, to serve them in their role. The consequence of this will be an employee wanting to do better than before out of respect for you and the company, rather than out of fear. People always do a better job when it's based on respect rather than fear.

Who among your global leaders or aspiring leaders is showing that they have great executive function? Who among them seeks to bring everyone together to get through hard times ahead? Conversely, who among them tries to divide and turn people against each other, in the knowledge that division and spreading anxiety and distress is the best way for them to get on? You don't want great leaders to create divisions; you want them to bring people together, for the more people work together the more hope you have of surviving and thriving. Teams are built by bringing people together of different skills and cultures, not by division and reliance on people of one type.

Throughout history there have been many leaders who used division to gain control. Hitler in Nazi Germany, Joseph Stalin in the Soviet Union, Mao Zedong in the People's Republic of China and the Khmer Rouge in Cambodia all used division to bring about control, ultimately persecuting large sections of the populations. The "gain" if any, was short lived, because they cared little for the long-term consequences of their actions. They all showed poor executive function, relying on instant gains and gratification, at a cost to their country and their people.

Alternatively, look at how the uniting leaders such as Ghandi and Mandela made great personal sacrifices to keep their people together. Through unity they achieved peaceful aims. In Ghandi's case it was to achieve independence from the British. In Mandela's case it was to achieve a united South Africa, seeking to use the skills of people of all colours to make a great country. In both cases they could have resorted to violence to achieve their aims.

There is the story that throughout his life Mandela always made his own bed. He did so in prison because that way he started every day with a good habit. He would also look his wardens in the eye and show he had dignity. However, he continued the practice when he was President of South Africa. He would say to his staff that he wouldn't ask them to do anything for their country that he wouldn't do. He showed great leadership.

Which of the above world leaders do you admire the most? Which of them do you want to emulate? Look to unite your people, not divide them. Look to make the most of diversity, and not to seek single-minded, narrow-minded people.

You have defined yourself as an executive seeking higher office by reading this book. With the search for high office comes responsibility, to put your leadership on the line. If you are working towards having good leadership you shouldn't allow bad leadership to thrive, nor keep your own leadership hidden. The better your leadership skills, the more you should put those skills to good use throughout your life, into and beyond retirement. Did Ghandi or Mandela retire?

In the UK, Tony Blair had good executive function. He saw that his political party, the Labour Party, had to undergo dramatic change in order to be relevant in the world. He led his party through a turbulent, but ultimately successful process; they were elected to government on three occasions and remained in power for 13 consecutive years, the longest period in the party's history. He increased investment into education and the health service. He continued the previous policy of John Major, his Conservative predecessor, and had secret talks with the "terrorists" in Northern Ireland, that ultimately led to the Good Friday Agreement and peace.

However, ultimately, on the world stage Blair failed because he decided to rely on a more powerful ally, George W Bush. Blair effectively deferred his executive function and left the attention of detail to President Bush and his US team. Blair wasn't in a position to influence the actions of his more powerful ally after the war had been won. Bush had used Blair to partially justify his actions to go to war and was not ready to listen to Blair after the war had been won. By then Blair was in a fix. By not fully thinking through the consequence of going to war, Iraq was left in a situation of complete uncertainty, with a leadership vacuum that was soon filled by evil. Iraq paid the consequence for the faith that Blair put in Bush.

Angela Merkel is often cited as one of the better leaders in Europe. She may be, but the system of leadership in Germany means that

German Chancellors have to rely heavily on the power located in their regions, the Länders. This is to ensure that Germany cannot elect the equivalent of another Hitler, who achieved absolute power. Thus, Merkel is often looking over her shoulder rather than planning for the future. She could be a great European leader, but her hands are tied, her wings clipped.

Surprisingly, perhaps the strongest world leader at present is Pope Francis, who has acquired a strong executive function since he became a bishop in his church. Reading his life story, he had something of a St Paul-like "Road to Damascus" moment which shook his beliefs. It didn't stop his belief in God, but it did make him think of the significance of a hierarchical, Catholic Church, imposing its will over its believers. His church was originally established 2,000 years ago to serve people, not to have them serve the Church. We can observe a change in the cognitive state of Pope Francis. He used to be supportive of the conservative Catholic Church, regardless. Now he is using his executive function in an attempt to build a sustainable strategy for his church, to bring about monumental change within it. Although up against strong opposition, he is courageous enough to stand up for his people, for humanity, for Christians and non-Christians alike. Without change, the Church could become a non-entity and wither and die. Time will tell if his executive function is strong enough to see through this change.

Pope Francis has an advantage over political leaders. Political leaders rarely have "executive authority"; they have to compromise because they have political parties that are involved in making decisions. The Pope has absolute authority from God. Other faith leaders are using their absolute authority in ways to destroy humanity, taking advantage of the weakness in cognition in many among us. There are many lessons to learn. Looking at people through the cognitive fitness prism can help.

Okay, so it's clear that to be a great leader you require a strong executive function, but what if your executive function isn't working at its best? Can you do anything to improve it? Initially you can look out for signs that your executive function is in need of help. These signs and signals display themselves in different ways.

The absence of executive function can see you employing short-term tactics that are not part of a long-term plan. This is when you don't really know where you are going or how to move forward. Sometimes you simply decide to tread water and stay where you are as everywhere you look seems worse. Or you may let your company float with the tide, not going in any specific direction.

You must also watch out for giving imprecise and "fuzzy goals", with a "that will do" approach, rather than deeply thinking about your plans and strategies.

These faults can come about when you continually work to a strict routine and have got into bad habits. If you find yourself repeating the same mistakes over and over again, this will certainly lead to personal and organizational hopelessness and despair; even depression in the long-term. You will undergo much pain and so will your company.

Look out for these signs and symptoms. This is something which you can talk about to a coach. You can even discuss it with a work buddy, provided they are honest with you. Your coach or work buddy can help you see your symptoms and you can use the exercises in this book to regain or strengthen your executive function, by building up good habits.

There are many strong executive function leadership habits. One of the best is the ability to see and help improve cognitive strengths in others, particularly in those who report to you. Too often when managers see staff with potential, they tend to fear that they may become competitors for their own position. The manager may try to hold them back, even finding opportunities to criticize them. Managers who do this are not worthy leaders. The best leaders, like you, hold out their hands to others to pull them up, nurturing their strengths, and helping them get on. Managers like this show their leadership through the encouragement of others and in doing so can go for higher leadership roles.

The cognitive function of an organization is like that of a person; it can grow stronger and bring about success, or it can grow weaker, bringing about demise. Even if you have a strong personal executive function, by working in an organization that has poor executive function, you may be influenced and pulled down by it over time. You may have difficulty maintaining motivation and difficulty in planning and initiating activities; you could even fall into deep depression yourself. Steve Jobs, when he returned to Apple, and Angela Ahrendts when she joined Burberry, both found organizations that were in decline due to poor executive function among the previous leadership. It takes exceptional talent, resilience, and stamina to stand up to an entire organization and take it to a better and stronger level.

For one thing, how do you uphold motivation in a company that is heading over the cliff? How do you prevent it from imploding even more quickly than it is? It requires an outstanding and extraordinary person to tell people how it is, while at the same time telling them how, despite the rough road ahead, all the pain is worthwhile on the way to the promised land. People who can do this are rare, but with determination more of you can reach those heights.

THE SCIENCE BIT

Good executive function provides the ability to strategically plan, act on the plan, and to change strategy if necessary. Executive functions may be considered as "supervisory" cognitive processes because they involve higher level organization and execution of complex thoughts and behaviours.[61]

Executive function plays a key role in virtually all aspects of cognition[62] and thus has a modulatory role over your other key cognitive fitness domains. The normal state of your brain is to rely on a whole series of habitual processes that you automatically use in everyday life.[63] Executive Function is particularly important for novel tasks for which one of these habits is not readily available or has not yet been formulated. For example:

- Executive function allocates resources, including your ability to either devote attention to a task, or to allow your attention to be captured by someone else.
- Executive function inhibits distracting or irrelevant information when using your working memory. It acts as a constant compass to keep you going in the right direction.
- Executive function enables you to formulate strategies for the encoding and retrieval of memories. It is used by you to attach a new memory to an older one, further encoding memories, and assisting in the recovery of memories when required.

Thus, executive function directs all aspects of problem-solving, decision-making, and other goal-directed activities. It has the power to override your habitual, automatic, or set behaviour where it decides it would not be sufficient for optimal performance, thus having an impact on:[64]

- planning or decision making;
- error correction or troubleshooting;
- responses which are atypical or contain novel sequences of actions;
- dangerous or technically difficult challenges;
- overcoming strong habitual responses or resisting temptation.

Historical scientific case study
Phineas Gage[65]

Phineas Gage would never have made the history books were it not for a horrific accident that occurred while he was working on building a railway. Like other historical examples that have been captured, his story allows us insight into the workings of the brain and, in doing so, uncovers some of the mysteries surrounding cognition.

The term executive function originally emerged from the concept of "frontal lobe syndrome" that also emphasized personality changes following anterior brain damage. Phineas Gage is perhaps the most famous case of having survived severe brain damage, and is the first case to suggest a relationship between personality and the function of the front of the brain.

Gage was the foreman of a railway construction crew cutting a railroad bed in Vermont. In September 1848, a charge that he had set accidentally exploded, propelling his tamping iron through his left cheek and out through the top of his head, landing several yards behind him. Even though most of the front part of the left side of his brain was destroyed, he survived.

Gage was successfully treated by Dr John Martyn Harlow and some months after the accident he was well enough to return to work. However, it's said that Gage was a totally changed man and the contractors would not reinstate him. Before the accident, he had been a capable and efficient foreman, with a well-balanced mind and shrewd business sense. After the treatment Dr Harlow said that Gage was fitful, irreverent, and showed little deference for his fellows. He was also impatient and obstinate, yet capricious and vacillating, devising many plans that were changed as soon as they were arranged. His friends said he was "No longer Gage".

Historical scientific case study
Ruth Penfield (RP)[66]

Ruth Penfield is the sad historical story about the sister of a neurosurgeon who tried valiantly to give his sister a normal life. Thankfully, the neurosurgeon included his sister in a series of case studies that have allowed a greater understanding of executive function.

The Canadian neurosurgeon, Dr Wilder Penfield, published case studies describing the psychological effects of frontal lobe surgery. His studies helped to make significant advances in the link between the brain and behaviour, and he is known for the discovery of a surgical treatment for epilepsy.

The operation to save his sister's life provides insight on the link between the frontal lobes and psychological function. Penfield's sister, RP, had suffered splitting headaches since an early age and, at the age of 20, experienced a Jacksonian seizure (a form of epilepsy that can involve alterations in movement). Several years later, she suffered a succession of seizures, which became increasingly frequent until she was diagnosed with a brain tumour. Penfield undertook the surgery, opting to remove almost the entire right frontal lobe.

Following a successful operation, there was no real change in her personality, but she displayed a profound difficulty in performing everyday household tasks (i.e. difficulties with planning and organization). Thus, she was confused by the simple task of preparing a meal. She was unable to plan complex tasks and to maintain the necessary steps in mind, leaving certain dishes unfinished and forgetting to begin other tasks at the appropriate time. After two years, her symptoms returned; the tumour had regrown and was successfully removed, but she died shortly after.

These two scientific case studies illustrate acute and severe changes to executive function that changed the behaviour of both subjects. The changes in behaviour came about due to the removal of large sections of their cortex. It is more often the case that similar changes will occur in people over a much longer period of time due to chronic but more subtle changes to cognitive fitness.

SHORT-TERM CHANGES CAN IMPACT EXECUTIVE FUNCTION

Even relatively short duration changes can affect your executive function. A very smart and intelligent college professor moved jobs and was working at a more challenging university, which was in the doldrums. The professor was certainly up for the challenge, but the new university was mired in the past and was known, like many academic institutions, to take years to change.

She had her work cut out in the first year, simply putting out the fires to all the objections being raised against why there couldn't possibly be any change in the college. It was at the end of this initial period that she measured her cognitive fitness and found her executive function was the lowest scoring of her five cognitive domains, whilst her processing speed was her best. Previously she had believed that her executive function was her strongest cognitive domain, but a year at the new university had eroded it. In its place the constant fire-fighting had enhanced her processing speed.

She used this new insight and delegated as much of the fire-fighting as she could to others. She found the time to give space and rekindle her executive function so that her vision for the university could come about and not be washed away in the daily workload.

You can see a change in your cognitive function when you experience significant changes in your life, like the college professor above. Moving jobs, getting married or divorced, a new house, having a baby; these and many other changes are significant life changes that can cause stress and bring about major shifts in your cognitive function. Stressful change is likely to be detrimental to your cognition and it's important to look out for the effect of these changes.

Moving to an institution that is unwilling to change can cause you to become depressed both in your energy and your thoughts. You have to be exceptionally cognitively fit to overcome the inflexibleness of the new culture.

ASSESSMENT OF EXECUTIVE FUNCTION
This is a manual exercise to quantify executive function.

Read the questions below and give yourself a score out of 25 for each answer.

1) **Planning and organizing:**

   a. When was the last time the company plan was considered, really looked at in depth? Do you simply consider the same old metrics, or do you make sure you leave no stone unturned? If not involved in the company plan, what about the planning within your own role?

   b. How often do you consider reorganizations of people and processes? Do you relate these to changes in the environment? Have you noticed any new competitors? How disruptive might they be? Do you consider them a flash in the pan, or might their disruptive influence last longer than you think?

c. Do you allow time for these activities, or do you think of them as luxuries? Is there time for planning? Do you take all of your holidays? Do you have time just to sit and think? Do you plan with likeminded people? Do you allow unorthodox people and non-traditional thinking into your work-life?

Score yourself out of 25 for planning and organizing. / 25

2) **Creativity and thinking out of the box:**

a. Do you get probed for new ideas, even in areas where you have no experience?
b. Do people find that you sometimes have outlandish, creative ideas, even if they like them?
c. Do you see competition from new quarters and do you see new opportunities beyond the obvious? Do you look to disrupt or do you prefer to leave alone?
d. Do you give your people the chance to be creative, too? Do you really let them take risks?

Score yourself out of 25 for creativity. / 25

3) **Undertaking new tasks:**

a. Do you relish undertaking new tasks? Do you reject the easy to do, but take on the distracting, challenging activities?
b. Do you crave challenges, constantly looking for new ways to do things better? Do you take the

opportunity to work in your communities where you are seen as an equal amongst other volunteers, giving you the chance to look at life from a new perspective?

c. Do you give yourself time to consider new applications and uses of your products and services?

d. Do you force yourself to do something entirely new every day or every week or every month?

Score yourself out of 25 for new tasks. / 25

4) **Thinking about the implications of actions:**

a. Do you always give yourself consideration time before sending off a potentially contentious email or work direction?

b. Do you ever stop before you say the first words that come to your mind? Do you often interrupt others before they have a chance to finish?

c. Are you intuitive – able to see what's about to happen? Do you think it's simply luck that you are good at predicting the future, or is it something you have to work at?

d. Do you get the best from your people because they respect you? Or do you get the best out of people because they fear you? What do you think works best; respect or fear? Which do you instil and how can you do more to bring about respect?

Score yourself out of 25 for intuition. / 25

_____

Add your scores for a total out of 100. / 100

Get a sanity check on the assessments above from colleagues, family, and friends, or a business coach or mentor. This is your executive function score and the first exercise to building a better you.

Later on in Chapter Three you can bring these together with other results to give a more complete picture.

REMEMBER

Executive function is strategic or forward-looking thinking, and covers the overall procedures that regulate, control, and manage most of the other cognitive processes.

Executive function allows you to plan, organize, and complete tasks while helping you to anticipate the implications of your actions before you make them.

By utilizing multiple thought processes, executive function allows you to manage your emotions and monitor your thoughts, so that you can work more efficiently and effectively.

This cognitive domain allows you to consider and appreciate "change" in your work practices. Many work behaviours requiring change are directly related to your planning and strategy capacity. Improved planning and strategy enables you to make more effective work plans, keep track of several tasks, engage in and lead group discussions, and evaluate and encourage ideas. It allows you to positively challenge your own thinking, that of team members, and of other leaders, so that you appreciate and become a catalyst for positive change.

You may find dealing with new tasks at work challenging but sufficiently rewarding. With further training you can continue to plan new tasks outside of your daily routine and be confident in accomplishing them with good effectiveness, possibly reducing stress and frustration.

Some examples of using executive function in the workplace include:

- planning and organizing tasks that may be new to you;
- prioritizing work;
- managing time with challenging demands;
- moving easily from one task to another and meeting deadlines;
- managing your emotions in stressful situations;
- planning future decisions, solving problems, and achieving goals;
- completing technically difficult tasks.

If your executive function needs improvement, you could be experiencing difficulties in the following:

- planning tasks and organizing resources;
- correcting mistakes or troubleshooting;
- working out how to complete new tasks or sequences;
- changing your normal ways of doing things with changes in rules or new processes;
- meeting multiple deadlines;
- managing your emotions in stressful situations;
- working without a clear structure.

EXECUTIVE FUNCTION CASE STUDIES
Case study
Angela Ahrendts – Burberry

Angela Ahrendts, an American businesswoman, is a senior vice president at Apple Inc., which she joined in 2014. Prior to that, she was the CEO of Burberry from 2006 to 2014. Ahrendts was hired by Apple for her "leadership". They paid her $73.4 million in cash and stocks in her first year because she had proven what great executive function she had at Burberry.

Angel Ahrendts was the former chief executive officer of Burberry. Ahrendts was from the midwest of America. What on earth was she expected to bring to this iconic British company? She brought amazing strength in executive function. She took a traditional British brand that was failing and transformed it into a digitally-savvy, international, successful powerhouse.

Ahrendts saw a brand that was dying and weak in a luxury market where the competition leaders were outselling Burberry ten to one. She focused on centralizing design behind the best of her designers. She insisted the franchised group had to follow the centre and make the brand strong and immediately recognizable again.

Every one of the leaders of the franchises had their own idea as to what was needed to make Burberry successful again. Ahrendts led them all in the same direction and convinced them that she had the right strategy for the organization.

The strength of her executive function outshone all others and took them through to a period of outstanding growth.

Case study

Peter Thomson – Peter Thomson International

Peter Thomson is one of the UK's leading strategists on business and personal growth. Peter has honed his executive function at the "coal face" of building and growing businesses and enterprises. He's taken some knocks, but has never been floored. He takes triumph and disappointment in the same stride, using experience from both to go on to greater things.

He reminds me of the great golfers who make things look easy, but you know that behind the scenes, he practises every bit of his delivery and ensures every step of every process is thoroughly thought through. He may take risks, but they are highly calculated risks, based on his experience, knowledge, and supreme executive function.

Peter started business in 1972 and built three successful companies, selling the last to a public company. This enabled him to retire at the age of 42... only he didn't. He has gone on to share his approach and his secrets with thousands of others who are wishing to emulate his achievements. His secret is based on enabling his clients to share their authentic messages with more people than they may ever reach on a one-to-one basis. This takes their businesses to greater heights than they may have imagined.

Peter has grown his expertise in the other cognitive domains, beyond the use of his skills in planning, organization, and creativity. He is able to use and share his wisdom, enabling himself and others to quickly climb the steepest of learning curves. He can focus his attention, while replying to questions with speed and accuracy. Like the best of batsmen at the crease, he appears to have all the time in the world to play even the most difficult of deliveries.

He has immense knowledge, but knows his limitations and leads a team with the best brains in social and content media, product development, design, and marketing. He forms an immediate bond with those he is working with using an uncanny memory of events, places, and people. He has an amazing gift of being able to hold an audience in the palm of his hand, while making them feel that he also has their individual, best interest at heart.

His team shares his passion of sharing their gifts and enabling their clients to achieve amazing things. He continues to propel his own business at such a pace, ensuring it captures new methods and new technical advances in product production and new innovated ways of marketing, so that it's always cutting edge. However, he ensures his business remains "family friendly", positive, generous, and market leading – and most of all, fun!! That is, "fun" with a serious intent.

Peter wasn't necessarily born with a great executive function. He built companies and sold them and learned by experience how to help others.

Case study
Julie Meyer – Ariadne Capital

Julie Meyer MBE is an American author, businesswoman, and entrepreneur. She is the CEO and founder of the London-based venture capital firm Ariadne Capital. Meyer is on a mission to enable small and large corporations to work with one another. She has the ability to merge the creativity and insights born out of a small company and link them with a larger organization, ready and willing to work with them, not exploit them. Her executive function enables her to see partnerships that others would overlook.

From following Meyer, you can tell she is cognitively strong and very resilient. She builds her leadership on the premise that to be a good leader, you must make sure you also look after yourself. This isn't being selfish; far from it. Only the healthiest of leaders can help others be their best.

Meyer drives herself; she will not let up. Living at the edge has its moments and there are times when Meyer has come unstuck and courted controversy. She is human, after all.

Her strength comes from several sources. Unlike most entrepreneurs of her generation, Meyer has a solid academic base including an MBA from INSEAD graduate business school. She also has depth in her experience as an entrepreneur, where she hasn't just climbed the mountain once, but several times. Furthermore, strength also comes from the relationship with her family and, particularly, her father. Together, these form the foundations of her physical, psychological, and spiritual leadership core, the basis of her executive function.

She highlighted the importance of fathers to women in

business when she founded the non-profit "Dads and Daughters Foundation". Her point is women can be as successful as men, and that many successful men are the fathers of daughters. By supporting daughters through this organization and sharing their experiences, fathers can enable their daughters to accelerate up the learning curve. They can impart confidence to their daughters so they can compete more fairly in an unequal world with men.

Meyer founded Ariadne Capital in 2000 and has positioned the company to support high tech entrepreneurs who want to make a difference to the world.

EntrepreneurCountry was founded as a subsidiary of Ariadne. This provides an environment where large, traditional enterprise businesses connect with entrepreneurs, offering financial and other support. Meyer calls it the, "Goliaths helping the Davids by using 'Ecosystem Economics'". All this and not a slingshot in sight.

Meyer is obviously on a mission, beyond mere business and commerce. She says, "Innovation for me is the search for excellence, and the ongoing quest for improving the way you live." One wonders where her executive function will take her next?

Case study
Richard Branson – Virgin

Sir Richard Branson is a British businessman, investor, and philanthropist. His Virgin Group comprises more than 400 companies. Branson showed an entrepreneurial spirit at the age of 16 years, setting up a student magazine. From this early age he also exhibited his talented executive function.

Virgin was launched as a brand that was different from everything around it. Branson used his executive function to see what other companies were not doing and filled the gap. His vision and creativity didn't necessarily invent new products, but redefined them for an audience fed up with the same old stuff. He did this with meticulous planning. He looks as if he was born with a robust executive function.

Branson saw that the market was changing, with a sufficient number of people wanting more excitement from the brands they were willing to purchase. His products have never been too different from the competition, be they music, aeroplane seats, or financial services. However, in each case these relatively standard products were brought to market with flourish and excitement. Finance and flying were sexy and electrifying again; air travel captured some of the excitement from the pioneering days, without any of the anxiety; financial services were something the young at heart now cared about; music and recording were passionate on a grand scale.

He managed to build a brand that crossed frontiers and excited the young and old alike. He continues to do so. He lives the Virgin brand as much as leading it. This living took him to circumnavigate the world in a hot air balloon (and almost dying in the process), as well as to establish a company to make space travel available to mere mortals.

WORKING MEMORY – THE HERO

INTRODUCTION

Working memory is the "workspace" in your mind. This is where you store relevant information that you can return to during the course of a mental comprehension or arithmetic activity. It is your ability to make decisions and solve problems.

Working memory allows you to comprehend complex reports, presentations, and financial accounts. A strong working memory is able to hold information, mentally manipulate it over a short time period, and to undertake continuous iterations of that process until you come to a conclusion or a decision with which you are comfortable.

Someone with a strong working memory builds trust. They are the people who think before they speak, but when they do it is worth listening to. They may not appear as slick as the person who can give an immediate answer to a question, but then again, people with an immediate answer to everything often only open their mouths to change feet.

A working memory that functions well enables you to be the "Hero", the person your people come to when there is a difficult or demanding question to answer or problem to solve.

In these cases people are not looking for a quick fix, but for a broad and deep assessment of all aspects of the challenge being presented. They know they can trust you in that regard.

A strong working memory is critical for great management. Great leaders are strong in both executive function and working memory.

THE ROLE OF WORKING MEMORY IN LEADERSHIP AND MANAGEMENT

Your ability to manipulate working memory involves the short-term storage of information. It is critical for your reasoning and comprehension and allows you to make the right decisions and solve problems. You do this by holding vital pieces of information in your short-term memory and manipulating them with additional information and data held in your cortex. You bring the parts together to come to a conclusion or decision. Once the initial round is completed, your mind may go through several iterations of the same problem, with slight changes in direction, perspective, or weighting until you are fully satisfied with the solution. Each turn of the brain takes seconds, but depending on the complexity and amount of data, the entire process could go on for some time.

An example of its use is the task of repeating a list of items in a different order, like when you are compiling a "to do" list, taking into consideration the priority of each item on the list.

Working memory is a strong management domain and it is relevant to everything that requires a calculation or decision-solving process. It is seen in people like Anne Mulcahy of Xerox, Paul Allen the Co-founder of Microsoft, J Patrick Doyle of Domino's Pizza and Harriet Green of Thomas Cook.

When it's at its best, your working memory makes you the Hero, the problem solver in your organization, great at decision making and an expert problem solver. You are involved in critical elements of forecasting and goal setting. You actively "think before you speak". You are the person your company needs in any complex crises.

Working memory is an extension of the concept of short-term memory. It is used to perform cognitive processes on the items that you temporarily store. Working memory is involved in the processes that require reasoning such as reading, writing, and numeracy. Thus, it is important and a critical managerial skill in support of leadership. Great leaders without a good working memory have to rely on people who have a great working memory to manage their leadership. Thus when running for President of the US, a leader may rely on an Agent with great working memory.

Those of you who have great working memory use it when attending meetings where an action is required. In the meeting you take in the data presented and manipulate it by comparing and contrasting it with other facts and information in real time, incorporating knowledge and data from others in the meeting as required. This enables you to make good decisions by triangulating all the possibilities, computing all the opportunities across all paradigms, rather than relying on a single or few sources.

Equally in meetings, it enables you to formulate questions, to clarify points made, to push the agenda along, and to create actions for others. Left to your devices, you manage meetings successfully and resourcefully.

Working memory is used when analysing and calculating financial data, such as share prices, exchange rate movements, profit margins, and cash flow. It enables you to see beyond the numbers and understand what they mean in a broader sense. Whether you work in finance or not, you are able to interpret financial and other data and see the trends, the covariates, and causations, the immediate and long-term consequences for your company.

You also use your working memory when negotiating the sale or purchase of a product or service, the sale of a company, or when negotiating staff salaries. It is also used when attempting to solve an intractable problem in a process. You utilize it for the deep, obstinate problems that others recoil from.

Working memory allows you to write and understand complex and intricate reports, to interpret these reports so that others understand them. When writing, you ensure that you break down the parts of a recommendation or action so that you don't lose people in the process. You may be able to quickly go from "A to Z", but you are cognisant that others require that you show them all the working through "B, C, D," etc.

What should you watch for when your working memory is not at its best?

The absence of working memory causes "cognitive paralysis", an inability for you to make decisions. Even simple decisions or problems that at one time you would stroll through, can become difficult. This may not be a sudden manifestation, but something that creeps up on you over a period of time. This makes it more difficult for you to notice weakness occurring. You may find yourself missing important facts. Rather than thinking comprehensively about a problem, you fall back on compartmentalized, simplistic, or overactive thinking, coming up with a solution before assessing all the facts.

In these circumstances you may become more socially isolated and withdraw from situations where decisions have to be made, where problems are solved. You avoid decision making meetings at work and the types of social get-togethers with friends where you'd normally look at all the "world's problems" together.

Alternatively, you may find yourself getting uncharacteristically angry and aggressive. You discover yourself blaming others and finding fault in their work for your inability to make a decision. Later we see how this aggression can turn to bullying, something all too common in the workplace.

Often, the cognitive paralysis that impairs your working memory is brought about by stress. Just as depression can undermine executive function, stress eats at your working memory, taking away your ability to be the Hero. Whatever the original cause of your stress, it impedes your working memory, disabling you from holding vital information in your short-term memory as you consider other data. This form of stress is cruel, because unchecked, it spirals out of control leading to disorder and breakdown. Unable to think clearly, you are easily confused. Where previously you'd spend hours or days on a project, now more often than not you cannot see a work project to the end. You have further decreased resilience to stress causing cognitive pain, which results in the unwanted behaviours of social withdrawal or aggression.

These are symptoms associated with ageing. Stress brings on the earlier signs of ageing and the symptoms of incapacity associated with it. However, you can combat stress, reduce its effects and, in doing so, diminish the impact of ageing within the workplace.

You have the means to measure your cognition and understand the strengths and weaknesses associated with your cognitive fitness. This can be scary, but it is important for your business that you can take control of this. Think of the fascinating insights this can give you – how it will change your management and leadership thinking for the better.

THE SCIENCE BIT

In over 200 years of psychological research, the concept of a "unitary short-term memory store" has been developed into that of a concept of a "multicomponent working memory system". Working memory provides a crucial interface between perception, attention, memory, and action. These were collectively termed the "central executive."[67] In the multicomponent models of working memory, as described by Baddeley, the core cognitive processes are summarized in a single model built around the concept of working memory, but which effectively comprises other cognitive domains and includes interactions with them. In this way, working memory is different to executive function. Working memory is represented as a system involving different cognitive processes, whereas executive function is the set of control processes carried out by the central executive.

In a narrow sense the "slave systems" are what we generally think about when we talk about working memory. The advantage of the multicomponent models is to underline how much executive function and working memory are related (not similar), all the way to constitute a unitary system.

The central executive acts as a supervisory system and controls the flow of information from and to the brain systems that feed into it, otherwise known as the "slave systems". It is responsible for the visuospatial sketch pad, which manipulates visual images and spatial information. It controls the phonological loop, which stores and rehearses speech-based information and is necessary for acquiring the vocabulary of a person's native language or a second-language, where this occurs. It controls the episodic buffer, which links information across domains to form integrated units of visual, spatial, and verbal information in chronological order, such as the memory of a story when used to illustrate how a decision was made or a problem solved. It is also thought to be linked to long-term memory.

In everyday life, for example, your phonological loop is activated when you repeat a phone number in your head or read or write, while the visuospatial sketch pad manipulates mental images of objects. Your central processor acts to select, initiate, and halt the routines of its slave systems when it decides it has sufficient information or when it requires further data on which to deliberate. This is when you delve deep into the memory to recall a piece of information (a date, a share price, an event) that you require as part of a decision making process. Sometimes you need the exact piece of information, whereas at other times a rough estimate is all that is required. Time and resources are taken into account by your working memory when doing this.

Neuroimaging studies suggest that the dorsolateral prefrontal cortex (DLPFC), which is involved in executive function, plays a role in the manipulation and updating of information in your working memory; the left prefrontal cortex is involved more in verbal tasks and the right prefrontal cortex involved in visuospatial tasks.[68]

Comparing working memory with executive function, it is clear that executive function "leads". This is because it gives the ultimate direction, sets the scene and parameters, whereas working memory acts more as a "manager" in ensuring that all the things that need to be done occur. Working memory brings leadership to life through effective management. You can be a greater leader if you also have a robust working memory, or if you can rely on someone on your team to supply these skills. Think of how many leaders have a confidant working on their behalf behind the scenes. When running for President of the United States, the most important appointment made isn't that of Vice President, it is that of his or her Election Agent, the person who manages their election to power and works behind the scenes to ensure everything gets done.

WORKING MEMORY IN CONTEXT

A characteristic of working memory is its capacity to handle information; how much and for how long can your short-term memory hold information. Your working memory control system tracks complex or convoluted problems. The characteristics of working memory's capacity were studied using functional magnetic resonance imaging (fMRI) in neurologically normal, healthy individuals.[69]

Subjects were asked to complete a working memory test that involved an increase in cognitive load, and ultimately led to a decrease in performance. The tasks (a variation of the n-back test[70]) required updating of information in the memory while responding to previously seen stimuli.

Areas within the DLPFC showed a specific neuro-physiological response as the cognitive load was increased and as working memory was put under greater challenge. With less challenging working memory loads, there was a tight correlation between performance and activation of the DLPFC, while at higher levels of challenge, this relationship fell apart.

The data suggest that there is a reduction of efficiency when loading working memory's capacity is approached, when it reaches the toughest level at which it is able to function effectively. Once the DLPFC reaches full capacity, brain areas outside of the DLPFC are recruited. These areas include the premotor cortex, parietal cortex, and thalamus. However, they also show capacity-constrained responsiveness. Thus, beyond normal capacity of the DLPFC there are variable limitations when the mind works across a wider network. This intuitively makes sense.

The implications for this are fundamental. Most of you know that you can run several projects at the same time by switching your mental resources across them. It's not so much that you multi-task, but that when switching between tasks you are capable of keeping sufficient knowledge of previous projects in your short-term memory. You can then return to the other projects and pick up where you left off without having to start from scratch. Unfortunately, for some it's not that you can't multitask, but that even to do one task properly is difficult because your working memory has limited capacity.

The important point is that everyone's working memory capacity can become overloaded. At this point of overload you can very easily drop all the projects for which you are responsible. Imagine the stress of having to pick up multiple projects from scratch at the same time because your capacity became overloaded?

All companies have employees who can cope with more projects than most, are good at their jobs, are reliable, and always say, "Yes", with a smile. These employees are worth their weight in gold. But these individuals can be highly susceptible to cognitive exhaustion. In particular, in times of austerity this is a common situation with more work being spread over fewer and fewer people. Many hard working employees use their strong working memory to run numerous projects, but rely on the executive function and good leadership of others to ensure they don't run themselves ragged and burn out.

These individuals can end up spending a substantial and costly time being on sick leave; with the right support they could continue to work efficiently in a more manageable and longer term way without burn out.

WORKING MEMORY AS YOU AGE

Functional neuroimaging studies suggest that different brain areas are activated differently in young and old adults, suggesting that the young and old perform working memory tasks differently,[71] including the recruitment of different areas of the brain, with varying control, as discussed above.

Three theories of cognitive ageing have been suggested in the context of working memory deficits.[72] The first is a reduction of all resources and this reflects a reduction in mental energy. Thus, tasks demanding high attention could show impairments as you get older, whereas those requiring little or no attention, or are habitually automatic, remain functional. Your working memory tasks are those requiring divided attention and manipulation and, therefore, they are more likely to put a strain on your limited resources as you get older.

The second theory of ageing relates to reduced speed of information processing. This is evidenced by the fact that older people are generally slower at information processing, and that the slowing of fundamental cognitive processes may have negative effects on more complex tasks.

Thirdly, you may see a failure of inhibitory control. The inability to inhibit irrelevant information in working memory may reduce its capacity and prevent access to relevant information. For example, age deficits could result in the failure to delete information previously learned from working memory, thus reducing the "working space" for new stimuli.

Working memory is a multidimensional cognitive construct that is thought to be involved in age-related deficits in a variety of cognitive tasks.[73] Older adults can show deficits in tasks that involve working memory, such as active manipulation, reorganization, or integration of data or information. Such deficits may have substantial impact on tasks that involve decision-making, problem-solving, and the planning of goal-directed behaviours. High functioning individuals who tend to work their cognition to full capacity may quickly notice when changes occur, whereas those less keen may be relatively unaware of a decline. Thus, it is common to see people with superior cognition have steeper falls in their cognition that occur later in life when compared to individuals with average cognition.

Most of the theories of cognitive ageing appear to implicate working memory.[74] In the working memory model of Professor Alan Baddeley, manipulation of information in short-term memory was proposed to be controlled by the central executive, and deficits in working memory were thought to be deficits in executive control. More recently, the workings of the central executive have been attributed to executive function, using cognitive functions above and beyond those associated with working memory. However, both cognitive domains are critical and both can fail with age.

ASSESSMENT OF WORKING MEMORY

This is a manual exercise to quantify your working memory.

1) Decision making:

   a. How good are you at making decisions?

   b. Are you looked on by others to make decisions in meetings and at times of crisis?

   c. Are you as good with numbers as you are with comprehension?

Score yourself out of 25 for decision making. / 25

2) Problem solving:

   a. Do you get asked to solve problems and are you called on when others have failed at solving problems?

   b. Do you have a good grasp of how long it will take to solve problems, or do you often underestimate or overestimate the time taken?

   c. Are you happy to ask others to wait until you are comfortable you have solved a problem?

   d. Do you break the solution down to help others see how you processed it?

Score yourself out of 25 for problem solving. /25

3) Understanding financial and numerical data:

   a. Are you good with balance sheets, profit and loss statements, cash flows, etc?

   b. Can you spot the important trends, correlates, and causations in a spreadsheet?

   c. Can you spot the difference between a cost and an investment for your business?

   d. Do you constantly have the "critical numbers" for your business in your head?

Score yourself out of 25 for financial data.   / 25

4) Negotiating:

   a. Do you naturally drive a good bargain? Do you enjoy the thrill of negotiating?

   b. Do you find yourself several steps ahead of others in deals, often having to fill in the details, even for those you are dealing with?

   c. Do you know when to turn away, when to stop investing, when to divest?

Score yourself out of 25 for negotiating.   / 25

Add your scores for a total out of 100.   / 100

Get a sanity check on your assessments above from your colleagues, family, and friends, or business coach/mentor if you have one. This is your working memory score and the second of the exercises to building a better you.

Later you can bring these together with your other results to give you a complete picture of your cognitive fitness.

CASE STUDIES
Case study
How poor working memory can create bullies.

Sally was a high flying senior executive. For years her company relied on her strong working memory to make decisions and solve deep problems. She was her company's hero. Then one day her sounding-board, Joe, left ship. Sally lost a mentor and also had all of his staff reporting to her as well.

For a while, Sally coped, but it soon began to get harder and more difficult for her to make decisions. The stress of more staff reporting to Sally didn't help and even simple decisions became challenging. Her people were no longer holding her in the highest esteem. She was "cognitively paralysed". The tipping point was when she erupted and threw insults at a team member during a meeting whilst trying to make a spur-of-the-moment decision. From that point she stopped managing and leading and, instead, bullied colleagues whenever she was in a tight spot.

Underneath it all, Sally hated the person she had become, but she got the chance to meet with Joe. He realized that she was clearly suffering, and advised her that she needed a new mentor, that she needed to delegate more and, importantly, to reduce her stress levels.

Sally got herself a mentor to replace Joe. She delegated more of her decision making, and worked with her PA to ensure that every meeting she attended was crucial. Sally stopped using electronic devices after 8pm every evening and not at all on Sundays. She ensured she got more sleep and reduced her stress. She also had her cognitive fitness assessed. The results were very telling. Her working memory was shot to pieces.

Now that the cause of her problem had been identified, Sally was able to do something positive about it. She undertook personalized training that exercised all five of her core cognitive domains, but worked more intensively on her working memory.

In time she again became the Hero within her company and she, her people, and her company were all the better for it.

Not all bullies are born that way. The state of your cognitive function determines your behaviour, good and bad. When your cognitive fitness fails, you often resort to coping mechanisms. In Sally's case it was bullying, as a result of her working memory failing. People like Sally with the same working memory problem, may become socially withdrawn instead. They avoid the spotlight, the meetings, and places where decisions are made. They no longer press themselves forward for extra responsibilities. They become a shadow of their former selves. They, too, are in pain and need help.

Case study
Anne Mulcahy – Xerox

Anne Mulcahy was the chairperson and CEO of Xerox Corporation. In turning around Xerox, Mulcahy endured a level of pressure that few corporate bosses ever face. Xerox were fortunate that in Mulcahy they had the best possible leader at that time and place with a supreme working memory to solve their problems.

The biggest crisis that Anne faced was when she was advised to file Xerox for bankruptcy. She didn't agree with her advisors; instead, she worked on finding a solution to the acute crisis, while at the same time looking for a longer term solution to ensure that Xerox became a high-tech player and didn't fall into this problem again.

She set up working meetings within the corporation and listened to her staff, making them believe that together they had the cognitive power to overcome the problems. Mulcahy met the top 100 Xerox executives personally. She delegated her workload with them, showing trust in their abilities. She created a sense of mutual trust and respect, and took into consideration all that was said and used their combined experience to make an effective choice. She clearly showed that it is when your business is struggling that you have to give everyone a sense of direction and resolution. In doing this Mulcahy expected full support from her entire workforce.

Through this process she saw Xerox in a new perspective and was able to understand the various defects that existed throughout the organization. She enhanced her teams' management skills and enabled them to see beyond the conventional data and fixed financial analysis.

This improved everyone's decision making and enabled her people at Xerox to take responsibility for their actions, set clear goals, and build a unifying roadmap to determine the company's direction. Along the way she was honest and transparent to the board, the shareholders, customers, and, most importantly, her employees.

The combined action of her team meant they could challenge the status quo and make the tough and difficult calls for the company's survival and ultimate success.

She was the ultimate hero who was able to give her best, when her company needed it most.

Anne Mulcahy showed that she had developed a robust and fully functional working memory. She initially used this to determine that the problems required more than her working memory alone could cope with. She recruited the best working memories from among her top employees and delegated sections of the problems to them, while maintaining excellent communication. Here is an example of someone using all her personal problem solving resources to utilize all her company's problem solving resources to reach the right solution.

Case study

Paul Allen – Cofounder of Microsoft

Bill Gates may have been the leader of Microsoft, but he relied on Paul Allen to provide management for Microsoft. In 1983, Allen resigned from Microsoft, having been diagnosed with Hodgkin's disease (Hodgkin's disease is a type of blood cancer that starts in the lymphatic system). He had seen his management of Microsoft make him a billionaire. Following several months of radiation treatment, he began to concentrate on other projects in sport, science, and philanthropy. He wasn't finished yet.

According to reports, Allen and Gates didn't get on well. Gates would focus on a single issue, while Allen was more of a generalist. In the early days, Microsoft needed both sets of skills to survive. In doing so it thrived and became very successful. Allen was needed to manage all the moving parts of the fast growing and considerably large organization Microsoft became. Allen would take the single minded vision from Gates and place it in the bigger picture, ensuring it meshed completely within the organization, with employees and customers alike.

Allen consistently used his working memory to keep a series of projects on the go, to ensure the dream he and Gates had would become a reality. It is no surprise that suffering from Hodgkin's disease would have a negative impact on his capacity to do this. What isn't clear is for how long the cancer was impacting his cognitive fitness before his diagnosis? Regardless, Allen decided to resign from Microsoft and in hindsight this was probably a very good decision. He had helped to set up one of the world's greatest companies and he left it in good shape to grow and dominate its sector. Had he stayed, he may never have overcome the stress of his disease, his relationship with Gates would have declined even further, and the foundation of Microsoft may have crumbled.

It isn't always easy to walk away, but in doing so Allen allowed himself the opportunity to get involved with and lead many great projects. To do this requires guts and a sense of one's cognitive fitness.

Allen's decision making and problem solving were essential in the early years of Microsoft. Taking time out allowed him to recover from a serious disease and come back into new businesses strong. Anyone with a less than resilient working memory may have failed miserably.

Case study
J Patrick Doyle – Domino's

J Patrick Doyle runs Domino's by working closely with the representatives of independent Domino's Franchisee Association, which focuses on the self-interests of its franchised members. Doyle ensures they are involved in all major decisions made by the company. Doyle is breaking the mould, using the power of his working memory to provide solutions to difficult problems. Usually independent associations of franchises wouldn't get a look in on running the business to which they belong. Yet Doyle sites this as one of the reasons for the success of Domino's.

Doyle managed several of the divisions within Domino's before he became the CEO. He had a lot of different jobs at the company and he understood the perspectives of all the different groups that make up the company. He knew how to manage all the moving parts to run a very successful company.

Doyle depends on surrounding himself with the best people. In business, you should always try to hire and work with people that are smarter than you. If you are the smartest in the room, you are in the wrong room. Doyle is smart enough to know that if he surrounds himself with the best of Domino's employees, as well as the best people from their franchisees, that he has the makings of an amazing team.

He takes these people and finds out how to incentivize and motivate them, as well as how to build trust with them. He started by understanding Domino's customers, franchisees, employees, and, ultimately, its shareholders. He managed to create value for each group.

He makes trust part of his leadership. He is open and honest with all stakeholders, so that even when he makes a decision that they don't agree with, they at least understand his viewpoint and that he has listened to them.

Doyle does not go out with a new program or new initiative without having thoroughly thought out how it is going to affect everybody. This is where he uses his working memory to the forefront. He has a huge capacity to hold information and manipulate it, before making decisions where all believe they have been heard. When his working memory capacity has been exhausted, he knows where he can go to get additional cognitive resources.

Listening, taking note, and explaining are key management skills that make effective leaders.

Case study
Harriet Green – Thomas Cook

Harriet Green took over at Thomas Cook in 2012, when it was the UK's least admired company. Few analysts thought it would survive and fewer still would have bet on its shares increasing tenfold before Green's departure in 2014. Thomas Cook chairman Frank Meysman reckons Green "can do any transformation job". It takes someone with a gifted mind and problem solving skills to have those skills.

Green states that one of her favourite quotes is from the American writer, Maya Angelou, that, "People will forget what you did and said, but never how you made them feel."

It is said that Green made a lot of her colleagues "feel" in a complete state of anxiety, living in fear of her public humiliations, suggesting that her leadership style is aggressive and divisive. But, she is also hugely charismatic, with an abundance of energy and drive, and she captured among her employees a lot of people who just wanted to work for her.

Green worked tirelessly with incredible levels of energy for the success of Thomas Cook. Green stated that the energy came from when her father died of a brain tumour when she was only 14. It made her strong, giving her enormous capacity and resilience. You had to be tough to keep up with her, but if you did, you really enjoyed the ride. She made sure she packed a lot into and made the most of every day, almost as though every day was her last. This is what was needed by Thomas Cook in 2012.

Critics said she was the most complex of individuals. In previous careers she had worked in Britain, the USA and Asia and spoke with an accent based on all three continents. She was a fusion of all three cultures. For example, in order to run sales in China she learned to speak Mandarin.

Her plan for Thomas Cook was to install a ferocious cost-cutting plan to save £440m by axing 2,500 jobs and closing 400 high street branches. To devise such a plan is one thing, but to manage its execution was almost incredible.

Green is an exceptional manager, not only for coming up with the plan, or for implementing it so dramatically, but also for leaving the company once all of this had been achieved. The last of these was probably more to do with Frank Meysman and his board. Green may not have wanted to leave when she did, but it was probably for the best. Green has the cognitive fitness that

can be put to much better use elsewhere now that Thomas Cook is on a firm footing.

REMEMBER

Working memory is the ability to carry out calculations and solve linguistic problems, utilizing short-term memory to recall multiple pieces of information in quick succession. You often use calculation and problem solving functions with numeracy and literacy. Poor calculation and problem solving indicates problems such as dyslexia, dyscalculia, and autism spectrum disorder (ASD) in some people. Higher levels of calculation and problem solving enhances your ability to retrieve, manipulate, and use information. Enhanced working memory results in lower levels of stress and reduced anxiety giving you even greater consistency of fault-free, decision making output. It gives you confidence to lead and manage projects. Improving your calculation and problem solving will help your decision making at work.

Working memory uses short-term storage of transitory information which can be manipulated including reasoning and comprehension. Some specific examples of using working memory in the workplace include:

- remembering and following verbal or written instructions accurately;
- performing mental arithmetic;
- accessing and manipulating short-term information for certain tasks;
- keeping a point in mind in a meeting when someone else is talking;
- using information from various documents to formulate a new document.

If your working memory needs improvement, you could be experiencing the following:

- having to re-read documents and paragraphs to remember the content;
- difficulty doing even simple mental arithmetic;
- needing to write notes to remember tasks or points.

EPISODIC MEMORY – THE CURATOR

INTRODUCTION

There is no such thing as a bad experience, provided you learn from it, and get stronger as a result. To learn from experiences, you must be able to recall them. Episodic memory is your ability to recall events, people, and places in context to a relevant situation. It is what helps you accelerate up the "learning curve" and impart wisdom to others in your organization.

Episodic memory includes the ability to retain information in the short term and continue to process it through the long term. Thus, you use episodic memory to ensure that new learning experiences complement the overall retention of information into your long-term memory. You don't just learn from a single viewpoint, but new things are coded across a range of perspectives, so that a single memory can be used in a broad range of situations, making the most of your experience and the most of your wisdom.

A strong episodic memory builds the foundation for strong leadership because it is critical for understanding the importance of people and the values of the company.

Within organizations, episodic memory allows you to remember everyone by their name. You know something about everyone around you; their families, their hopes, and their struggles. You know the importance of people and you value them above all else. You thoroughly understand the values within your company. You hold yourself and others accountable to these values. You see your company with a sense of historical perspective that sees the trends, fashions, and styles that have helped to form it.

You are able to recall what previously worked and what didn't. You are the valued historian and connector within your organization and are seasoned enough to know your partners and competitors equally well.

You are critical to setting agendas for meetings, workshops, and team bonding. You are called on to help create solutions where your wisdom is required. You know the value of "team work" and are active in team development and in the retention of the best people. You are fiercely loyal to your company and what it stands for and will not let its values be diluted. You demand loyalty from others.

Within your organization you are the "Curator", your company's historian, connector, and custodian of its values.

THE ROLE OF EPISODIC MEMORY IN LEADERSHIP AND MANAGEMENT

Episodic memory, as seen in leaders like Mark Parker of Nike, Howard Schultz of Starbucks, Alan Sugar at Amstrad, and Warren Buffet at Berkshire Hathaway, is evidence of your wisdom. Their "wisdom" grew and became more evident as each of them continued "round the block" a few more times, building their experience reservoir as they went using their strong episodic memory to accumulate wisdom quicker than their peers.

Episodic memory is the ability to recall specific events, their outcomes, and the people and places associated with those events. With a strong episodic memory, you are the person who people turn to in order to recall what happened the last time the company faced a challenge or opportunity. You know who was there, what was said, and what action was taken. You know who was informed, how the shareholders were told, and how the share price was protected. You not only have the knowledge of one of these events, but you are able to combine the details of several similar events, building a critical mass of wisdom, a composite of memories and experiences.

Episodic memory is the wisdom you use to form the basis of your "corporate memory". You know the long-term values, processes, and practices within the company. You know why the company was formed, what goals and objectives it set out to reach. With this wisdom you are able to connect the people in your organization to be a part of the company's mission and vision. Through your articulation they can sense what your company is trying to achieve, why it was brought into life in the first place, even long after the founder(s) has gone. People want to learn from your experience to give them the edge and a better chance of success. You also seek out equally wise workers to assimilate their knowledge with your own, to build solid strength within the company.

Therefore, as a leader and manager with strong episodic memory you radiate confidence, creating confidence in your teams and colleagues.

Our episodic memory can begin to fail for a number of reasons. Brain diseases and disorders can affect your memory, preventing it from laying down new memories. For a time, you may be able to get by through using various coping mechanisms but eventually people will notice that you are not as up-to-date as you should be. They begin to question the relevance of your wisdom and lose confidence in your word.

Your own confidence is dampened through the inability to recall relevant information, facts, and data that was previously at your fingertips. You become afraid of talking in public in case your forgetfulness makes you look foolish. You begin to forget the names of people, especially newcomers in the organization. You eventually begin to repeat mistakes. You find yourself reliant on the skills of others to overcome even modest challenges. As a result, there is a huge inconsistency in your relationships; people no longer trust you and you don't trust them in return. Your status as the Curator wanes. You question the company values you once fought to maintain. You don't trust yourself and seek to retire.

People are living longer and, as a consequence, are working longer too. In the knowledge economy this ought to be a good thing. The longer a person has worked in a company the more time they have to develop their wisdom. These people can be invaluable in many ways because their episodic memory is based on the company's memory. This allows them to more fully understand the values of the company and to use those values to the greatest extent. They use their experiences most effectively when trying something new, because their wisdom allows them to start the new task further up the learning curve than someone new to the company. They are the source of knowledge within the company and those with the best episodic memory will never say, "We tried that and it will never work... don't bother." Instead, they are likely to say, "We tried that and with these changes it should now work... let's do it."

The trouble is these experienced people can also be among the most stressed. They are sought out and used by everyone in the company, seeking their wisdom, management, and leadership skills. In time they can be overused and when this occurs they are tempted to walk away.

Giving these people access to good cognitive fitness perks can help the company and help them. The measurement will identify where their cognitive function is underperforming and interventions can be put in place to improve their function, including cognitive fitness training.

With this support, work can become less stressful. The experienced staff will feel happier to stay longer. Retaining a key member of staff benefits the company hugely in economic terms. The employee is also better off, as their cognitive function benefits from working longer in a caring company, ensuring that their cognitive function will retain its resilience over a much longer period of time.

THE SCIENCE BIT

Episodic memory, also known as autobiographical memory, enables you to remember events that you personally experienced at a specific time and place.[75] Examples include the date of an event, the meal that you ate yesterday, and the name of a previous work colleague. It is a division of long-term memory.

The recollection of episodic memory is thought to be a reconstructive process rather than retrieval of a single whole record.[76]

Episodic memory focuses on past experiences, and enables mental time travel, i.e. the past, present, and future.[77] This allows you to remember previous experiences and to think about possible future ones.

Nerve components of episodic memory are made up of a widely distributed network of cerebral cortical and subcortical regions of the brain, which overlap with and extend beyond the networks also serving other memory systems.[78] Episodic memory tends to be more vulnerable than other memory systems to neuronal dysfunction, such as Alzheimer's disease.

Episodic memory is one of two assumed subdivisions of declarative memory.[79] The other is semantic memory, which enables you to acquire and retain factual knowledge about the world. Semantic memory is your knowledge base, which includes the memory of the meaning of words, as well as rules and concepts.

The two are intricately linked and episodic memory is thought to have evolved from semantic memory.[80] In fact the operation of episodic memory is dependent on semantic memory; it cannot function without relevant components of the latter. However, semantic memory is not dependent on episodic memory in its operations and can function without it. Thus, when you assess episodic memory, you are also ensuring that semantic memory is present.

Features or properties unique to episodic memory[81] include the memory of personal past happenings. It allows you to be self-centred, with a conscious awareness of yourself as an independent entity that is separate from everything else. It is also a conscious awareness of knowing when you are remembering and not perceiving or imagining an event, although lack of sleep and other impairments to cognitive fitness can impair this ability.

Episodic memory requires activation of a special kind of mental state called 'episodic retrieval mode'. It is relatively late in developing, in that children must gain experience and knowledge about their environment (through semantic memory) before they can be aware of their own past personal experiences.

Historical case study
Patient KC[82]

The case of KC, a Canadian patient with a memory disorder, is used to demonstrate the role of episodic memory. KC lacked episodic memory with respect to his entire past but retained his semantic memory. Semantic memory refers to general world knowledge that you have accumulated throughout your life; it is intertwined with experience and is dependent on culture.

In 1981, aged 30 years, KC suffered a traumatic brain injury in a motorcycle accident. KC experienced epileptic seizures and was unconscious. He had severe injury to his medial temporal lobes and almost complete bilateral loss of the hippocampus (situated within those lobes). The neurological damage hindered KC's ability to form new episodic memories (personal experiences), although his semantic memory (memory of meanings, understandings, concept-based

knowledge) was unimpaired. Thus, he was unable to remember emotional details of past events, such as his brother's death, but he could recall factual information that he learned before the accident, such as scientific and geographical facts. In conversation, KC used his semantic memory to retrieve facts, e.g. knowing that funerals were sad events, he used this knowledge to say his brother's funeral was a sad occasion. He was unable to imagine future events and would lose any memory of his current actions.

The accident also left KC with severe anterograde amnesia. This made it impossible for him to remember both new personal experiences and semantic information, along with temporal retrograde amnesia, which was somewhat an anomaly as his ability to recall events before the accident was dependent on when those events occurred.

Historical case study
Henry Molaison (HM)[83]

HM was an American patient with a memory disorder. He is used as a case study to demonstrate how particular areas of the brain may be linked to specific processes thought to occur in memory formation.

HM suffered from intractable epilepsy, attributed to a bicycle accident before he was 10 years old. His neurosurgeon localized the epilepsy to HM's left and right medial temporal lobes. Surgical resection of these brain regions (including hippocampi and amygdalae) was carried out in an attempt to cure the epilepsy. Following the surgery, HM suffered from severe anterograde amnesia. He could not commit new events to memory and was impaired in his ability to form new semantic knowledge. Once he stopped thinking about an experience, it would be lost forever. He also suffered moderate retrograde amnesia, whereby he could not remember most events shortly before surgery or up to 11 years before surgery. However, his working memory and procedural memory were intact; he was able to complete tasks that required recall from short-term memory and procedural memory but not long-term episodic memory.

EPISODIC MEMORY AS YOU AGE

As you age you are often in the mindset that your memories for distant events are better than your memories for recent events. However, it is likely that your older memories have become more semantic, whereby the basic information is retained while the detail is lost.[84]

The context or source of information appears to be more of a problem than the items being remembered. For example, you can remember seeing a multi-coloured bus, but have difficulty recalling where or when you saw it.[85] The encoding and retrieval of specific and peripheral details for past events may be particularly demanding on all resources, and there may not always be the necessary cues for retrieving the information.[86]

Age-related deficits in memory may be reduced for emotional events, such as the death of a loved one or a big win on the races.[87] This may form important variables in episodic memory, particularly in shared memories where the memory means more to one person than another (can you and your spouse recall what you were both wearing on the first occasion you met?).

There is evidence to suggest that age-related deficits in episodic memory may involve deficiencies in encoding, storage, or consolidation, and retrieval processes.[88] New information may be encoded with less elaboration, so the memory is less distinctive, and thus more difficult to retrieve. Alternatively, as you age you may attend to important information only, disregarding peripheral detail and context. Many common everyday memory lapses experienced by normal older adults, such as forgetting where they put their keys, may represent poor encoding. Storage or consolidation, is thought to include binding of event features into a composite memory trace. It is possible that the extent of binding is impaired in older adults. Additionally, evidence suggests that retrieval causes episodic memory problems in older people. Consciously controlled memory processes (i.e. recollection) appear to reduce with age, whereas automatically controlled memory processes (i.e. assessment of familiarity) are unaffected.[89]

Patients with Alzheimer's disease develop difficulty in retrieving individual words and general knowledge.[90] Thus, in tasks that require naming and describing objects, these patients show a loss characteristic of semantic memory. Initially, they lose the ability to discriminate between fine detail which, over time, extends to broader categories. For example, initially, they may distinguish a peach from an apple, but with further decline over time, it is all fruit.

MINDFULNESS AND LEADERSHIP

Many people today are looking at other ways to understand their thinking and have used techniques such as mindfulness. Mindfulness can be very powerful. Through meditation you bring your mind and senses to consider your current situation; you bring yourself to "now". Mindfulness brings your mind to the present and effectively says, "Here and now you are in a good situation, so stop worrying about the past and future." The technique works for millions of mindfulness practitioners, but be careful, there may be a price to pay for being in the "now".

Episodic memory is your ability to recall specific events and to recall the outcomes, the people, and places associated with those events. It is your wisdom and increases as you go round the block a few times, building your experience reservoir as you go. However, with a strong episodic memory you find you accumulate this wisdom quicker than your peers. You are the Curator of your company's values and knowledge.

With an effective executive function, you are the Pilot, the visionary and strategist within your organization. Executive function is your ability to plan and organize, to think out of the box, to attempt new tasks and be creative. It is also your ability to inhibit actions because you are able to consider the consequences of them on yourself and on others.

The price you may have to pay with mindfulness is that, by being in the present, you blunt your episodic memory and executive function. By blocking your rumination and catastrophizing, you may also block some of the wisdom and creativity in your cognitive skill set. Mindfulness may still bring you many benefits, and people who get those benefits should continue with it. But you should use it knowing there could be an opportunity cost. Where the positives outweigh the costs, mindfulness is powerful and many of you have benefited from it.

ASSESSMENT OF EPISODIC MEMORY

This is a manual exercise to quantify your episodic memory.

1) **Reciting vision and values:**

   a. Do you pay lip service to these or truly live them?
   b. Do you hold others to account when they forget the values?
   c. Do you burst with pride when you talk of your company's accomplishments?

   Score yourself out of 25 for company vision
   and values. / 25

2) **Knowing colleagues and staff:**

   a. Do you know as many as possible by name? When they started, their family circumstance, their drives, and ambitions?
   b. Do you make everyone in the company feel special? That their contribution is as great as anyone's in taking the company forward?
   c. Are you good at spotting the right hire for the right job in your company, using your experience to seek the A-list people you need?

   Score yourself out of 25 for how well you
   know your people. / 25

3) **Learning new tasks:**

   a. Do you have sufficient experiences to use them across a range of tasks, even if they are new to you?

b. Are you experienced enough to be able to share this gift with your team, exuding confidence to them?

c. Are you able to accelerate the uptake of new procedures and processes?

Score yourself out of 25 for shortening learning curves.   / 25

4) **Making the most of good experience and the best of bad experience:**

a. Do you have a strong foundational base of all the good that you have achieved within your company?

b. When things haven't gone to plan, have you been able to see why so as to not repeat the mistake again?

c. Do you say, "That will never work," or do you encourage others, saying, "This is what you learned last time," to give you a better chance of success this time?

Score yourself out of 25 for experience.   / 25

_____

Add your scores for a total out of 100.   / 100

Get a sanity check on your assessments above from your colleagues, family, and friends, or business coach/mentor if you have one. This is your episodic memory and the third score towards building a better you.

Later on in Chapter Three you will bring these together with your other results to give you a complete picture.

CASE STUDIES
Case study: *Mark Parker – Nike*

Mark Parker has 27 years of extensive Nike experience across a broad range of leadership roles, from product design and development, to marketing and brand management. He has built up a wealth of experience that he uses to maintain Nike's values, as well as to encourage the development of new and exciting brands. He is known as one of the world's most creative CEOs. He has an uncanny ability to appear as comfortable meeting with investors on Wall Street as he is hanging out with street artists and contemporary design legends. He knows them equally well, what inspires and motivates them. They, in turn, trust his leadership. Parker takes episodic memory to new levels.

He not only understands the inner workings of the company, but is fanatical about the sports they support, knowing many of the stars personally. He wants the stars to endorse Nike products because they value them as much as he does, not just because they are sponsored to wear Nike.

Parker is inspired by visual stimulation. He uses his episodic memory to recall and visualize the designs of all Nike's footwear range across all sports and the athletes they support. When he discovered that Nike's research and development were working on a total of 350 new ideas, he got them to reduce this to 50. He recognized that too many projects would cause too much stress, resulting in too few of those ideas actually coming to market.

Many believe that the extraordinary growth of Nike is down to Parker. He brought this growth about through continual expansion. Parker knows what to look for in new employees in order to stay ahead of the competition. He is passionate about Nike's culture and values, through which Nike attracts "smart, curious, and highly creative employees". Every employee must be focused on serving the athlete, the customer of the company. This is regardless of whether that customer is at the top of their sport or simply wears the shoes because they like the Nike swoosh.

Parker himself seeks employees who can continually build on their experience and learn from the knowledge of those around them. Parker's experience and mastery of his episodic memory drives new thinking across the company, to ensure both the employees and the company grow.

To complete his episodic memory and sustainability credentials, Parker is committed to ensuring that Nike remain environmentally aware, with Nike launching the first "Green Shoe" that adheres to the principles of sustainability.

Parker has been totally loyal to the values of Nike, to their board, shareholders, employees, and customers. He seeks total loyalty in return.

Case study
Howard Schultz – Starbucks

Howard Schultz is the chairman, president and CEO of Starbucks Coffee Company. He has built a company noted for the balance it strikes between profitability and social conscience. Originally leaving the company in 2008, Schultz was concerned that Starbucks had lost its way. He was determined to return the company to its core values and restore not only its financial health, but also its soul. This was evident in how he used his episodic memory.

Schultz joined Starbucks as its director of retail operations and marketing. During a buying trip to Italy, he was struck by the romance of coffee and the sense of community that existed in the coffee and espresso bars. He returned with this sensory experience and wanted to create a new brand of coffee bar under the Starbucks brand. This venture was unsuccessful, despite a successful pilot of the café vision; the original Starbucks' founders were not comfortable with it. Schultz left Starbucks in 1985 and a year later opened his own café, called Il Giornale.

Two years later Schultz was able to buy Starbucks and merge it with Il Giornale to form Starbucks Coffee Company, which now owns some 17,000 stores worldwide. At its peak, Starbucks was opening a new store every 12 hours and serving up to 44 million customers a week.

Schultz has a transformational leadership style based on his experience to give customers the best possible experience in coffee. Loyal customers do not just buy a coffee; they buy the whole Starbucks experience.

His experience has led him to have compassion for, and

commitment to, customers and staff alike. This was explained in depth in his 1999 book *Pour Your Heart into It*, where he states, "If you treat people like family, you will make them loyal and encourage them to give their all."

Schultz' compassion has also bequeathed a strong sense of social consciousness. In 2011 he announced his "Create Jobs for USA Program". He wants his experience and values to do the best and his private fund lends money to small businesses across the United States, especially in underprivileged areas.

He is proud of his awards for commendable conduct and for Ethics in Business, but only because they exemplify his passion for what business can do to help people. In 2011, he was named *Fortune* magazine's "Businessperson of the Year"

for his initiatives in the economy and job market; in 2013, he was awarded the Kellogg Award for Distinguished Leadership. The list goes on.

Schultz believes that business should put people first. Customers and employees should be treated with the utmost respect. Schultz is an inspiring and engaging leader. He serves his people because it is they who count.

Case study
Alan Sugar – Amstrad

Lord Alan Sugar is the Chairman of Amstrad, the company he founded in 1968. Not being born with a silver spoon in his mouth, he entered business the hard way and learned much in doing so. His episodic memory and his wisdom may appear to come from his gut feelings, but his business choices are borne of much cerebral thought and deliberation, taking every ounce of experience into account.

He is an inspiring, motivational, driven, opportunistic, intuitive, and, some would say, autocratic manager and has gained celebrity status through *The Apprentice,* the reality TV show where potential business partners are tested to the limit.

Beyond the television, Lord Sugar is a commendable role model and a leader who takes full responsibility for his company's successes and failures. He relates strongly to his early experience, coming from a poor background. He admires others who are in a similar situation, who also have the same determination to succeed. Life has taught him that you must be honest, straightforward, and to not beat around the bush.

He shares his experience, "Tell it how it is. It might not be what people want to hear, but in the end they'll respect it. Fly-by-nights are exactly what they are – they don't last. Opportunists don't last. You have to have morals and self-discipline and put your head on your pillow at night and think 'I'm happy with myself'. And that's important." [91]

He is also careful not to stray away from his core strengths and gives this advice to those who want to go into business.

"Stick to what you know. Business is a risk. There's no such thing as the Harvard Business School module where you open the book and by page five you've got a successful business."[92]

His autocratic management style works and is an advantage to his companies. It allows Lord Sugar to make decisions without disagreements, simply because the respect for him is so high. He came up the hard way and uses his experience to inform his decision making, but he also imparts it to his people. He helps all of them to get up their individual learning curves that little bit quicker and that makes all the difference.

He was not the wealthiest of people when he was younger, but to achieve what he has now will have inspired a bunch of youngsters even in the worst of circumstances.

Case study
Warren Buffet – Berkshire Hathaway

Warren Buffett, the American businessman, investor and philanthropist, is considered the most successful investor in the world. He is the chairman, CEO, and largest shareholder of Berkshire Hathaway. His success has made him among the world's wealthiest people and in 2012, *Time* named him as one of the world's most influential people. He has learned from experience and has a sharp memory for details.

How did Buffet amass his fortune?

Buffett buys stocks in companies with strong cash flow that appear to be undervalued. He buys them for the long-term, not short-term gain. He has lived through share price crashes and times of expansions. He has studied the markets over a long period of time and uses his experience to spot those companies to buy. Experience counts, and in the case of Warren Buffet to the tune of $61 billion.

As a child of eleven years old, he bought three shares of Cities Service Preferred for $38. Shortly after buying the stock, it fell to around $27 a share. He remained resilient and held his shares until they rebounded to $40. He then promptly sold them, but they soon rose to $200. The experience taught him one of the basic lessons of investing that he never forgot. When it comes to stocks and shares, patience is a virtue.

REMEMBER

Episodic memory is based on the experiences of your life and that which you can glean from others.

A good episodic memory is where you combine good experience memories with similar ones. In doing so you build good, strong connections and you are more likely to recall these memories when required. You can also use the good experience more often, seeing its relevance in several situations.

Episodic memory is critical for leadership. It helps you understand and fully appreciate the importance of your people and your colleagues. You understand their hopes, fears, and aspirations. This helps to make you a better manager of people. You are able to connect people with people, and people with ideas.

In the same way, episodic memory is important in recalling the values of your company and the combined strength, stamina, and durability of these values. In effect, why it is that they have survived the test of time. As the Curator, you are the company's historian, the custodian of these values.

Ultimately, episodic memory is wisdom. You share this broadly within and across your company, community, and family for the greater good.

Episodic memory is your ability to recall people, places, and events that are relevant to the current situation. Some specific examples of using episodic memory in the workplace include:

- remembering and following verbal or written instructions accurately;
- performing mental arithmetic;
- accessing and manipulating short-term information for certain tasks;

- keeping a point in mind in a meeting when someone else is talking;
- using information from various documents to formulate a new document.

If your episodic memory needs improvement, you could be experiencing the following:

- your recall is fuzzy, unclear, or incoherent;
- you get lost in detail of a day's, week's or month's work;
- you may sometimes repeat actions that have already been done because you do not have full recall of doing them the first time around;
- you may sometimes appear slightly socially aloof due to your difficulties with remembering shared events;
- you may present with poorer confidence in your abilities.

ATTENTION
– THE COACH

INTRODUCTION

Attention is the ability to concentrate and focus. Attention involves many cognitive functions that are interrelated allowing you to selectively focus on a task even when being distracted. Thus, you can painstakingly absorb a complex report, listen to a colleague with the utmost intensity, or conscientiously focus on the driest of presentations.

There is an opportunity cost in paying attention. If you give your attention to one point, it diminishes what you can give to another. Therefore, do you continue to write that "important email" during a colleague's performance review? Or should you take that moment in time to focus entirely on what they have to say?

There are two main forms of attention. There is the attention you devote to something; a task, a test, a person. There is also the attention you allow to be captured, as when someone calls your name. How do you know when to devote your attention or have it captured? How do you know what to focus on?

Your executive function controls where and how you pay attention, and determines what is important at that moment in time. It sifts through the information with which you are bombarded on a daily basis and decides what your need is, based on your motivations and interests, and what results you need at that particular time to achieve your overall objectives. Your executive function decides how to direct the attentional system and what level of intensity is required. Executive function drives your attention, but it's also reliant upon it.

You can still be independently strong in either executive function or attention, but both are limited if there is a weakness in the other.

Working memory and episodic memory are also reliant on attention. The perception, processing, and storing of information are optimal when you have a strong attention.

A durable attention that can be devoted and captured drives for results, making you the "Coach", the person you go to for instruction and training.

Attention underpins great leadership and management.

THE ROLE OF ATTENTION IN LEADERSHIP AND MANAGEMENT

The ability to concentrate on tasks at hand and filter out secondary noise and stimuli depends on the ability to pay attention. As a leader, attention makes you the Coach, keeping your team focused on the game plan and driving for results, despite multiple disruptions.

Attention allows you to focus on the most important tasks in your company. Applying this level of focus means that you have the reputation among your peers not to get distracted when there is an immediate task at hand. With supreme attention, you are known for your laser-like focus on the most important tasks in your company. You are known to keep going when others falter and fall by the wayside. You are the Coach, driving for results. You are the resource for the most demanding and challenging of projects. Nothing will derail you and you are known for your staying power and ability to keep going until you have accomplished your mission.

There are occasions where you decide to "devote" your attention to a single task and block out all forms of distraction, but there are also times when you allow others to "capture" your attention, when you are in listening mode, a critical skill in leadership. Your cognition realizes that there are times when you need to allow others to "capture" your attention, like in board meetings, when you are facilitating an advisory meeting of experts or when listening to your customers. You want everyone at meetings to contribute and you want everyone to have the opportunity of capturing your attention. When you are in listening mode, this is a critical skill in leadership.

The strength of your cognition allows you to understand the balance between devoting your attention and allowing it to be captured. This allows you to know how to be the Coach within your organization, staying on track to reach the right destination, regardless of the bumps in the way.

The ability to devote attention can be vital in some areas of work where you are called upon to do tasks that require attention to detail. For example, reading highly complex documents and immediately bringing the attention of your peers to what is critical and what can be discarded.

Alternatively, there are times when you allow others to capture your attention. This is important when you are working as part of a team, or attending a training workshop or meeting from which you need to learn. Equally, as a good facilitator of a meeting, you allow your attention to be captured by the participants of the meeting to ensure a fair hearing of all points of view. Therefore, you are not overly enamoured by the sound of your own voice; you give others a chance to have their say and you listen. You don't want to miss the opportunity to allow your directors to impart vital information to you and to each other.

Successful executives such as Lizanne Falsetto of thinkThin, Marissa Mayer of Yahoo, and Jørgen Vig Knudstorp of Lego, understand the term "to pay attention" infers an opportunity cost. That is, when paying attention to one task, you are not able to fully undertake another. They get their companies to focus on what matters. This is really insightful on their part and ensures that they prioritize tasks carefully, taking account of the time required to do them. Thus, by paying attention to "task A" they are making the decision not, at that moment, to pay attention to "task B". They are thus the best at presenting plans, highlighting what needs to be done by whom and when. They are great at providing feedback to staff and peers alike and because of their attention to detail their criticism is always considered. They set the bar high for themselves and are a great example to the workforce.

Listening is an essential attention skill for leadership. As leaders you spend more time listening than talking – how else do you find out what's really going on? How often have you attended meetings with a manager but they continue to write their emails? You know full well they are not really listening and the meeting is a waste of time. This is poor leadership.

Knowing when to "devote" attention and knowing when to allow attention to be "captured" is a fundamental skill that is a direct result of the strength of your cognitive function.

When your attention goes wrong it can seriously blunt your ability to perform. It will blunt your ability to switch from "devoting" your attention to allowing it to be "captured". This has consequences for the leadership roles you undertake. If you can no longer switch attention modes this will simply cause heightened stress, which will worsen your cognitive fitness.

Poor attention will see you having to read the same paragraph in a report over and over again to understand it. Poor attention will see you phasing in and out of important meetings and even one-on-one discussions with a colleague. You often joke about not listening to your spouses or partners, but that too can be a sign of poor cognitive function, for they are among the most important people in your lives.

If you cannot concentrate in the work environment, cannot keep track of events, and are easily distracted, then you are no longer the Coach, no longer driving for results.

THE SCIENCE BIT

Attention is the cognitive process of selectively concentrating on one thing in the environment whilst filtering or ignoring other information. Attention is considered to be the most concrete of all cognitive processes because of its strong links with perception – seeing (visual) and hearing (auditory). For example, attention is when you hear what someone is saying over other conversations in a crowded room.

Attention is a complex cognitive process with many sub-processes specializing in different aspects of attention processing.[93] In one form or another, it is involved in almost all other cognitive domains (excluding tasks performed automatically). Thus, any decline in attention can affect many aspects of daily functioning.[94]

We can divide attention in a number of ways,[95] but the most extensively investigated in normal ageing include selective, divided, and sustained attention.

Selective attention is the ability to attend to a stimuli while disregarding others considered irrelevant to the current task. For example, to visually search for a target letter (e.g. letter "E") amongst non-target letters (e.g. letter "F"). Divided attention requires attending to two or more sources of information, or two or more tasks at the same time. Sustained attention is the ability to maintain concentration on a task over an extended period of time. For example, people may have to monitor the environment for a relatively infrequent signal, such as a blip on a radar screen.

There is also spatial attention which can be overt or covert. Overt attention is that of directing your senses (sight and listening) towards a source of stimulus, while covert attention is when you mentally focus on one of several stimuli. Covert attention is thought to be a neural process that increases the signal from a particular area of the sensory field.

Attention is implemental in engraving information into memory and determines what will be encoded into it. When attention is divided it prevents conscious memories from forming. While complex, unconscious memories can be encoded – even when there is another concurrent task – the stimuli to be encoded must be selected from other competing stimuli. Attention is also guided by memory from past experiences. Moreover, brain areas that are important for memory, such as the hippocampus and medial temporal lobe structures, are operative during attention tasks.[96] Attention deficits can, therefore, substantially reduce memory performance.

HOW ATTENTION CHANGES WITH AGEING

Older people exhibit significant impairments on tasks that require dividing or switching of attention among multiple items, or tasks where the attention demands of the two tasks are complex.[97] These tasks tend to require flexible control of attention, which is associated with the frontal lobes of the brain. Additionally, older adults seem less able to allocate resources appropriately according to task priority,[98] which is usually explained in terms of declining processing resources associated with ageing. Thus, resources are exceeded in older adults when attention has to be divided among more than one source.[99] Similarly, their performance is slow relative to that of young adults when attention must be switched from one task to a totally different task.[100]

On the other hand, older people maintain their performance level on tasks that require the selection of relevant stimuli (selective attention), are no more impaired by distraction than younger adults, and are able to maintain concentration for an extended period of time (sustained attention).[101] These observations might be driven by the needs of the individual and, as such, older people may not be driven by the same needs and goals as younger people. However, that older adults appear to be slower than younger adults in responding to selected targets indicates that any deficit can be mainly attributed to a general slowing of information processing rather than to selective attention deficits.[102]

In everyday life, attention deficits can have a significant impact on the ability of an older person to function adequately and independently.[103] Key to independence and affected by attention problems is the task of driving, which requires a constant switching of attention in response to changing circumstances. A driver's attention has to be divided amongst driving, monitoring the environment, and filtering out what is relevant from the many continuous stimuli.

PUTTING ATTENTION INTO CONTEXT

Hemispatial neglect is a condition following brain damage whereby patients fail to be aware of items to one side of space (i.e. the side of space opposite to the brain damage). Neglect is most pronounced and long-lasting after damage to the brain's right hemisphere, such as after a stroke, when individuals often become unaware of objects on their left. Thus, individuals may eat from only one side of a plate, copy only half a picture, write only on one side of a page, or shave only one side of their face (i.e. the same side as brain damage). Hemispatial neglect has classically been associated with damage to the right posterior parietal cortex, although other areas may be implicated (e.g. subcortical areas and frontal lobe).

Cases of hemispatial neglect were reported in a study[104] in which two Italian patients were asked to imagine being in the Piazza Del Duomo in Milan, and describe what they saw from one end of the square. The description they gave was of features that would have been to their right while only a few on the left were recalled. When asked to describe the image from the opposite end of the square, most of the features were the ones to their left. Thus, knowledge of features in the square gained before these individuals became ill was in their memory but they were unable to access all of it normally.

ASSESSMENT OF ATTENTION
This is a manual exercise to quantify your attention.

1) **Strength of focus:**

    a. Can you spend hours or days on a single task to ensure its completion?
    b. Can you work even when distracted by others or on less arduous tasks?
    c. Are you known to sometimes work long into the evening until you get something right?
    d. Are you good at prioritizing tasks and keeping to them?

    Score yourself out of 25 for focus.   / 25

2) **Presenting plans and feedback:**

    a. Do you have the ability to cover all the detail in a plan?
    b. Are you able to present detail simply, without jargon and self-importance?
    c. Can you criticize without causing discomfort when giving feedback?
    d. Do your team and peers value your thoughts on their performance?

    Score yourself out of 25 for presenting and providing feedback.   / 25

3) **Devoting and capturing attention:**

    a. Are you able to determine when you must attend

to something to the exclusion of everything else?

b. Are you also able to determine when the company will benefit best by having your attention captured?

c. Can you easily switch between these two states, to ensure you are at your most effective?

Score yourself out of 25 for devoting and capturing attention. / 25

4) **Listening:**

a. How much time do you spend in listening mode vs talking mode?

b. Do you only listen attentively to those in authority?

c. Do you find time with your team to talk on a one-on-one basis?

d. Do you ensure the listening time is quality time? That is, time when you are not undertaking other activities?

Score yourself out of 25 for listening. / 25

Add your scores for a total out of 100. / 100

Get a sanity check on your scores from your colleagues, family, and friends, or business coach/mentor if you have one. This is your attention score, the fourth on the way to building a better you.

Later on in Chapter Three you will bring these together with your other results to give you a complete picture.

CASE STUDIES
Case study
Lizanne Falsetto – thinkThin,

Lizanne Falsetto is a Business and Wellness guru. She launched thinkThin in 2000, after a career of international modelling. She was fascinated by food and was driven to analyse everything she ate, looking for the recipe that would enable great nutrition. She demonstrated not only great attention to producing a series of great products, she also clearly allowed her attention to be captured by the customers to whom she sold these products.

Lizanne not only created a high protein nutrition bar, but she also developed it for a specific market niche; active women on the go. In both aspects she displayed intense levels of attention, firstly to creating a food that was good for you, and secondly by focusing on a growing, but as yet untapped, market of the go-getting female executive. She steered her company and her nutritional bars to become household names and a national brand.

Since selling her company she has concentrated on a movement to empower women entrepreneurs to be "resourceful, leverage their innate personal qualities and both manage and grow a successful business".[105] She pays attention to human traits that are often devalued in the hurly-burly business world. She encourages kindness, intuition, instinct, and wellness. She wants to shift the executive mindset, promoting traditionally feminine qualities in running a business.

She has taken her attention to detail on the modelling runway with her into business and concentrated her executive power to enable others to succeed.

Case Study
Marissa Mayer – Yahoo

Marissa Mayer is a computer scientist and business executive. She joined Google in 1999 and was their twentieth employee and their first female engineer. At Google she became known for her attention to detail as she developed and designed their search offerings.

Among her many achievements at Google she helped to develop their AdWords. This uses complex algorithms to enable advertisers to target what products consumers want. AdWords amounted to 96% of the company's revenue in the first quarter of 2011 and is still a major money-maker for the company.

Mayer also conceived the Associate Product Manager program, a mentorship program to recruit and cultivate new hires and train them for leadership roles. The two-year program includes assignments and intensive evening classes, which require great concentration.

During her time at Google, she taught introductory computer programming at Stanford University, again showing her attention skills.

In 2012 Mayer became President and CEO of Yahoo!, her vision is to "make the culture the best version of itself". She saw that employee morale was not well within Yahoo! and instigated an online program to collect complaints, allowing them to vote for those the staff felt required attention.

Mayer controversially imposed a ban on remote-working employees, making them return to office-based responsibilities. Her view was that the skill of the workforce needed to be concentrated, bringing greater attention into the office.

Another controversial act was the institution of an employee performance review system. This was based on using binomial distribution (bell shaped) ranking of employees. Those on the low end were fired. She was heavily criticized by *The New York Times* and other newspapers.

Mayer is paying an opportunity cost for focusing her attention so powerfully on employee-related matters, looking for solutions to problems such as productivity. By not thinking through the implications of her actions, she might be causing more problems going forward. By focusing so much on productivity, she is paying the price for missing what is really go on within Yahoo!.

Case study
Jørgen Vig Knudstorp – Lego

Jørgen Vig Knudstorp is the Chief Executive of the Lego Group. He led Lego from the brink of financial collapse to become the world's biggest toymaker by sales. Knowing where to pay attention to his business has enabled Knudstorp to resurrect the ailing toy company. He ensured great product design continued within the company, while at the same time cutting all peripheral and unnecessary costs.

Concentrating on designing, developing, and selling essentially one product, Lego is bigger than toy companies such as Mattel and Hasbro who have multiple brands such as Barbie, My Little Pony, and Transformers.

His model for innovation isn't that far removed from Apple and Steve Jobs. Both businessmen and their companies concentrated on marketing few products to their target customers.

To bring about the turnaround, Knudstorp cut costs, sold off peripheral businesses, and got Lego to concentrate on its core competencies. He said that he got his inspiration from being a pre-school trainee teacher. "My dad says that's where I learned everything I needed to know about leadership. If you can be a leader with kindergarten children, you can be a leader anywhere."[106] The attention that children demand was a great training ground for the young Knudstorp.

Case study

*Jan Leschly – former Chairman of SmithKline Beecham
and tennis player, and John Robb – Chairman and
CEO of Wellcome Pharmaceuticals*

Jan Leschly never forgot his tennis playing days. Tennis influenced his leadership and taught him to always "keep score", otherwise you were "only practising". His attention to detail was centred on ensuring the best return on investment. However, his approach to leadership wasn't simply about numbers. He took a year out of running pharmaceutical companies to study Theology. Leschly said the break gave him a unique perspective on leadership that he could never have acquired through other means.

Despite his insistence on keeping score, on paying attention, and being driven, he was also very much a "people person", highly regarded and liked by peers and staff alike. His "humane" approach to leadership didn't leave him looking soft or an easy touch. He managed to remain humane yet solid and respected in an industry somewhat noted for its cut-throat approach to management. His time out of the industry gave him qualities that set him apart as a leader.

John Robb became CEO of Wellcome Pharmaceuticals in the 1980s, not long after the company was floated on the stock market by the Wellcome Trust, the world renowned global charitable foundation. Robb made a solid start to his leadership and quickly got the company on a more profitable setting, with cost cutting and selling off non-core businesses to focus on pharmaceuticals. He was successful at this, focusing on making the company profitable. But once all major costs had been cut, he kept up the pressure on the bottom line and wouldn't consider investment opportunities. At the time a colleague told me that Robb, having exhausted all areas of cost-cutting, had now resorted to banning sandwiches at lunch time meetings.

Robb had difficulty seeing the difference between a cost and an investment. He also lost favour with the Trust, who began talks with Glaxo; in 1995, Glaxo bought a majority share in Wellcome and took over the company. Robb paid the price for not being able to allow his attention to be captured by the Trust. He didn't see that Wellcome could be taken over if the Trust so wished.

One of the differences between Leschly and Robb was that Leschly invested time to acquire skills and new perspectives on leadership, devoting his attention to these new skills. Robb was immensely successful when in cost cutting mode, but couldn't adapt to the new circumstances when an investment mindset was required.

REMEMBER

Attention is the measurement of focus and concentration. This is the skill you use to concentrate when working on a task. If you have poor concentration, you are easily distracted and will not be able employ the other cognitive domains effectively. This can cause frustration to you and your co-workers as you may disrupt their work. Improving concentration means better focus on tasks, improved productivity, and greater abilities in the management of your work.

Concentration is necessary for higher cognitive function to be optimal and so it is important to ensure it is maintained at high levels. Some examples of attention in the workplace include:

- completing tasks within a work environment with noise or lots of visual stimuli;
- listening intently to someone speaking within a noisy environment;
- completing individual tasks on your to do list.

If your attention needs improvement, you might experience:

- becoming distracted by noise in an open plan office;
- not completing tasks on your to do list;
- drifting off when someone is speaking to you;
- switching between tasks without completing them;
- problems reading detailed reports;
- difficulty in listening to a complex presentation;
- difficulty in listening in a one-to-one conversation.

PROCESSING SPEED – THE JUDGE

INTRODUCTION

Processing speed is the rate and accuracy at which different cognitive operations are executed. It impacts your verbal fluency and articulation, the rate at which you are able to engage thinking processes.

Processing speed is responsible for the variability of cognitive performance across a wide variety of tasks. It is your ability to respond with speed and accuracy, to make quick assessments, and to appear as if you can keep "many plates spinning".

It enables you to do things without necessarily thinking specifically about the task in mind. It relies on beliefs and habits and enables them to be used when decisiveness is to the fore, when a quick read on a situation is more important than deep deliberation.

Processing speed is a fundamental cognitive domain. It is for when you are firefighting, not strategizing. Strength in this domain makes you decisive; within your organization you are the "Judge".

THE ROLE OF PROCESSING SPEED IN LEADERSHIP AND MANAGEMENT

Your processing speed is your ability to energize and enable sequences of tasks with fluidity, accuracy, and pace. As a leader, your processing speed helps you to be the Judge – thinking quickly on your feet, responding rapidly to situations, initiating new tasks, and communicating decisions.

Processing speed allows you to respond with speed and accuracy, with smoothness and coordination. With this cognitive skill, you know when to put more emphasis on the speed of the task in hand versus the accuracy of it. When time is precious, you can make the most of a "quick and dirty" solution. You are out in front and frequently the first to make a comment, have a plan, and are able to assess the circumstances for a quick resolution or direction. You are decisive and you are the Judge within your company.

You are the live wire in team meetings, keeping the agenda going and ensuring all points are covered. You are great for adapting processes, especially when there are a lot of moving parts. You are also very good at proactive problem solving, when a quick answer is required.

Some roles require more weight on speed, and others more weight on accuracy. You can excel in both and switch when required. Brian Chesky of Airbnb, John Martin of Gilead Sciences, Jeff Bezos of Amazon, and Mark Zuckerberg of Facebook all have amazing processing speed. They can rapidly scan information when a quick decision is required, when they know you have to be roughly right because sometimes speed is more important than accuracy. However, they also appreciate the need for accuracy and will find the extra time (and extra people and resources) to achieve precision when it is required.

This is important when you bring "time" into the equation. When time is precious, you know how to weigh speed over accuracy. Equally, when allocating a task, you take into account the need for speed over accuracy when allocating the time in which it is done. You often ask for a "quick and dirty" solution when you know time is short. You know when to put more emphasis on the speed and when to put more on the accuracy, thus discriminating between them.

Processing speed comes into play with your ability to be orally articulate, as when having to immediately reply to a question. You may have to talk to board members, potential investors, or to the media. Good processing speed enables you to "think quickly on your feet", but have the ability to be "roughly right" most of the time; you also need to give your questioners confidence in your answers.

Thus, in the workplace you demonstrate calmness and confidence, yet appear lively, energetic, and, most of all, decisive. You can switch tasks and direction when required, with smoothness and coordination. You appear to maintain control of several "spinning plates" at the same time because you are able to efficiently switch from one task to another. Therefore, you are often sought after to look after the complex processes. When at your best you realize this skill can easily take you out of reach of your peers. You know when to slow down to bring them back in line with your thinking, so that they are still owners of the processes you are working on.

The absence of good processing speed confines you to roles that have fewer responsibilities, fewer thought processes, and less complex tasks. You have difficulty in sequencing and coordinating tasks and as a result there is a lack of decisiveness in your words and actions. You will seem slow, ponderous, and lacking in energy, no longer decisive. You will avoid the meetings where there will be intense questioning or interrogation. You will seep into the background and become a wallflower rather than amidst the scene of the action. Your colleagues and friends used to love being around you because you exuded energy and dynamism, which they could lap up. Now, they feel their drive being diminished and so avoid wanting to be with you.

Social isolation will simply make your cognitive function worse. You become more erratic, responding unpredictably even to simple requests. As you increasingly feel misunderstood, you see around an over reactive culture. The smoothness and precision, the decisiveness of the Judge has gone.

THE SCIENCE BIT

Processing speed is the coordination of a sensory or thinking (cognitive) process and a motor activity.[107] It is the degree of skill demonstrated by a person when completing a task. The accuracy of motor response depends upon the speed with which the brain makes decisions to produce the response.

At the lowest level this is the innate ability to react to a stimulus in the environment. With learning and experience, this develops into various motor behaviours that are coordinated, timely, and appropriate responses to the sensory input. Thus, with increasing complexity, processing speed progresses from a simple innate reflex response (e.g. after touching something that is hot), through simple behaviours (e.g. picking something up, riding a bike) to complex behaviours (e.g. riding a bike through an obstacle course).

PHASES AND CHARACTERISTICS OF PROCESSING SPEED

Processing speed may be divided into three phases:

- cognitive phase: learning about "what" to do, but not necessarily "how" to do it. The learner makes awkward, slow movements that need to be thought about and require conscious control. Performance is generally poor.
- associative phase: learning the skill. Although not yet automatic, less time is spent thinking about every detail of the movement, which is associated with movements already known. Performance is smoother.
- autonomous phase: the skill is perfected and performed automatically, rather than with thought. Learning is near completion, although the skill may be continually refined through practice. Movements become spontaneous and do not require thought.

Characteristics of processing speed include:

- accuracy: precision in which the skill is executed;
- speed: rate and confidence of the movements;
- efficiency: amount of resources used and spare capacity available;
- timing: accuracy of timing and correctness of the order;
- consistency: regularity, constant results;
- anticipation: speed of expectation of events and appropriate response;
- adaptability: amount of adjustment to current circumstances (situation or condition);
- perception: amount of information obtained from cues and signals.

ASSESSMENT OF PROCESSING SPEED

This is a manual exercise to quantify your processing speed.

1) Responsiveness:

    a. Are you happy to take questions, anytime, anywhere?

    b. Can you respond even when under duress, even on subjects where you don't have 100% understanding?

    c. Do you appear lively and energetic? Do you bring energy to a meeting?

    d. Do you come across as decisive or dithering?

    Score yourself out of 25 for responsiveness.   / 25

2) Accuracy:

    a. Do you have the ability to be accurate when required?

    b. Do you know when it's best to slow down a process to ensure it is spot-on?

    c. Do you know when to bring in other brains to ensure the accuracy of a task?

    d. Can you switch tasks and maintain control?

    Score yourself out of 25 for accuracy.   / 25

3) Adaptability:

    a. Can you spot the vital details that others overlook?

    b. Do you know when to slow down and when to press ahead?

    c. Can you keep others up to speed with your line of thought, to keep them in the process rather than losing it?

    Score yourself out of 25 for adaptability.   / 25

4) Crisis management:

    a. When others are running around like headless chickens, are you still able to see the wood for the trees?

    b. Are you able to step in and take control, even at awkward moments, sticking to the process, working from the checklist?

    c. Do you build confidence in your team at these times, ensuring that, whatever the problem, you will overcome it?

    d. Even when working at the greatest haste, do you appear cool, calm, and collected?

    Score yourself out of 25 for working in a crisis. / 25

    Add your scores for a total out of 100.   / 100

Get a sanity check on your scores from your colleagues, family, and friends, or business coach/mentor if you have one. This is your score for processing speed, the final assessment to building a better you.

Later on in Chapter Three you will bring these together with your other results to give you a complete picture.

CASE STUDIES
Case study
Brian Chesky – Airbnb

Brian Chesky's biggest challenge is the sheer amount of information he has to process while growing a fast-moving organization. A self-taught CEO, businessman, and leader, his management style has evolved since he established Airbnb. He has learned rapidly to lead and manage with speed and accuracy.

He likes to talk fast and sees his role as CEO as the captain of a ship. He has many things to think about. He must ensure the ship stays afloat, by checking below the waterline, and he has to cover the important areas above the waterline that add value to his company. He has chosen product, brand, and culture. He empowers leaders within his company, and only gets involved when there are holes below the waterline.

Chesky has become the poster child for the so-called "sharing economy".

Chesky has sought advice from of a long list of leaders since co-founding the home-rental website, because, as he says, paraphrasing Robert McNamara, the 1960s US Defence Secretary, "There's no learning curve for people who are in war or in start-ups."

Chesky is described as intense, focused, and really, really, really curious. He learned to run a company by two processes. Firstly, by trial and error, allowing himself and others to make mistakes. Secondly, by teaching himself how to go deep on subjects fast. He uses a method he calls "going to the source". He goes straight to the people he regards as experts in various fields and he has gone to many of them.

He processes vast amounts of information quickly, not always accurately, but is roughly right enough of the time to make the right decision and be the best of leaders.

Case study
John Martin – Gilead Sciences

John Martin, of Gilead Sciences, has positioned his company as a leader in fast-paced drug development. Gilead is the new "go-to partner" for any biotech looking for a deal. Martin has made sure that Gilead works at speed and is able to partner smoothly with smaller, more agile companies.

Gilead, already a world-leader in HIV medication, has diverged by buying into hepatitis C and cancer drugs, both growing markets with unmet needs.

The pharmaceutical industry is full of organizations known for not taking risks. Martin is challenging that philosophy and has been willing to spend generously, making Gilead one of the industry's top partners of choice.

Martin has helped model a style of leadership, processing masses of data in search of quick, dramatic results, accelerating development within his company, and striking quick deals outside of it.

Compare this to Pfizer, where everything was staked on achieving a low tax status by attempting to merge, first with Astra-Zeneca and then with Allergan. Both were failures and as Plan A and Plan B failed, it was clear that was as far as the thinking at Pfizer had gone. Their leadership was incapable of attempting to develop more than one strategy at a time. Pfizer has failed in trying to replace Lipitor, the biggest single selling pharmaceutical product in history, and looks set to spend a considerable number of years competing with generics rather than flourishing with branded pharma interventions. It is almost as if Pfizer scientists have poor morale, and no drug to take for it.

Martin has taken risks that have helped improve terms for every seller in the industry. He has set a pace that others will try to mimic, an energizer for an industry crying out for bold leadership.

Case study
Jeff Bezos – Amazon

Jeff Bezos of Amazon is a technology entrepreneur and investor, as well as a leader in the growth of e-commerce. He is the founder and CEO of Amazon, the largest retailer on the World Wide Web. He has always had a remarkable talent for managing a host of different projects and enterprises. He is the epitome of sharp minded, quick thinking, and has the energy of two fit people.

Bezos had an early love of computers and studied computer science and electrical engineering at Princeton University. As a child, Jeff Bezos showed an early interest in how things work, turning his parents' garage into a laboratory and rigging electrical contraptions around his house. It was while at high school that he started his first business.

His original work was in finance, but he gave up this extremely lucrative career in a risky move into the as yet untapped world of e-commerce, opening an online bookstore in 1994. He developed software for the business. It should be no surprise to find out that he named his company after the meandering South American river, which is pretty much how his thinking works. He has a butterfly mind and will float from topic to topic seeing links and opportunities that others pass by because of their more logical, directed, sense of thinking.

Bezos started with books, but soon saw opportunities in a wealth of diverse products. In 2006, Amazon.com further diversified into a "video on demand service". This was followed by the launch of Kindle, which is not only a brilliant idea in its own right, but is also a raging conduit for sales from the Amazon website.

As if all that were not enough to contend with, Bezos invested in Blue Origin, which offers space travel to customers. He also bought *The Washington Post* and other publications. Bezos told *The Post* employees, "There is no map, and charting a path ahead will not be easy. We will need to invent, which means we will need to experiment. Our touchstone will be readers, understanding what they care about... and working backwards from there. I'm excited and optimistic about the opportunity for invention."[108]

Bezos caused a stir when he announced a new, experimental initiative, Amazon Prime Air. This service uses drones to deliver products to customers. Bezos says that Prime Air could become a reality within as little as four or five years. Where many see mayhem, Bezos sees possibilities.

With all his ideas and energy, Bezos is not short on making mistakes. The Fire Phone, launched in 2014 was criticized for being too gimmicky and was discontinued in 2015. But that will not deter him from processing further sets of amazing business ideas.

Case study
Mark Zuckerberg – Facebook

Mark Zuckerberg is a programmer, entrepreneur, and philanthropist. He is the chairman, chief executive, and co-founder of Facebook, which was established in 2004. He likes a lot on his plate, a lot to do at work, and at home. He would get easily bored if he couldn't delve into the detailed workings of Facebook.

Every year, Zuckerberg takes on a personal challenge to learn new things and to grow outside of his work at Facebook. In recent years he has set himself the task of reading two books every month, learning Mandarin, and meeting a new person every day.

He is very much into the possibilities of Artificial Intelligence, seeking to explore every prospect for this new form of technology. He is processing all the possibilities, including voice and face recognition. He will use it for simple functions, for example, controlling music, lights, and temperature. He will also explore the possibility of using it to look after children and vulnerable people, as well as ways in which it can help organizations be more effective.

This will involve him working with engineers and he loves nothing more than getting deep into the details of the technical projects his colleagues face. He's involved in many projects, including the physics of building solar-powered planes. He is investigating how to expand internet access to parts of the developing world currently without the service. To do this he is discovering how you might be able to power satellites with solar power and use them to beam down the internet to inaccessible locations.

He is hands on with projects whenever he can. It is not so much the coding that excites him, as all the things he can do with the code. His brain power is immense and his processing speed is off the scale.

Conflict case study

When your processing speed is off the scale

The cognitive fitness of senior executives in many organizations has been assessed. We will now look at an unusual circumstance when assessment was used in a conflict resolution.

Tom (not his real name) was an energetic and lively leader in a telecommunications company. He was brought into the company because of his reputation for designing new products. He was welcomed into his new company and, at first, everything seemed to be going well. Then we got a call from his Chief Executive. Supriya couldn't say what the problem was, but the symptoms were telling. Tom was destroying morale in his team and she was losing patience with him. She asked if we could help.

We took Tom through the LeaderThink program and he was pretty impressive across all five domains. However, his processing speed was astonishing, one of the highest we had observed.

It was also almost 20 points above his next highest score.

This led to an in-depth discussion with Tom about his work practices and we began to delve into how he used his processing speed power. It turned out that Tom saw every product challenge as a problem. Each time, he quickly surveyed the situation and immediately came up with a solution; before the rest of his team could take a breath, he had implemented the solution, leaving everyone in his wake.

We asked him how his team must be feeling about this. At first he thought they should be pleased to be led by someone so smart and he'd wanted to impress them from day one with how good he could be. After further questioning on this subject he admitted it might leave some of them feeling a little overwhelmed. He finally admitted that he could now see that many of them were feeling helpless and deficient in his presence, as though he was simply unmasking their faults.

We put together a simple strategy to help Tom and his team, and put him back in Supriya's good books. The strategy was that Tom wouldn't do anything without talking and walking at least one of his team through his thought process as he took on the product challenges.

This was going to slow Tom down, but that wasn't a problem. By slowing down and informing members of his team, he was coaching, mentoring, and training them, all at the same time. This enabled them to feel part of the process and even to make suggestions and make good use of their experience.

They began to respect Tom and feel that they were being led, not being pressurized and hurried. Their morale improved measurably within a very short period of time.

Supriya now fully appreciates Tom's skills and knows how to manage him at his best. Whenever there is a need for decisive judgement, she calls on Tom and lets him rip. For all the other occasions, he now knows how to temper his processing speed and everyone benefits.

REMEMBER

Processing speed describes the ability to co-ordinate thinking with a physical task and perform sequences of movements with speed, fluidity, and accuracy.

Some examples of using processing speed in the workplace include:

- remaining articulate, even under constant questioning;
- responding quickly to others' requests;
- reacting to emails popping up in your inbox;
- completing your work accurately;
- completing familiar tasks quickly and accurately;
- speaking with fluency and knowing the right words to use in conversations and emails;.

If your processing speed needs improvement, you could be experiencing the following:

- not being as quick to respond to requests;
- making some errors in your work;
- not being able to think of the right word to say in a conversation;
- being slower to formulate and edit documents.

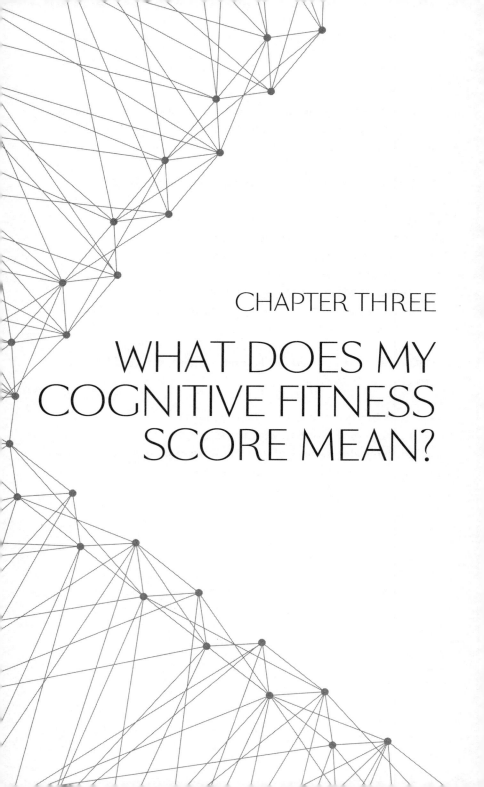

CHAPTER THREE

WHAT DOES MY COGNITIVE FITNESS SCORE MEAN?

INTRODUCTION

In Chapter Two you used a manual assessment of five cognitive domains and their impact on the power of your leadership and management thinking. You can take the average of those scores to give your overall cognitive score, which will provide an insight into your overall cognitive fitness.

This manual exercise is very useful, especially if you seek the thoughts of your coach, mentor, work colleagues, and family. In addition, the code in this book gives you access to LeaderThink online, which will use measurements of your behaviour to more accurately gauge your cognitive fitness and LeaderThink score. If you haven't done it, go online now and see how the measured score compares to the manual score.

If there are major differences, this is probably because the manual score is based more on your belief of your cognitive fitness, whereas the online assessment measures your actual behaviour, which is a closer representation of reality. Just like the college professor who changed universities and couldn't see her executive function eroding, depending too much on your beliefs when self-assessing can lead to errors. Thus, if you have over- or under-estimated your manual score, you should reflect on why this is the case.

Regardless, if you have manual scores, add the five together and divide by 5

Average overall cognitive score: _____ out of 100

You can now understand the five key cognitive domains more fully and how they relate and apply to your leadership and management. You can identify your highest score, which is your strongest domain. Equally it is important to know how balanced you are across all domains and if there are any in which you are particularly weak, or in need of development.

Cognitive Domain	Key Skill	Manual Score	Cognitive Score	Ranking*
Executive Function – The Pilot	planning and strategy			
Working Memory – The Hero	calculating and problem solving			
Episodic Memory – The Curator	remembering			
Attention – The Coach	concentration			
Processing speed – The Judge	decisiveness			

Band Label	Score Range
Lower	0 to 25.99
Lower Middle	26 to 41.99
Middle	42 to 57.99
Upper Middle	58 to 73.99
Upper	74 to 100

*We rank the cognitive scores according to the bands in the table left. Use these bands to look up the description of your cognitive profile for each domain later in this chapter.

As well as ranking the results, you can calculate the difference between your highest and lowest score, thus:

Highest Score_____ - Lowest Score_____ = _____

INTERPRETING YOUR SCORES
– HIGHEST VS LOWEST

If all of your five cognitive domains are within 15 points of each other, your scores are similar, showing a leadership profile that is balanced.

Action: Think about how you could improve all domains in current leadership situations, while keeping them balanced.

If the five domains have a difference of less than 40 but greater than 15, your scores show a leadership profile with some variation across the domains.

Action: Begin improving results, match the individual higher or lower scores below to the needs of your leadership situation.

If the five domain scores have a difference greater than 40, your leadership profile has a lot of variation.

Action: Improve on these results, concentrate on strengthening weaker domains as these will be having a marked impact on your leadership and management.

INTERPRETING COGNITIVE FITNESS SCORE BY DOMAIN

EXCUTIVE FUNCTION – THE PILOT

**EXECUTIVE FUNCTION
– UPPER BAND (SCORE 74 – 100)**

If the self-assessment score for the executive functioning domain was in the upper band, this suggests that you are likely to possess very good executive function skills. The results are within the higher range for adults and indicate that at present you are able to think strategically, plan and organize tasks, move easily from one task to another, make decisions, and manage stressful situations. You control emotions and behave appropriately towards your colleagues.

Strategic planning and organizing are vital leadership strengths, and you have them.

Impact: The Pilot – thinking ahead and moving easily from one difficult situation to another make you a powerful leader.

People with very good executive functioning skills tend to show greater strengths in the following areas:
- generating ideas and strategizing;
- demonstrating good long-term problem solving skills;

- learning from their mistakes following good coaching guidance or mentorship;
- changing their approach or thinking about things in a different way;
- demonstrating selective and sustained attention;
- planning, organizing, and managing their time;
- practising self-control, managing emotions, and thinking of the implications of actions before implementation.

EXECUTIVE FUNCTION – UPPER MIDDLE BAND (SCORE 58 - 73.9)

This baseline score is upper middle and the results are within the upper middle range for adults. This indicates that at present you are able to prioritize work, think strategically, plan, and organize tasks reasonably well. But there is room for improvement. You think quite well strategically which enables you to plan goals and organize tasks.

Impact: You need to score higher. Anything you can do to improve this leadership ability will pay off quickly.

Adults with good executive functioning skills should be able to do the following at or above an age appropriate level:

- practice self control;
- generate ideas and strategize;
- demonstrate good problem solving skills;
- learn from mistakes following parental guidance;
- change approach or think about things in a different way;
- demonstrate selective and sustained attention;
- plan, organize, and manage time.

EXECUTIVE FUNCTION – MIDDLE BAND (SCORES 42 - 57.9)

This baseline score is in the middle band and the results are within the average range for adults. This result indicates that at present you are able to think strategically, plan, and organize tasks to the same level as most other people. This is not exceptional, but a good starting place.

Do you need improvement in planning and organizing competing tasks?

Impact: This thinking is essential to leadership. Improved results will follow quickly through simple improvements.

Adults with adequate executive functioning skills should be able to do the following at an age appropriate level:

- practice self control;
- generate ideas and strategize;
- demonstrate adequate problem solving skills;
- learn from mistakes following parental guidance;
- change approach or think about things in a different way;
- demonstrate selective and sustained attention;
- plan, organize, and manage time.

EXECUTIVE FUNCTION – LOWER MIDDLE BAND (SCORES 26 - 41.9)

This baseline score is within the lower middle range for adults. This result indicates that at present you are able to plan tasks, but may have some challenges with prioritizing some work; you may benefit from creating structure at work.

Impact: Re-examine the way meetings are structured and be open to support from team members.

The assessment suggests that you are likely to experience some weaknesses with executive functioning skills and this may present some of the following difficulties:

- lack of thinking through the implications of actions, plans, and strategies;
- initiating behaviour;
- lack of cognitive flexibility, i.e. some difficulties in changing behaviour / problem solving;
- selective and sustained attention and distractibility;
- somewhat poor academic progress;
- controlling impulsive and inappropriate behaviours (e.g. shouting out).

EXECUTIVE FUNCTION – LOWER BAND (SCORES 0 - 25.9)

This baseline score is in the lower range for adults, indicating that at present you may have difficulty being able to plan tasks and may have some challenges with prioritizing or working out how to go about new tasks. You may benefit from more structure. You may experience difficulty initiating and leading change.

Impact: Executive function is in a poor state, the organization could end up "in a rut", unable to move or change direction even when there is a compelling reason to do so.

Adults with weaknesses in their executive functioning skills may exhibit some of the following types of difficulties:

- lack of thinking through the implications of actions, plans, and strategies
- initiating behaviour;
- lack of cognitive flexibility, i.e. difficulty changing behaviour / problem solving;

- poor selective and sustained attention and distractibility;
- poor academic progress;
- controlling impulsive and inappropriate behaviours (e.g. shouting out).

WORKING MEMORY – THE HERO

**WORKING MEMORY
– UPPER BAND (SCORES 74 - 100)**

This baseline score is in the upper band – the higher range for adults. This result indicates that at present you are able to access and utilize various pieces of information very well to make leadership decisions.

Impact: You are the Hero in problem solving situations because you understand everything that is going on and remember what success looks like.

Adults with very good working memory skills should show greater strengths in the following areas when compared to other adults their age:

- retaining information in the short term and use it to support their current thinking;
- following multi-step instructions;
- completing work-based tasks that require retaining extensive amounts of information;
- processing and understanding complex instructions;
- carrying out a number of different tasks at once.

WORKING MEMORY
– UPPER MIDDLE BAND (SCORES 58 - 73.9)

The baseline score is in the upper middle band and is within the higher middle range for adults. This result indicates that at present, you are able to access and utilize various pieces of information completely in your head to get leadership decisions made.

Impact: It could be better. Try focusing on a simple leadership process, like weekly team meetings, and begin tuning personal individual performance.

Adults with good working memory skills should be able to do the following:

- retain information in the short term and use it to support current thinking;
- follow multi-step instructions;
- complete work-based tasks that require them to retain moderate amounts of information;
- process and understand complex instructions;
- carry out a number of different tasks at once.

WORKING MEMORY
– MIDDLE BAND (SCORES 42 - 57.9)

This baseline score is in the middle band and within the middle range for adults. This result indicates that at present you are able to access and utilize various pieces of information to complete tasks, suggesting that you are likely to have adequate working memory skills. You could improve the way you access and use information to complete tasks and make decisions.

Impact: Things may be getting lost. A deeper understanding of the use and communication of information will help.

Adults with adequate working memory skills should be able to:

- retain information in the short term and use it to support their current thinking;
- follow multi-step instructions;
- complete work-based tasks that require retention of moderate amounts of information;
- process and understand complicated instructions;
- carry out a number of different tasks at once.

WORKING MEMORY – LOWER MIDDLE BAND (SCORES 26 - 41.9)

The baseline score results are within the lower middle range for adults. This result indicates that at present you are able to access and utilize some information, but may have some challenges with using and remembering a lot of data.

Impact: As a leader, you must use your team members more. You must distil information to the few critical things you can more easily recall.

Adults with weaknesses in their working memory skills may present the following types of difficulties:

- retaining information in the short term and using it to support their current thinking;
- following multi-step instructions / carrying out a number of tasks at once;
- completing work-based tasks – specifically those that require you to retain lots of information at once;
- processing and understanding complex instructions. Often it may appear that they have not paid attention, when in fact they have simply forgotten what it is they have to do;

- wanting to ask a question, then finding that they have "lost" or "forgotten" the question "held" in their "working memory";
- undertaking mental maths or tasks such as interpreting complex reports that require "heavy" mental manipulation in the mind.

WORKING MEMORY – LOWER BAND (SCORES 0 - 25.9)

The baseline results are within the lower range for adults, indicating that at present you may have difficulty accessing and utilizing information and may have some challenges with remembering more than a little data. You benefit from taking notes.

Impact: You need to bring more structure to your decision making so that important things are not omitted. You can try to use your team's memories.

Adults with weaknesses in their working memory skills may exhibit the following types of difficulties:

- retaining information in the short term and using it to support current thinking;
- following multi-step instructions / carrying out a number of tasks at once;
- completing work-based tasks – specifically those that require them to retain lots of information at once;
- processing and understanding complex instructions. Often it may appear that they have not paid attention, when in fact they have simply forgotten;
- wanting to ask a question, then finding that they have "lost" or "forgotten" the question "held" in their "working memory";
- undertaking mental maths or tasks such as interpreting complex reports that require "heavy" mental manipulation in the mind.

EPISODIC MEMORY – THE CURATOR

EPISODIC MEMORY – UPPER BAND (SCORES 74 - 100)

The baseline results are in the higher range for adults, indicating that at present you are able to apply your past learning and experiences accurately and very quickly to current tasks. These skills are a great strength in leadership

Impact: You are the Curator – accessing information from the past to shape a far better future. Does understanding the past ever limit your ability to think about the future?

This suggests that you are likely to have very good short-term visual memory, i.e. good visual processing, encoding, and retrieval skills.

Adults with very good memory skills should show greater strengths in the following areas when compared with other people their age:

- processing, encoding, and recalling visual information;
- recognizing and remembering patterns in numbers and data;
- recalling experiences and events relevant to the current situation;
- learning new tasks quicker and accelerating up the learning curve;
- imparting information to others so they can also accelerate up learning curves.

EPISODIC MEMORY – UPPER MIDDLE BAND (SCORES 58 - 73.9)

The baseline score in episodic memory and the results are within the higher middle range for adults. These indicate that, at present, you are able to apply past learning and experience to current leadership tasks in good time and with few errors. You have good visual processing, encoding, and retrieval of data.

Impact: You know how to structure use of historical information to the future benefit of your organization and yourself.

Adults with good memory skills should show strength in the following areas when compared with other people their age:

- processing, encoding, and recalling visual information;
- recognizing and remembering patterns in numbers and data;
- recalling experiences and events relevant to the current situation;
- learning new tasks quicker and accelerating up the learning curve;
- imparting information to others so they can also accelerate up learning curves.

EPISODIC MEMORY – MIDDLE BAND (SCORES 42 - 57.9)

The baseline results are within the middle range for adults and indicate that at present you are able to bring your past learning and experiences to your leadership work, but could do more to sustain focus and relevance. You have adequate short-term visual processing, encoding, and retrieval of data.

Impact: You can structure how you use some historical information to the benefit of your organization and yourself.

Adults with reasonable memory skills show some abilities in the following areas when compared to other people their age:

- processing, encoding and recalling visual information;
- recognizing and remembering patterns in numbers and data;
- recalling experiences and events relevant to the current situation;

- learning new tasks quicker and accelerating up the learning curve;
- imparting information to others so they can also accelerate up learning curves.

EPISODIC MEMORY
– LOWER MIDDLE BAND (SCORES 26 - 41.9)

The score is within the lower middle range for adults. The results indicate that at present you are able to apply your past learning and experience to current tasks, but may require a little more time to complete tasks accurately. This suggests that you are likely to experience some weaknesses with your memory, i.e. somewhat weaker visual processing, encoding, and retrieval of data.

Impact: Shaping conversations to avoid old mistakes is your job. You can use your team to sustain greater relevance in discussions.

Adults with weaknesses in episodic memory skills may exhibit the following types of difficulties:

- getting lost easily as they cannot always easily remember places visually;
- repeating actions that they have previously done because they do not remember doing them the first time around;
- giving details about what they have done at work that day;
- appearing slightly socially aloof due to their difficulties with remembering shared events;
- having lower confidence in their ability.

EPISODIC MEMORY –
LOWER BAND (SCORES 0 - 25.9)

The baseline score is within the lower range for adults. This indicates that at present you are not always able to apply your past learning and experience to current tasks but may require help with new tasks. You have weak visual processing, encoding, and retrieval of data. You are not yet fully applying past learning from events and conversations in your leadership. You may have difficulty remembering past events and conversations that are important to your job.

Impact: Consider a radical overhaul of the way you lead so that the information needed is readily available. You have much difficulty structuring how you use some historical information to the benefit of your organization and yourself.

Adults with weaknesses in episodic memory skills may exhibit the following types of difficulties:

- getting lost easily as they cannot always easily remember places visually;
- repeating actions that they have previously done because they do not remember doing them the first time around;
- giving details about what they have done at work that day;
- appearing slightly socially aloof due to their difficulties with remembering shared events;
- having lower confidence in their ability.

ATTENTION – THE COACH

ATTENTION
– UPPER BAND (SCORES 74 - 100)

The baseline results are in the upper band for adults, indicating that at present you are able to concentrate very well on tasks, despite distractions within your environment. You are able to complete tasks. The power to stay focused and filter out noise, and to give your full attention to your people, is a great leadership strength.

Impact: You are the Coach – sustaining your organization's dedication to the ongoing game plan. Do distractions ever annoy you?

Adults with very good attention skills should show greater strengths in the following areas when compared with other people their age:

- strong focus and ability to listen intently;
- ability to pay attention to a task for a long period of time;
- strong ability to focus on results;
- not being easily distracted;
- taking in everything that is going on and around them in the environment;
- retaining information;
- completing work-based tasks, e.g. seeing tasks through to completion;
- believing that everything is achievable.

ATTENTION
– UPPER MIDDLE BAND (SCORES 58 - 73.9)

The baseline score is in the upper middle range for adults. The results indicate that at present you are able to concentrate well on tasks despite distractions within your environment. You are reasonably able to focus and listen when motivated. You can pay attention to a task.

Impact: Consider how you can develop this into a real leadership strength. Focusing is a very powerful leadership ability within your reach.

Adults with good attention skills show strengths in the following areas when compared with other people their age:

- strong focus and ability to listen intently;
- ability to pay attention to a task for a long period of time;
- strong ability to focus on results;
- not being easily distracted;
- taking in everything that is going on and around them in the environment;
- retaining information;
- completing work-based tasks, e.g. seeing tasks through to completion;
- believing that most things are achievable.

ATTENTION
– MIDDLE BAND (SCORES 42 - 57.9)

The baseline results are average and indicate that at present you are generally able to concentrate on tasks despite distractions.

Impact: Do you find the volume of distracting situations is increasing? This is the signal for learning more about the way you can stay focused.

Adults with reasonable attention skills have some strengths in the following areas when compared with other people their age:

- reasonable focus and ability to listen;
- ability to pay attention to some tasks for a period of time;
- ability to focus on results;
- are sometimes distracted;
- taking in what is going on and around them in the environment;
- retaining some information;

- completing most work-based tasks, e.g. seeing tasks through to completion;
- believing that some things are achievable.

ATTENTION
– LOWER MIDDLE BAND (SCORES 26 - 41.9)

The baseline scores are in the lower middle range for adults and indicate that at present you are sometimes able to concentrate on tasks but you experience attention challenges where there are multiple competing demands.

Impact: How can you reshape your work environment so that you don't lose focus on tasks?

Adults with poorer attention skills are likely to experience some weaknesses in the area of "attention" from time to time. Barriers to learning that might show in the work-based environment would include:

- difficulties completing work, sustaining attention;
- inattentiveness / distractibility;
- difficulties retaining information as they may not be fully listening;
- difficulties completing work-based tasks as their concentration span is short, e.g. not seeing tasks through to completion, due to limited perseverance / focus on longer tasks;
- struggling to complete activity completely if they feel it is too long and the task is seen as not achievable;
- taking short cuts.

ATTENTION
– LOWER BAND (SCORES 0 - 25.9)

The baseline scores are in the lower range for adults and indicate that at present you are not able to concentrate on tasks; you experience attention challenges when there are multiple competing demands. You are not hitting your targets hard enough.

Impact: Can you do something simple to reduce distractions immediately?

Adults with poor attention skills experience weaknesses in the area of "attention" from time to time. Barriers to learning that might show in the work-based environment would include:

- difficulties completing work, sustaining attention;
- inattentiveness / distractibility;
- difficulties retaining information as they may not be fully listening;
- difficulties completing work-based tasks as their concentration span is short, e.g. not seeing tasks through to completion, due to limited perseverance / focus on longer tasks;
- struggling to complete activity completely if they feel it is too long and the task is seen as not achievable;
- taking short cuts.

PROCESSING SPEED – THE JUDGE

PROCESSING SPEED
– UPPER BAND (SCORES 74 - 100)

The baseline results are within the higher range for adults. Your results indicate that at present you are able to respond to tasks quickly and display high levels of accuracy. These skills are a great leadership strength.

Impact: You are the Judge – you make wise decisions by understanding how time and accuracy plays into the way you get things done.

Your strength in processing will help with the following:

- taking in new pieces of information, reaching a judgment about it, and formulating a response;
- responding to questions with speed and accuracy;
- switching and staying on task;
- thinking on your feet quickly;
- processing visual and auditory information quickly when problem solving.

PROCESSING SPEED – UPPER MIDDLE BAND (SCORES 58 - 73.9)

The baseline results are within the higher middle range, indicating that at present you are able to respond to tasks within good time and with accuracy. Do you experience overload when too many tasks are on your plate? You may be able to complete timed activities quickly as you are able to process information well.

Impact: Simple improvements in running meetings and delegating tasks will pay off for you.

Having high "average", "psychomotor" speed would help you with some of the following:

- taking in new pieces of information, reaching a judgment about it, and formulating a response;
- responding to questions with speed and accuracy;
- switching and staying on task;
- thinking on your feet quickly;
- processing visual and auditory information quickly when problem solving.

PROCESSING SPEED
– MIDDLE BAND (SCORES 42 - 57.9)

The baseline score in processing speed is within the middle range for adults. The results indicate that at present you are able to respond to tasks within a reasonable time and with reasonable accuracy. A score in the average range suggests that you have age appropriate skills in this area.

Impact: Lack of speed can limit your effectiveness. Think about improving the conduct of your meetings and accelerating task completion.

Your assessment score for the processing speed domain was in the "average" range, meaning you should be adequate across some of the following abilities:

- integrating new pieces of information, reaching a judgment about it, and formulating a response;
- responding to questions with speed and accuracy;
- switching and staying on task;
- thinking on your feet quickly;
- processing visual and auditory information quickly when problem solving.

PROCESSING SPEED
– LOWER MIDDLE BAND (SCORES 26 - 41.9)

The baseline score in the lower middle band indicates that you could respond to some tasks with more speed and you may need to improve your accuracy.

Impact: You will improve your career by training yourself to go quicker, especially in meetings.

Adults with weaknesses in their processing speed skills may

exhibit some difficulties in the following abilities:

- taking in new pieces of information, reaching a judgment about it, and formulating a response;
- responding to questions with speed and accuracy;
- switching and staying on task;
- thinking on your feet quickly;
- processing visual and auditory information quickly when problem solving.

PROCESSING SPEED
– LOWER BAND (SCORES 0 - 25.9)

The baseline score in the low range suggests that you may experience great weaknesses with your psychomotor processing speed and reaction times. This is the rate at which you can take in a new piece of information, reach a judgment about it, and formulate a response. Your results indicate that at present you may be able to respond to tasks, but may take longer to do so or may need to improve your accuracy to reduce errors. Taking too long to respond to important tasks may limit your leadership role.

Impact: Consider finding new ways to trade off thoroughness for response rate.

Adults with weaknesses in their processing speed skills may exhibit some difficulties in the following abilities:

- taking in new pieces of information, reaching a judgment about it, and formulating a response;
- responding to questions with speed and accuracy;
- switching and staying on task;
- thinking on their feet quickly;
- processing visual and auditory information quickly when problem solving.

WHAT NEXT?

These results should give you clear insights. It is as important to know where your leadership and management need development as much as it is to know where they have strength.

The great thing is that, because of neuroplasticity, you can develop and grow new neurones and new neuronal pathways to improve your cognitive fitness and make up for any deficiencies. You can also seek out people that complement your strengths with theirs. The best board of directors, the best executive team, the best financial, operations, or marketing teams will have people with clear strengths across all five domains, with a clear knowledge as to who excels in each domain.

Good people are not always in abundance. Therefore, if you have good people in your company, you should do everything you can to improve their cognitive fitness. You can inspire them and encourage others to motivate them, even if they see them as a threat. By acknowledging strength in someone else, especially in someone who reports to you, and by helping them to nurture that strength, you are showing true leadership.

Knowing the cognitive strengths of your team, your peers, your entire company, will help establish their leadership and management strengths. Where their strengths are lacking, if they are willing, you can help them develop skills to make up for any shortfall.

The next sections consider 50 training habits that you can practise to help you grow in each of the five cognitive domains. There are ten per domain and the idea is that you should try to run through a new habit each week. Within a year you could have 50 new or strengthened habits, giving you more durable and resilient leadership and management skills.

CHAPTER FOUR

IMPROVING COGNITIVE FITNESS THROUGH GOOD HABITS

INTRODUCTION

Keeping cognitively fit is essential in order to compete in the executive world. You need to be at your best for as long as you can and as often as you can. You never want to have a poor day, and want to know that you can perform at your best even when under stress.

You want to be a true professional and set a great example for everyone. Not just your colleagues, but for your community, family and friends as well. You can only consistently achieve this with a healthy and fully functioning cognition. This can be achieved by ensuring that you take a personalized approach to training.

You cannot begin to train without assessing your cognition first. A personal trainer will not attempt to improve physical function without first doing a physical fitness check. That's why the first part of this book is about assessing cognitive fitness.

Nowadays, there are plenty of brain-training programs, but few ask you to comprehensively understand and assess your cognition first. This is where cognition training is different. Brain-training is like going to the gym and not really knowing what to do; attempting some exercises but not really knowing if they are doing you any good. In the worse example, it's like lifting a heavy weight only to put a joint out.

Cognitive-training, on the other hand, begins with an assessment and is like having a personal trainer to ensure that you have a personalized, bespoke, and targeted training experience. Training your cognition in areas where you are the weakest takes you out of your comfort zone. You have to find a way to make the training engaging and palatable, like adding sugar to nasty tasting medicine. Simply approaching training through puzzles may not work; given the choice between two puzzles, you are more likely to choose the one you are best at performing. In doing so you continue to train the domains where you already have strength and forego those that are weaker; those that actually require training.

The problem with most of today's brain-training programs is that they are not personalized. Many people tend to train the areas where they are already strong and forego those parts of their cognition that require training. This is because training the weaker areas will take you out of your comfort zones. That is why before training you should be assessed.

GENERAL HEALTHY HABITS FOR COGNITIVE FITNESS

INTRODUCTION

The good news is that even though the inevitable stress from the workplace can lead to reduced performance due to poor cognitive fitness, this can be combated and prevented through exercise, a good diet, a good sleep regimen, drinking alcohol in moderation, not smoking, avoiding addictive behaviours, and even cognitive fitness training. The best leaders in history look after themselves.

According to studies,[109] [110] [111] regular physical activity is considered one of the best methods of promoting cognitive fitness. Exercise stimulates brain cell growth, maintains brain function, and cognitive efficiency. It can help prevent the loss of cognitive fitness in ageing. The effects of exercise on the hippocampus can boost learning and memory and help your emotional state.

Exercise is a stress reducer, so a proper exercise and relaxation schedule can reduce stress from the workplace. It could be used alongside cognitive training to further reduce the negative effects of the stress.

Interestingly, mental stimulation from social contact, participation, and engagement in challenging, cognitive fitness tasks can protect you against age-related declines in cognition and maintain high cognitive fitness.

To maintain a good state of health, you should consider the following:

- Keep healthy to positively impact overall cognitive performance.
- Exercise routinely, with good sleeping habits, nutrition, and hydration.
- Work with some stress, being careful not to let this pull you down.
- Ensure you are in a good environment and are not taking on too much.
- Manage life events, but don't be afraid to talk to someone if you suffer an adverse event in your family or home life. Help is available.

EXPERIENCES INFLUENCING BRAIN DEVELOPMENT

A wide range of experiences influence brain development and plasticity.[112, 113]

Regular physical activity indirectly stimulates brain cell growth. It maintains brain function and cognitive efficiency; hence, it can help prevent loss of cognitive efficiency in ageing and neurodegenerative diseases. Therefore, physical activity is perhaps one of the best ways to promote cognitive health.[114] More specifically, exercise can boost learning and memory through its effects on the hippocampus. Physical exercise also increases cerebral blood flow, bringing oxygen and nutrients to the brain, which in turn promotes nerve cell growth. Additionally, exercise, along with relaxation, may be beneficial in reducing stress. Minimizing stress may have a beneficial impact on the brain, as exposure to high levels of stress hormones can impair memory.[115] Chronic stress can also contribute to depression and anxiety disorders, which also impair cognition.

The following sections look at how your lifestyle impacts your cognitive fitness and, ultimately, your leadership skills.

NUTRITION

About 10,000 years ago, we learned how to become farmers and agriculture enabled us to develop the sophisticated lives we now lead. However, 10,000 years in evolutionary terms isn't a long period of time. Diets changed too rapidly from depending on scavenging, where you would eat basically anything and everything, to one that is predominantly based on cereals. Our intestines still haven't evolved sufficiently to take advantage of such a cereal-rich diet and many people have problems because of such a diet. These problems extend to those of cognitive fitness, as well as the digestion process.

In the last few hundred years, there has been a significant increase in our consumption of meat and sugar. Yet again, on an evolutionary scale our bodies haven't had much opportunity to adjust and beneficially deal with the growth in consumption of these food stuffs. This has resulted in increases in the rate of obesity, diabetes, and poor cardiovascular health. There has been a further knock-on negative impact to cognitive fitness. Good nutritional habits will enable you to lead a healthier and a more cognitively fit life.

BALANCING YOUR DIET

It has been shown that a good balanced diet can have an influential role on cognitive fitness by acting on molecular systems or cellular processes. These are vital for maintaining cognitive fitness. For example, there is evidence that omega-3 fatty acids reduce cognitive deficit, and folate has positive effects on memory performance.[116] Conversely, a poor diet high in saturated fat and sugar has been shown to increase the rate of cognitive ageing, hence reducing cognitive fitness. Moderate caloric restriction could protect the brain, as research indicates that an excessive intake of calories might counteract the positive effects of otherwise "healthy" diets.[117] What you eat and drink affects your health and if you have a healthy diet, you are more likely to have a healthy cognition.

Nutrition is, therefore, a critical factor in maintaining and improving cognitive fitness and will help keep you safe against cognitive decline.[118] Eating a healthy diet counteracts cognitive ageing and improves cognitive fitness (see Table 3).[119] This includes a diet rich in: antioxidants, found in fruit (e.g. berries, apples) and vegetables (e.g. spinach, broccoli); omega 3 fatty acids, found in nuts and oily fish; vitamins and minerals (e.g. B vitamins, zinc); and other compounds such as flavonoids and choline. Conversely, the absence of these nutrients can impair learning and memory; in the long-term they can even increase your chances of neuropsychiatric disorders.

Table 3: Selected nutrients affecting cognitive fitness (various sources)

Nutrient	Potential effects on cognition/emotion	Sources
Omega-3 fatty acids	Amelioration of cognitive decline in the elderly; basis for treatment of mood disorders Cognitive improvement in traumatic brain injury; amelioration of cognitive decay in Alzheimer's disease	Oily fish, flax seeds, kiwi fruit, walnuts
Curcumin	Amelioration of cognitive decay in traumatic brain injury and Alzheimer's disease	Turmeric

Nutrient	Potential effects on cognition/emotion	Sources
Flavonoids	Cognitive improvement in the elderly Cognitive enhancement with exercise	Cocoa, green tea, citrus fruits, wine, dark chocolate
Vitamins B	B6, B12 or folate: enhances memory performance in women B12 improves cognitive impairment	Various natural foods, e.g. oily fish, meat, spinach, banana, yoghurt
D	Preserves cognition in the elderly	Oily fish, milk, mushrooms, grains
E	Reduction in cognitive decay in the elderly – amelioration of cognitive decay	Asparagus, avocado, spinach, nuts, seeds, vegetable oils, olives, wheat germ
Combination of C, E, & carotene	Antioxidant vitamins delay cognitive decline in the elderly	C: citrus fruits, green vegetables, liver; E: as above; Carotene: sweet potato, carrots, squash
Choline	Causal relationship between dietary choline and cognition – reduction of seizure-induced memory impairment	Egg yolk, meat, lettuce

Minerals	Effects on cognition/emotion	Sources
Calcium	High levels are associated with faster cognitive decline in the elderly	Dairy produce
Copper	Low plasma levels correlated with cognitive decline in Alzheimer's disease	Oysters, red meat, Brazil nuts, molasses, black pepper
Iron	Iron treatment normalizes cognitive fitness in young women	Red meat, fish, poultry, lentils, beans
Selenium	Life-long low levels are associated with lower cognitive fitness in humans	Nuts, cereals, meat, fish, eggs
Zinc	Reductions in diet reduces cognitive decline in the elderly	Oysters, nuts, seeds, whole grains

[Adapted from Gómez-Pinilla 2008]

INTESTINAL FLORA

It is not only what you eat that is important, but the contents of your intestines also have a major impact on your health and cognitive fitness. The weight of your flora is about 1.5 kg, the same as your brain. You find the same biochemical transmitters being used to send signals to adjacent cells in the gut as you find in the brain. There has always been evidence that demonstrates the importance of the gut and, with new techniques, more is being learned about the influence of the gut on cognitive fitness.[120]

The human body is populated with indigenous microbes after birth, and colonization of the gut has been found to impact on brain development and subsequent adult behaviour.[121] The gut microbes influence signalling pathways, neurotransmitter turnover, and the production of synaptic-related proteins in the cortex and striatum. This suggests that microbial colonization initiates signalling mechanisms that affect neuronal circuits involved in motor control and anxiety behaviour.[122] It is important that you look after your gut flora, replenishing the good microbes on a regular basis by consuming foods rich in Lactobacillus and Bifidobacterium. Fermented foods such as sauerkraut, kombucha, and kimchi could improve health generally and cognitive fitness specifically.

PHYSICAL ACTIVITY AND EXERCISE

There is growing scientific evidence linking the benefits of exercise to neuroplasticity. You can take advantage of this. By maintaining a physically active lifestyle you can achieve a wide range of positive health outcomes, including benefits to cognitive fitness. It is suggested that some effects of aerobic exercise on brain structure occur via a more global mechanism, such as increased grey matter density in the frontal, temporal, and cingulate areas of the brain[123] and the number and intricacy of blood vessels in the brain.[124]

Exercise alone may not be the complete answer. Environmental enrichment (living and working in an interesting, uplifting, and stimulating environment, as opposed to one that is drab) has been shown to produce exercise-related structural changes in motor areas of the cerebellum and cerebral cortex, and in regions of the hippocampus which play a role in learning, memory, and navigation.[125] This is because while neurogenesis (neuronal cell growth) in the hippocampus has been shown to increase physical activity,[126] many of the new neurones produced do not survive. Thus exercise increases the rate of brain growth, and "environmental enrichment" is required to increase the number of new neurones that survive and get incorporated into the existing neural network.[127] Exercise is like a priming mechanism. It's not surprising that athletes make great business-people and leaders if they use the grey matter that they are nurturing in an intellectual way.

LIFELONG BENEFITS

Neuroimaging studies have demonstrated the efficacy of physical activity in improving cognitive fitness across your lifetimes. Aerobic fitness protects you from age-related loss of brain tissue[128] and physical activity in later life has been linked to less cortical atrophy, better brain function, and enhanced cognitive fitness.[129] The effects of physical activity on the ageing brain are widespread; however, as mentioned previously, exercise must be linked to environmental factors (or other stimulating activities) to fully cement the improvements.

BRAIN-DERIVED NEUROTROPHIC FACTOR

The link between the benefits of exercise (and diet, i.e. food/energy restriction), and neurogenesis and cardiovascular function may be provided by the brain derived neurotrophic factor (BDNF). BDNF is a protein produced to enhance the growth and development of nerve (brain) cells. BDNF plays a significant role in the development of the autonomic (involuntary) nervous system and in the control of cardiac function.[130]

Exercise and energy restriction (from food intake) provoke an increase in the activity of neuronal circuits and mildly stress the cells in the nervous system. This stimulates the production of BDNF and its release. BDNF promotes growth of neurones. It enhances synaptic plasticity and it increases neuronal resistance to injury and disease. In the hippocampus, BDNF promotes neurone production and survival from progenitor stem cells, and integration of new neurones into existing neuronal circuits.

It is interesting to note that exercise (via BDNF) also influences glucose metabolism and body fat composition. Diabetes mellitus, which results from inadequate insulin release and/or reduced insulin sensitivity, has the potential to induce neurological complications, including cognitive deficits.[131] Signals from insulin receptors are important for many nerve processes, such as neuronal survival, dendritic outgrowth, circuit development, and synaptic plasticity.[132] It is important to note that obesity is associated with BDNF deficiency.[133]

THE IMPACT OF EDUCATION ON COGNITIVE FITNESS

Education tends to be considered as an activity that occurs between the ages of 4 to 18 years old, or to 21 years old, at a push. All of you should become involved in life-long learning, because while activities like exercise produce new neuronal cells, these cells will die unless they are stimulated. Continuous education is a great way to ensure stimulation, together with the benefit of the learning itself.

Higher education tends to be associated with higher levels of cognitive performance later in life. Most longitudinal studies have found a direct relationship between education levels and age-related cognitive decline. Individuals with lower education levels tend to be more at risk of poor cognitive fitness and performance.[134]

Studies have shown that a longer time in education is related to better initial performance on cognitive tests across a range of cognitive domains, and higher levels of education are associated with a slower decline in mental status.[135] There appears to be differences in the rate of decline linked to education, working memory, and episodic memory. It is suggested that education may both increase cultural competency and improve brain function by increasing the number of synapses.[136] Thus, cultural knowledge appears to be especially sensitive to education.[137]

STRESS

Without some level of stress many of you wouldn't get out of bed in the morning. Some of you produce your best work when under stress. As seen above, some level of stress is required to stimulate the production of BDNF and its release, and all the benefits flowing from that. It seems that just as you have to put muscles under stress to improve physical fitness, the same can be said for cognitive fitness. For both forms of stress to be beneficial, recovery periods are required.

However, there is a cost to pay if you are under constant, chronic stress. Stress over a prolonged period of time will damage cognitive fitness, not enhance it. Your bodies, and particularly your brains, were not designed to be under stress 24/7.

During stress, a wide variety of hormones, including glucocorticoids, are released through and regulated by the system known as the hypothalamus-pituitary-adrenal axis. Repeated or prolonged exposure to glucocorticoids will have a detrimental effect on your brain function, and probably contribute to age-related decline in your cognitive fitness.[138]

Stress and glucocorticoids have profound consequences for learning and memory, and synaptic plasticity, and contribute to neuronal atrophy, changes in rates of neuronal turnover, and eventually to neuronal death.

Stress inhibits adult neurogenesis (growth of nerve cells) in the hippocampus, a key area of the brain that is central to emotion, memory, and learning. The changes exhibited in the hippocampus include a reduction in the volume, neuronal size, and density of neural cells. Thus, stress causes actual physical changes to this part of the brain. Undergoing stress for a prolonged period translates into a decreased brain reserve and actually alters cognitive fitness through memory impairment, attention deficit, and altered exploratory and emotional behaviour; it also increases psychopathologies such as schizophrenia, ADHD, depression, and drug addiction.[139]

LOWERING STRESS

It is not easy to directly measure stress and it is even more difficult to try to establish levels that are optimal for individual performance. It is easier and more useful to measure cognitive fitness, which shows brain health and, therefore, how you are coping with stress. Over time this measurement can show if you are moving in the right direction and allow you to adjust your work practices accordingly.

Some people can cope (and actually thrive) under more stress than others and this is reflected in their workload and their ability to cope. Currently stress is measured in a very non-scientific manor, almost by luck as people are given more and more work until they drop. Too much stress can cause serious health problems over a long period of time; working memory becomes paralysed, making it difficult to make rational decisions or even causing serious illness.

By having the courage to allow cognitive fitness measurements in the workplace, leaders will find that employees have the ability to shine further. It is better to find an optimum level of work specific to each individual, and keep slightly below this.

Emotions are also governed by the hippocampus. However, as you know, emotions are personal feelings and also very difficult to assess as they differ greatly from one person to the next. You can measure emotions in many different ways, but few of these are known to correlate with one another and none give a true picture of your cognitive fitness until they reach extreme proportions. Measuring cognitive fitness directly is, therefore, the best way to understand, work, and live in a good emotional state.

SPECIFIC HEALTHY HABITS BY DOMAIN

INTRODUCTION

In the previous section you looked at lifestyle changes that can have a general impact on overall cognitive fitness, making general improvements to your leadership and managerial thinking.

In this section the focus is on specific habits for each of the core domains. There are ten habits per domain, 50 in all. These habits are designed to be taken on a week at a time, giving you roughly a year of good habits to acquire.

EXECUTIVE FUNCTION

Executive function is a key domain in leadership and management. Even if this is a strong domain for you, it's a good idea to practise these habits continually and acquire them as part of your personal development. It is good practice to share these with your teams and encourage them to practise areas where they can benefit the most.

EXECUTIVE FUNCTION HABIT 1:
ONE-PAGE PLAN - PUBLIC DISCUSSION AND DISPLAY

As a leader you are in control of the direction that your company takes. Depending on your position your "hand on the wheel" may have more or less influence, but regardless, you have influence.

Leaders must produce plans for their companies, sections, departments, or teams and themselves, and share these with all colleagues. This shows your leadership, whatever level you are in the organization. It shows you are proactively looking to take the company forward.

Undertake an exercise to capture and distil the salient points of a one-year plan. The art will be to keep the visionary aspects of the plan, along with near-term objectives, in an easily digestible format; hence, it is suggested to keep this to one page.

This will be a test of understanding the key elements within the plan. It will also be a great exercise in editing the vision. Think of it in terms of an extended elevator pitch, perhaps as much as three minutes. If you can lay out your vision on one page, whilst keeping the content solid, then you have the basis to communicate it time and again to many different audiences, as well as posting it for all to see.

Encourage feedback on the plan and aim to undertake regular updates (say, every two months). Refer to the plan in team meetings, highlighting the objectives that have been achieved; how they were achieved; with what resources; who was involved; why it was important.

During team meetings encourage further discussion of the plan and how it is used to flow out to your teams to enable them to keep plans and share objectives. This exercise will help to keep on top of work flows, ensuring that the overall vision is still the main target.

Giving yourself a week to produce the first one-page plan should be ample time. Keeping the plan up to date is important, but shouldn't require as much time.

EXECUTIVE FUNCTION HABIT 2:
AFTER ACTION REVIEWS

How often do you hold meetings where actions are set? In reality, almost every meeting, beyond those to disseminate information, should have actions. But how often do you undertake "after action reviews"?

As a leader it is essential that you keep the momentum going, that you are able to assess the best use of resources required to meet targets.

After action reviews are a good habit to get into. Rather than just tag these items on to the end of the agenda at other meetings, make these a specific meeting in their own right. There are several direct benefits from doing this:

1. The learning:
   An after action review gives sufficient time to explore all that can be learned from undertaking the action.

2. The commitment:
   Colleagues will immediately see how committed you are for everyone (including yourself) to complete their actions. Their commitment will grow accordingly as the reviews take place. No one wants to be seen to be letting the team down.

3. Knowing what's important:
   Actions will take on a new lease of life. When setting actions, everyone will consider how important it is to the overall vision, how much time, and how many people it will take to complete. The whole action setting process will work more effectively, with fewer, but better actions being set. The more important actions will rise to the surface.

4. Create a checklist to capture the above, listing the steps involved in each task.

5. Generate meeting summaries, regular employee acknowledgement, and frequent team evaluations.

No one likes adding meetings to already busy workloads, but these action reviews needn't be stand alone. They can be incorporated into existing meetings, provided they are given sufficient emphasis on the agenda. Or they can be included in daily or weekly huddles as appropriate. Ask one team member to come up with a suitable template to improve the process by ensuring there is continuity among the actions.

A good leader gets work done. After action reviews will increase your leadership skills.

EXECUTIVE FUNCTION HABIT 3: TOUGH AND TRUTHFUL DECISION MAKING

Sometimes it's easier to take the well-trodden path when it comes to decision making. The best leaders know when they have to make tough and truthful decisions for the good of their company, workforce, clients, and shareholders. This comes about by thinking plans through to the end, to be able to see where the road will get bumpy, and to know what contingencies to put in place. A good and clear vision requires commitment, and truthfulness when you have to depart from it.

One of the toughest decisions leaders have to make is when to let someone go. Most companies put people through a tough hiring process to allow the candidate to show their strengths. But this process should also show their weaknesses.

The process should also allow for gender variations; in general, men overstate their skills more than women, believing they are more intelligent for example.[140] Getting candidates to complete and present a case study is a good way to even out that inequality and understand their strengths and areas of weakness.

However, once you take someone on you want them to perform well. If they don't, it's often because you haven't conducted the interview process correctly.

In these circumstances it is better to admit you made a mistake than allow a person to continually fail in their job. This is a miserable position to be in and over time can even bring about poor health. As leaders it is your responsibility to be tough and truthful and let the person know that you are going to let them go. However, don't just cut them adrift. You can help them find a new position, more in keeping with their skills, by getting in touch with contacts either within or outside your organization.

By endeavouring to help them move on you make a tough process more achievable. You also get the chance to show that compassion is a good strength. Not only will the person you let go admire you, so will all your staff, and work better as a result. They will realize that you will stand by them at times of difficulty.

Not all tough decisions involve firing people, but whenever you have to make a tough decision, think about it from every point of view and see how to make it achievable, while creating other opportunities for those involved.

In every case, be honest with yourself. Leaders don't shirk from their responsibilities.

EXECUTIVE FUNCTION HABIT 4: PLANNING EVENTS

It's especially important to nurture planning and strategy skills. You often rely on others to set up all your meetings, but if you rely on others too much your sense of planning will diminish.

Therefore, think of a series of events that would be good for the team. You may have an international team, based around individuals who all have expertise in their region. Running events to get each one to present on their country in turn would be a good way to inform all of them about the contrasts and similarities across the markets. This would lead to more efficient working.

You could plan these as breakfast/lunch/evening time seminars and either supply food at the event or ask people to bring and share their own. Perhaps the food theme can be based on the country in question to make that a feature of the event.

This could also form the basis of a team-building exercise, where new skills such as cooking, photography, painting, or creative writing could be used as a catalyst to build the team. It needs to be a new creative activity that would be of interest to all.

A similar initiative could be used to encourage networking across the organization when employees/teams are geographically apart. And "geographically apart" can mean on different floors of the same building. It's amazing how a single flight of stairs can keep people from networking almost as much as a sea or an ocean. You could ban the sending of emails or phone calls within a department, encouraging people to get up (a good thing to do in any case) and actually go and speak to someone in person. Don't think of this as time wasting. Think of the time saved in numerous emails or phone calls, going back and forth, when a quick discussion would have done.

Leadership is about getting the best from people. Think of events that will do just that. This habit will also improve your planning skills and creativity.

EXECUTIVE FUNCTION HABIT 5:
WORKING WITH OTHERS OUTSIDE
YOUR ORGANIZATION

As leaders you can get too comfortable working with the same people in the same circumstances. Working with other people outside of the organization can stretch and show you things that you wouldn't normally see.

There are numerous organizations that need voluntary leaders to enable them to function. This is a great way to get involved in the local community. Not only does it show that you care, but it also shows that you think long term about resources within the community and keeping them going for those that need them.

It's also a great opportunity to work with people who are motivated by volunteering as opposed to being paid. The skills developed from volunteering can provide new ideas for your organization. It's a new and different way to see how to get the best out of people.

Leaders can also join any of of the numerous professional organisations geared towards small- and medium-sized enterprise (SME) leaders or entrepreneur leaders. As well as learning opportunities, these organizations provide an opportunity to get involved, to use your skills, and to help others within the organization. By giving your time you get ten times back in experience, knowledge, and understanding.

The great thing about working in these organizations is that you are working alongside your peers, as opposed to having people reporting to you. The skills required to motivate peers will be different to motivating employees, but if you want to get to the top you have to understand how to do this.

You can also look at obtaining additional qualifications. Although the MBA doesn't seem to be as attractive as it once was, it's still worth considering to accelerate leadership.

EXECUTIVE FUNCTION HABIT 6:
MAKE TIME FOR PLAY

Playing certain types of games with your children will provide challenges, practice, and the self-regulating skills associated with executive function. You can steadily increase the complexity of the games and activities you give them and offer opportunities to help them grow, learn, and mature without getting bored.

It's the same at work, except the games and activities take on a different meaning. But, it doesn't hurt to see work as a game or activity. Playing games keeps the brain in good cognitive fitness. Playing manages stress levels and boosts the immune system.

Being happy is also good for you. Research suggests that laughing encourages people to think more creatively. Studies reveal that people who laugh a lot get ill less often.[141]

There are lots of times when the mind goes off in strange directions, and this is okay. There are many cognitive benefits in letting the mind wander, including increased creativity and problem-solving abilities.

EXECUTIVE FUNCTION HABIT 7: ENCOURAGE CONSTRUCTIVE ARGUMENT AND CRITICISM

You should routinely critically analyse your "actions" and the way that you have behaved towards other people and colleagues; you should consider the implications of your actions on the way people work and respond. Think about the long-term benefits your actions bring about. Should you change any of your work habits to benefit your team and organization? For example, shouting at a staff member may scare them into doing the right thing, but a calmer approach will make a better staff member in the long term. Giving them the right to challenge your thinking will empower them, bringing out their leadership and management skills.

You could actively encourage others to argue against your opinions. This will be a strong test of your convictions. It will help you hone your opinions and practise your strategy skills.

This is why it's important to always hire people that are smarter than you. Smarter people will help make you and your company stronger. The art of conversation requires that you think on your feet, and conversing with someone smarter can be a fantastic exercise in quick thinking, as well as an opportunity to learn something new. Seek out interesting people and engage them in conversations, however brief, and if they are truly smart, offer them a job.

EXECUTIVE FUNCTION HABIT 8: TRY NEW IDEAS/EXPERIENCES TO SHARPEN THE SAW

The last of Covey's famous seven habits[142] was to continually sharpen the saw, to never let cognitive fitness or leadership be blunted. You must continually open yourself to new ideas, new ways of doing things, new experiences.

You should encourage and collate "out of the box" ideas in the work environment; allow consideration of these ideas and the means to implement the best of them at appropriate times. You can document how you will put new ideas into practice. This avoids the routine and creates a culture that allows innovative ideas.

You should attend external strategy seminars and encourage others to do so too. You can try different working practices and allow others to practise new ways to do things.

You could travel to work by different routes, by different means, try different food, seek the unusual such as unusual sporting activities, new challenges, new hobbies.

Life-long learning is something you should all do. The day you stop learning is the day you die. You can start a new qualification at night school or online.

You could plan your family activities, weekends away, holidays, ensuring that you do something different. You must play challenging strategy games with your kids and your parents, their grandparents. Three generations can challenge each other.

Travelling enables your brain to adapt to a new environment, experience unknown challenges, and make explorations. To increase brain activity, new experiences and learning environments are a must and travelling can provide such opportunities.

You must make sure that you do something you love every day. If your brain is constantly bogged down in work, it has no time or space to explore creative, fun ideas and concepts.

If the barman at the pub, or the barista at the local coffee shop, or the waitress in the restaurant all know what "I'll have the usual" means, it's definitely time for a change. Just stop and consider something (anything) different. Try wearing a watch upside down or brushing your teeth with a non-dominant hand. Try giving employees a hand written thank you instead of an email. Employees will appreciate the hand written note far more. Hand-writing can also help to improve cognitive skills like learning and memory by the physical act of writing words by hand.

You can sharpen the senses by challenging the brain to involve all senses in routine activities, like eating with your eyes closed and placing more emphasis on taste and smell.

EXECUTIVE FUNCTION HABIT 9: PRACTICE EMPATHY

I am often asked about Emotional Intelligence. I certainly believe in connections between the gut and the brain, and between the heart and the brain. I also believe in Neuro-Linguistic Program-ming (NLP), a specialist behavioural technology practice, through which a set of guiding principles can bring about great benefits.

I believe that all behaviour depends on the state of your cognitive fitness and that it is ultimately through cognition that you exhibit good and bad behaviour. The best part is that you can meas-ure cognitive fitness, using psychometric tests to assess various aspects of your behaviour. Through this you will get a quantita-tive understanding of your leadership and managerial thinking. It is, therefore, your cognitive fitness that ultimately controls your ability to exhibit empathy.

Empathy is a strong leadership skill. Knowing how to read some-one is vital if you want to get the best out of them. How can you practise empathy? You could try to be more empathetic to all your work colleagues, to talk to colleagues with whom you don't usually have a conversation. To say "thank you" to the cleaners when they empty your bins. Chat with them, find out what's important in their lives, plus others you don't normally talk to. Perhaps make tea for your personal assistants or other colleagues when they are hard pressed. To find as many ways as possible to "lead" by "serving".

By practising empathy you will open your mind and be more creative and open to ideas.

It's also a great way to practise your listening skills. You never know what you might learn.

EXECUTIVE FUNCTION HABIT 10:
REST WITH YOUR FAMILY

Spend time with your family, your spouse or partner, your friends, and loved ones. Do what they want to do.

This habit is good for you and for your family. It shows your commitment to them, that you really care about what they want (above your own interests), and that you are willing to give them your time.

It's also another good way for you to turn off and let your mind wander on to new and surprising areas of thought. New ideas will emerge as a result of this. Current ideas will bed down.

However, also spend this time to reflect on how lucky you are to have a supportive family and friends. Time passes so quickly and before you know it your children are leaving home or your best confidants have passed away. Every second of life is precious. Don't spend the majority of those seconds in the boardroom.

WORKING MEMORY

Working memory is ultimately about trusting yourself to be able to make good decisions and solve big problems. The following 10 habits will help to improve working memory.

WORKING MEMORY HABIT 1:
CHECK OUT YOUR DIARY WITH A FRIEND

One of the biggest problems leaders have is that their diaries are packed with meetings. Sitting in meetings all day prevents you from "working" and, if they are not action-orientated meetings, they can erode working memory.

How can you change this?

To overcome this you need to find someone you can trust, a workmate. And they must trust you too, because you are going to share your diary secrets with them.

This habit must be performed every Friday. It is the one meeting every week that you must not delete, because it is the one meeting that will save you from madness.

Every Friday meet with your workmate and talk through your diary for the coming month and, particularly, for the following week. For each meeting try to justify why you must attend and why you can't ask for the minutes and catch up that way, etc.

Your colleague must do the same with you. You must aim to reduce your diary entries by 25%. You can use this extra time for your decision making and problem solving tasks from the next habit (Working Memory Habit 2).

WORKING MEMORY HABIT 2: MONDAY MORNING "DECISION MEETING"

Do you jump out of bed on a Monday because you can't wait to get back into the office? If you enjoy your work, there is no reason why you shouldn't look forward to it. If you enjoy your work, you should also want to catch up with the people you work with. A meeting on a Monday is a great way to set up the week.

If possible, try to start the meeting early because that way you avoid the commute problems that build up on a Monday.

Set aside five minutes for people to talk about their exciting weekends. You want some of that weekend energy in the office.

This should be an action-oriented meeting. For example:

- What actions were set last week that need your attention this week?
- What actions are required this week?
- Who needs support to close a big sale?
- Who needs help with the latest social media campaign? How is recruitment going; internship planning; company training plans?
- What is the biggest decision to be made this week? This month? This quarter? This year? And do you have your best people working on each of them?

Keep a record of all the actions set and use this to set a personal agenda for the week. Allocate time to think about and make the decisions for the actions allocated. This will only be possible if you have been smart and not allowed your diary to be fully choked with meetings (see Working Memory Habit 1).

You can also use this meeting to personally thank someone for something exceptional they did last week.

WORKING MEMORY HABIT 3:
EXTERNAL LEARNING INVESTMENT

Lifelong learning is for everyone. Try it yourself and set a good example to your team. In some ways it doesn't have to be connected to work, so long as it challenges the brain cells.

There are dozens of online courses and many are free. Look out for those that give you accreditation for your work. Spend some time this week and find one suitable for you and get into the habit of learning again.

You can learn just about anything online – even on a mobile device. Whether it's on your transport to work, on your lunch break, or in the five spare minutes you have between meetings. Commit to learning something that requires a little investment in time now and again, but one that can be built to into a substantial learning project.

See if you can convince your colleagues or even your spouse to join you.

WORKING MEMORY HABIT 4:
SLEEP

Find time to relax; get sufficient sleep. For most people, a solid seven hours of sleep is important to maintain cognitive skills such as learning, concentration, and memory. But be careful. Oversleeping on a weekend could end up feeling like jet-lag, without the fun of a holiday.

There is a big difference between the amount of sleep you can get by on and the amount you need to function at your best. The truth is that over 95% of adults need between 7.5 to 9 hours of sleep every night in order to avoid sleep deprivation. Even skimping on a few hours makes a difference! Memory, creativity, problem-solving abilities, and critical thinking skills are all compromised.

Sleep is critical to learning and memory in an even more fundamental way. Research[143] shows that sleep is necessary for memory consolidation, with the key memory-enhancing activity occurring during the deepest stages of sleep. It can help with those deep problems you are working on.

The following are some tips to help you develop good sleeping habits:

- Get into a regular sleep schedule. Try not to break your routine, even on weekends and holidays.
- Avoid all screens for at least an hour before bed. Don't allow them in the bedroom. Plug them in overnight as far away as possible.
- Buy a simple alarm clock to wake up to.
- Reduce caffeine intake. Caffeine affects people differently. Some people are highly sensitive, and even morning coffee may interfere with sleep at night. Try reducing your intake or cutting it out from 2pm in the afternoon or entirely if you suspect it's keeping you up.
- Are you allowed power naps? Some research suggests even a few minutes can increase alertness. But don't let them replace the necessity of a good night's sleep.

WORKING MEMORY HABIT 5:
PRACTISE COMPLEX PROBLEMS

Your brain is like a muscle. If you don't exercise it, it will get weaker. Varying your activities will stimulate the release of dopamine, which increases motivation and through other mechanisms, the growth of new neurones. It's important, therefore, to practise complex problems or comprehension, but be sure to choose something enjoyable and stick with it. There are many ways to do this:

- Keep the brain active through studying a new subject; history, geography, the classics.
- Play "logic games" with your kids (and parents).
- Do your personal finances. Check your bank or accountant is getting it right.
- Try a variety of puzzles because you soon get used to the same techniques.
- Take a new route home and go back to reading maps and planning journeys, rather than relying on your smart phone navigation.
- Go orienteering in the woods with a map and compass.
- Learn to read music; play a musical instrument, which will help to develop your motor control, hearing, and visuospatial skills.
- Keep giving yourself (and others) positive reminders. A positive mindset is a healthier and more creative and smarter mindset.

1) Visualize the problem to support visual-spatial and verbal working memory. Research demonstrates that visual-spatial working memory is a crucial component of many higher-order mathematical skills. Ask your team to create a mind picture to represent information and then to draw a picture that represents the information and explain it. Eventually the goal would be to have them describe the picture they have in mind, rather than needing to draw it. It may be helpful to give them cues to

create this mental image such as who, what, where, when, colour, size, shape, number, texture, mood, movement, and sound.

2) Practice, practice, practice. Repeated practice can reduce the strain on working-memory capacity. Strategies that make a process automatic, such as over-learning multiplication tables, reduce the brain's need to keep things in mind, helping you to improve working memory and math skills simultaneously. Memorizing or over-learning a task allows you to work something out like second nature, which is less taxing and frees up memory capacity. Have "attention breaks" where you can take a break from the assigned material for a couple of minutes. This helps to maintain focus and not drift off-task, lessening the effectiveness of over-learning. Repeated practice helps you to maintain information, and by practising and repeating what you have learned, you will continue to stretch your working memory capacities.

3) Summarize your life. Recount an experience in a concise and orderly fashion. Mathematics requires organization, precision, and keeping track of information, particularly with word problems. Recalling a recent experience can help you learn to retain information while actively organizing it.

WORKING MEMORY HABIT 6: COMPREHENSION SKILLS

Undertake activities that will enhance your comprehension skills. There are many you can choose from:

- Take up a debating or public speaking hobby.
- Read a non-UK, English written newspaper (e.g. if you live in the UK, *The New York Times*) to get a different slant on the international news.

- Do homework with your children that involves mental arithmetic and literacy comprehension.
- Read those difficult novels that intellectuals go on about.
- Encourage deeper processing and test comprehension to improve working memory:
  o One strategy to promote deeper processing is thinking aloud. Instead of reading text in your head, find two or three main points to read out loud.
  o Promote discussion of it. What someone has read or heard often stimulates more thinking about it than simply re-reading it.

WORKING MEMORY HABIT 7: GET ORGANIZED

Organizing your thoughts will help you to use your working memory to the maximum. Break complex problems down into their constituent parts and assess each one in time. Create checklists for your most complex procedures at work. Checklists work for airline pilots and others in critical roles.

Clear the desk and the mind at the same time: an organized workspace may help improve cognitive skills. Put the empty desk space to good use by using creative diagrams and pictures of the problem in hand.

Take your organization skills out of work. Mentally rehearse the most efficient route around the supermarket and visualize the items you wish to buy. When you are in the supermarket, you'll find your memory is prompted.

WORKING MEMORY HABIT 8: REDUCE UNNECESSARY STRESS

Stress is necessary, but chronic stress will damage us. Stress interferes with attention and your working memory. It prevents you from storing items in your short-term memory. The thing that is stressing you replaces your intended short-term memory, breaking your ability to undertake working memory problems.

To avoid stress, try to minimalize it where possible. The "always on" culture of many workplaces nowadays means that most people find it hard to switch off. Try to:

- have "no smart phone" weekends;
- ban phone usage during meetings;
- don't allow smartphones or similar devices in the bedroom;
- put in place an IT moratorium (e.g. no emails before 8:00 or after 21:00 during the week);
- reduce time allowed for watching television.

Equally, there are things you can positively do to avoid stress, such as:

- when stress builds up take a series of long, deep breaths;
- take regular breaks away from the computer and your desk;
- take a walk outside... walk on the grass;
- consider meditation – it can help improve memory, decision making, and attention span; all of these are good for working memory;
- but don't over-meditate – if you spend all the time in the "now" state, you may compromise your executive function and episodic memory.

WORKING MEMORY HABIT 9:
TEACH

Improve working memory by teaching others. Before teachers relay information, they process what they have learned in a way that prepares it for departure. This illustrates the common axiom, "To teach is to learn twice." Teaching is a process of consolidating information and archiving it, while at the same time making way for more long-term memory.

Make learning and memorization a social experience. Study with your friends. Do a "text test" with them, exchanging short questions and short answers. Students quizzing each other is often much more successful when memorizing for a test. This is not always helpful, as the social nature of studying together can deteriorate into socializing rather than studying, so try and have a good mixture of fun and learning. In addition to the verbal and interactive components of memorization, another person's perspective on what is important to remember can be very useful in learning and test-taking.

WORKING MEMORY HABIT 10:
READ A TRASHY NOVEL

Just for once, read a trashy novel that doesn't tax your brain.

If nothing else, this will have you running back to your science journals and intellectual pursuits in no time.

Seriously, everyone needs a little balance in their lives and something like an easy read will give you that respite. A constant bombardment of problem solving and decision making isn't necessarily good for you. Just as a muscle needs time to recover, relax, and unwind, your working memory needs time to let neuronal processes and pathways reach a point at which they can bed down and consolidate.

EPISODIC MEMORY

Episodic memory is the measurement of recalling past events that are relevant to the current situation; it's your wisdom. The good news is that if you keep it healthy, the potency of this domain will increase with age. By using your memory to recall experiences of previous outcomes, you can complete your current work more effectively and efficiently. Using experience (and not simply giving advice) is a great way to direct others in your team, giving increased confidence to those around you.

With further training you can build the extensive neural networks involved with episodic and other memory systems. This builds brain resilience and enhances the ability to record, recall, and reuse episodic memories with more effectiveness, leading to improved overall cognitive function and wisdom.

EPISODIC MEMORY HABIT 1: LOOK AFTER YOUR HEALTH

Do you feel that your memory has taken an unexplainable dip? If so, there may be a health or lifestyle problem to blame.

It's not just dementia or Alzheimer's disease that causes memory loss. There are many diseases, mental health disorders, and medications that can interfere with memory:

- Cardiovascular disease and its risk factors, including high cholesterol and high blood pressure, have been linked to mild cognitive impairment.
- Studies show that people with diabetes experience far greater cognitive decline than those who don't suffer from the disease.

- Women going through menopause often experience memory problems when their oestrogen dips. In men, low testosterone can cause issues.
- Thyroid imbalances can also cause forgetfulness, sluggish thinking, or confusion.
- Many prescription and over-the-counter medications can get in the way of memory and clear thinking. Common culprits include cold and allergy medications, sleep aids, and antidepressants. Talk to your doctor or pharmacist about possible side effects.

Emotional difficulties can also take a heavy toll on the brain. In fact, mental sluggishness, difficulty concentrating, and forgetfulness are common symptoms of depression. The memory issues can be particularly bad in older people who are depressed – so much so that it is sometimes mistaken for dementia. The good news is that when the depression is treated, memory should return to normal.

EPISODIC MEMORY HABIT 2: GOOD NUTRITION

Good nutrition and a healthy, well balanced diet can help to maintain a good episodic memory. Below is a list of foods that are great for cognitive fitness. There must be something here you can eat. Think of ways you can incorporate some of these foods into your regular diet. Think of the foods that are not so good for you (e.g. sugars) that can be replaced by these.

- Omega-3 fatty acids reduce cognitive deficit and folate has positive effects on memory performance.[144] These fatty acids provide health benefits. Salmon is a top source of omega-3, so are walnuts and flaxseed oil.
- Spices like cinnamon may help preserve memory. Try it in coffee, smoothies, or pasta.

- Leafy green vegetables; if you don't like them, try liquidizing them with half a lemon, a banana, and some non-dairy milk. Add protein powder if you really want to go to town. Spinach and other leafy green vegetables are filled with vitamins and minerals. Plus, the antioxidants in these lean greens may offer powerful brain protection.
- Nuts and seeds give you nutrients that boost cognitive performance. Zinc in pumpkin seeds may improve memory; the vitamin E in nuts may enhance cognitive skills.
- Try a multi vitamin and see if you can see any benefits after three months. If you can, carry on. If you can't, your diet is cool. Try to get your parents to do this too.
- Complex carbohydrates can help boost alertness by offering energy that lasts all day.
- Apples are a great fruit. They contain vitamin C. It's best to eat them with the skin on. They are extremely rich in important antioxidants. They also contain flavanoids and dietary fibre to help keep your gut in a good condition. The phytonutrients and antioxidants in apples may help reduce the risk of developing neurodegenerative disorders, cancer, hypertension, diabetes, and heart disease. Remember, an apple a day keeps… your grocer happy.
- Dark chocolate is loaded with organic compounds that are biologically active and function as antioxidants. These include polyphenols, flavanols, catechins, among others. They can help your cardiovascular system feed your nerve cells and help protect them. Rich dark chocolate is best.
- Chicken and eggs are both high in protein and choline, which is a precursor of acetylcholine, which helps memory.
- Our brains are mostly fat and water, so drink plenty of water and eat good fats.

EPISODIC MEMORY HABIT 3:
USE IT OR LOSE IT

"Use it or lose it" is a common expression and there is a lot of truth in this.

- Life-long learning – don't be afraid to take up a new qualification, to keep the "knowledge reservoir" stacked up.
- Attend or speak at seminars on subjects of interest and expertise – this will also help to keep up to date on subjects.
- Get involved with local colleges to help them produce new courses on subjects you know as an expert.
- Relate your information through stories, anecdotes; this makes them easier to recall and has a greater impact.
- Take up singing, dancing – the rhythm of these activities helps the rhythm of the stories you tell.

EPISODIC MEMORY HABIT 4:
THINK IN PICTURES

Practise memory – use mnemonics and other tools:

If you're trying to remember a list of things – items you want to recall in a non-scripted presentation – conjure up an exotic image of them all together and you'll find it much easier to recall. For example, if you're trying to remember a country, sales, products, competitors, partners, distribution chains, and profit margins, conjure up an image for each one in your mind and a picture that encapsulates all of the individual elements – and you'll find that you readily remember the items when required. This mnemonic imagery technique is up to three times more effective than trying to learn by repetition.

An alternative is to remember the items as part of a poem or a song. Again, your ability to recall them will be far more efficient.

This is why people spoke in prose and verses before the advent of printing enabled you to write things down.

EPISODIC MEMORY HABIT 5: MEMORY TECHNIQUES

The following are memory techniques you can use to help you with your episodic memory:

Business cards. You might find that you have problems with remembering:

- people's names;
- dates;
- what was said in a meeting yesterday.

To help with this, make use of the business cards you get. Make notes on the back of every business card you get of details such as date, place, event, feelings, follow-up actions, etc.

House the information. To remember items in a specific order, for example, the different errands you have to do today, try the ancient Greeks' technique of the "method of loci". Here images are assigned to information or actions and they are placed in the rooms of a familiar house or building, in the required order. To remember the order, you simply "walk" through the house in your mind.

Divide and conquer. It's easier to remember information if it's broken down into more manageable segments and linked to a story or something personal. For instance, if you need to remember a phone number like 0181 21963 it is easier if you 'chunk' the information into 0 1812 (like the overture) and 1963 (the year JFK was shot). Everyone's approach will be unique as they will be using their own experiences and personal frame of reference to help them.

Songs, rhymes, and images. You may remember a list more easily if you create a song or make up a rhyme. Others find that visualization helps them remember multiple items. When you are heading home from work, visualize yourself stopping at the supermarket, picking up milk, cheese, bread, and yoghurt. Imagine going to each section of the supermarket, and see what it looks like. Because images are more powerful than words, you are able to remember everything you need at the store as you follow your visualization.

Using emotions. Try to connect an emotion to something you want to remember. Studies suggest that making a meaningful emotional connection to something, or attaching a strongly held opinion to what you are trying to remember, makes you more likely to commit that information to memory.[145] Sometimes it might be useful to generate an emotional response, such as finding a reason to be happy about a meeting event or to think of something that is scary from a presentation.

EPISODIC MEMORY HABIT 6: MAINTAIN RELATIONSHIPS

This habit is probably the most important of them all. Those of you with good relationships will live longer and have a greater quality of life than those that don't.

If you haven't done already, make a habit of telling someone you love them, every day. Make an even better habit… by showing that you love them. Don't take people for granted. Don't let others take you for granted.

There actually is some research that suggests that sex can improve cognitive fitness. More than just the physical exertion, sex raises levels of serotonin, improving creativity and logical decision-making, and sex increases the hormone oxytocin, related to problem-solving ability.

But the reason good, positive relationships are in the episodic memory category is because they can help protect against memory loss. Just don't forget who it is you really love and be monogamous. Sharing your love too thinly will weaken the power of this habit.

EPISODIC MEMORY HABIT 7:
MOST MEMORABLE LISTS – MUSIC, SMELLS, AND TASTES

There is a UK radio programme called *Desert Island Discs*, where guests choose eight pieces of music they would like to have if they were ever stranded on a desert island.

It is a great format to interview a celebrity, politician, businessman, or whoever. The programme has been running for over 70 years. The interesting thing is that the show reminds you how memorable music can be. How a few notes or a melody can take you back to an unforgettable incident or event.

This habit is to take your treasured memories beyond desert island discs by compiling not only your eight most memorable pieces of music, but also your eight most flavoursome foods, your eight most evocative smells, and so on.

Make this week's habit one of keeping a list of the "most memorable items of the week". You can choose whatever categories you like and share them with your family.

Display the list in your office and when asked, relate some of the memorable moments from your list.

EPISODIC MEMORY HABIT 8:
END OF DAY ACTION LIST

At the end of every business day, think of the three actions you have to complete to make your company more successful. Write these down and keep that list going. Ensure you refer to it on an ongoing basis to keep you on track. Take the list to meetings, delegate responsibility where you can, but don't stop until you have completed each action.

Keep notes on the successful outcome of each action. Post these publicly within your company where possible.

EPISODIC MEMORY HABIT 9:
GESTALT – SHARE EXPERIENCE, DON'T GIVE ADVICE

There is a form of conversation where you only talk from experience, this is called "gestalt". There are two main benefits from using gestalt. Firstly, when speaking from experience, you speak in much greater gravitas because the problem was real to you. Your answer is truly authentic.

Secondly, listeners know they are hearing a real experience and it means so much more to them. Simple, made up advice doesn't come close.

EPISODIC MEMORY HABIT 10:
SPEND TIME WITH YOUR PARENTS...

And learn from them. If you haven't got a parent, another elderly relative will do. If there are no elderly relatives... adopt a parent at your local elderly peoples' home.

A good episodic memory is one where you put events into context. Who best can give you that context than your parents?

Why do you think about certain things the way you do? Your views on politics, on religion, on society? Where did they come from? What influences did your parents give you and where did they get theirs?

If you don't have parents, think of visiting another elderly relative or someone from their generation. You can learn so much from the recent past.

In addition, it's another way of giving back, of showing your love and respect for the generation that looked after you and brought you up.

My own parents lived through the Great Depression of the 1920s and 1930s, the General Strike; through real poverty. They lived through the Second World War, nuclear bombs and the Cold War; through fear and anxiety. They lived and loved their way through all this.

You can learn a lot from the experience of your parents.

ATTENTION

Remember with attention… you can devote attention to something and you can have your attention captured.

Make sure you practise both types.

ATTENTION HABIT 1:
DON'T GO LEAN, GO GREEN (WITH SOME QUIET SPOTS)

"Lean offices", devoid of distractions and clutter, are a popular model designed to focus employees on the task at hand. These cater well to those who need a quiet spot in the office to minimize distraction, away from large screens, noisy people, and other distractions.

However, working in an office with plants and more furniture is actually healthy and good for the mind. This intuitive idea has recently been borne out by scientific research: the 2014 'Green versus lean office space' report[146] found that working in sight of plants was associated with 15% higher productivity levels than working in minimalist offices. You could change the look of your office, breathe healthier air, and boost your employees' mental function and productivity, with minimal costs.

It's also important to consider work positions, both while working and in meetings. Do you always have to sit down? Could you consider standing during short meetings? Could you stand at your desk? What makes you more alert without being tiring? Researchers think certain body postures might make you more insightful.[147]

ATTENTION HABIT 2:
THE THREE WORK OBJECTIVES (PLUS PERSONAL)

As part of your planning process, you should determine the top three work objectives that you must achieve. You should write them down and, if you like, add a personal objective to the list.

You should then allocate time and focus to the most difficult of the objectives and aim to complete these as soon as possible. Then reallocate time to others. It will help if you publish these and encourage your staff to do so too. That way you can keep track of your progress and see how, as a team, you can help each other.

Where required, it is beneficial to break down big objectives to their constituent parts. This makes tasks more achievable and concentration on smaller topics can be more manageable. Delegate parts of the objective, as and where appropriate. Help others by taking on some of the responsibility where appropriate.

Don't forget the personal objectives. By helping your staff to develop you are increasing the productivity in the office without having additional hires.

ATTENTION HABIT 3:
GIVE CLEAR INSTRUCTIONS AND FREQUENT FEEDBACK ON COMPLEX PROJECTS

Be sure to provide commentary and feedback on the attention and focus of others regularly, thus enhancing their awareness of this strength.

Run regular, short, sharp, meetings to get feedback on the progress of complex projects. Use the meetings for fact and agreement checking. Ensure project managers give short, clear instructions to those involved in the process.

Provide clear, consistent expectations, directions, and limits, as well as updates on resources. A complex project can tax everyone's concentration and it helps if everyone knows exactly what others expect from them.

Where possible, proactively reward prolonged efforts focused on getting the project completed. Celebrate successes, no matter how small. Make an effort to be engaged with all the elements of the project.

Continue to keep the project team part of the office. Sometimes long-term projects can cause cliques and break up team members. Watch out for this.

ATTENTION HABIT 4: ENCODING, STORAGE, AND RETRIEVAL – THE DEVIL IN THE DETAIL

Psychologists divide the process of learning new information into encoding, storage, and retrieval. IT specialists helping you with big data projects will do the same. Here are some tips for your survival through the process.

The first stage requires that you pay complete attention to the overarching items of the project. Test yourself by making a picture of the work or write a checklist and see what you can recall without referring to it. By paying attention to details, your memory will perform more effectively.

Be organized, use a separate "in-tray" and file storage for the big data project. Make sure you empty the tray each day. Don't allow items to build up.

Retrieve the data on a regular basis. Know where to look for each component of the project and regularly discard previous "work-in-progress" versions of old documents, spreadsheets, or presentations.

Determine key questions to ask team members and get guidance on how they should structure the data to answers these questions. This is to ensure consistency when retrieving data. This is well suited to many common business processes and recurring reports, and remains a key part of a speed-driven data infrastructure.

However, to ensure there is capacity for adopting different practices, be flexible and prepared to maximize the potential of big data and advanced analytics. IT colleagues should create a platform that consolidates all sources of information and enables creative discovery, so you can explore the data for ideas. Companies have achieved this through having an integrated data warehouse and more than three quarters of these have invested in data acquisition capabilities to support sourcing the wide assortment of data they collect.

ATTENTION HABIT 5:
THE OFFICE ENVIRONMENT

You need to consider the impact on attention of the environment in which you work. The following points need to be taken into account:

- Impact of noise and music in the vicinity of where you work – would wearing headphones make an improvement? If yes, what style of music played is best suited to paying attention?
- Room temperature – what temperature is best for comfort vs best to keeping alert?
- Lighting in the office can affect your attention – try different levels to see what works best.
- Risk of dehydration – ensure to keep well hydrated by drinking plenty of water.

ATTENTION HABIT 6:
CARDIOVASCULAR FITNESS

When stuck reading a report that is boring, try acute rapid exercise (e.g. run up and down the stairs where you work).

Cardiovascular fitness has been shown to increase functioning in the attentional network of the brain during a cognitively challenging task.[148]

Aerobic exercise is good for cognitive function. Listening to music while exercising can make the activity more fun and can improve cognitive fitness. Cardiovascular rehabilitation patients who exercised to music performed better on a test of verbal fluency than those who exercised without music.

Dancing is a great way to meet people and a great way to listen to music and to exercise. The best of all worlds. Listening to classical music can improve spatial processing and linguistic abilities.

Strength training can also boost cognitive fitness. That's because lifting weights may cause moderate stress and increase levels of BDNF, which controls the growth of nerve cells.

Sports like golf can be social, giving you time to talk as well as exercise and take in the sunshine. A few rounds of golf may do more than just work out the arms. Golf might improve your motor control and spatial awareness, as well as your cardiovascular fitness.

ATTENTION HABIT 7:
LIFESTYLE

Living a good, healthy lifestyle is very important. Be sure to:

- Get a good night's sleep.
- Avoid alcohol
  - o Enjoy that glass of red wine. Drink a little red wine regularly, it may also have neuroprotective properties. The key is moderation.
- Avoid drugs.
- Don't smoke.
- Eat a healthy diet
  - o Avoid too many high-fat, sugary foods that have no nutritional value.
  - o Avoid sugar rushes from fruit juices.
- Taking care of your teeth is also good for brain health. The plaque that accumulates can actually trigger an immune response, preventing arteries taking nutrients to the brain.
- Say "thank you" and "excuse me" on the underground. Be polite, but assertive.
- Take a break: you can benefit from taking a five-minute break every 60 minutes or so.

ATTENTION HABIT 8:
LISTENING

Listening is a great leadership skill. The greatest of leaders spend more time listening and learning than they do talking.

Practise listening with a colleague. Let them practise on you.

John Simpson spoke of the time he first met Nelson Mandela. Mandela greeted Simpson as though it was his honour to have him in his home. Although being interviewed, Mandela wanted to know all about Simpson and his views on world affairs, then to give his own. Mandela was always in listening mode. Here is how Simpson described Mandela:[149]

> "Right from that moment I understood what it was about Nelson Mandela that made people worship him. It wasn't just the humility, it wasn't even that extraordinary forgiveness and lack of bitterness. It was the way he looked you straight in the eyes... Once, at a grand banquet in his honour at the Guildhall in the City of London, my wife... greeted him in her native Afrikaans as he made his way past us. He stopped and talked to her in his own courtly Afrikaans for an agonisingly long time, ignoring the frozen smiles behind him, showing a real interest in her. "We need you back in South Africa," he said. "When are you coming home?"
>
> My warmest memory comes from a visit he made to my old college at Cambridge... his minders... tried to cut our interview short, but as ever Mandela was interested... in the person holding the microphone; I found myself having to steer the conversation back to him all the time."

Learn from the Master. Learn to listen.

ATTENTION HABIT 9:
STAY HYDRATED, BUT DO GO TO THE LOO

Treat your brain like a garden and ensure it never dries out. A 2% decrease in hydration can lead to a 20% loss in energy, and in the capacity to memorize and think correctly.

Hydration is essential to keep the brain working properly, and research suggests being thirsty can distract you from cognitive tasks.[150] The research shows the importance of being hydrated at all times and not, for example, just during exercise.

Lawrence E. Armstrong, a professor of physiology in UConn's Department of Kinesiology in the Neag School of Education, states:[151]

"Our thirst sensation doesn't really appear until we are 1% or 2% dehydrated. By then dehydration is already setting in and starting to impact how our mind and body perform. Dehydration affects all people, and staying properly hydrated is just as important for those who work all day at a computer as it is for marathon runners, who can lose up to 8 % of their body weight as water when they compete."

Note, the air conditioning in our offices can be as dehydrating as lying in the sun.

Another study showed that Japanese Americans who drank fruit and vegetable juice three times a week were significantly less likely to develop Alzheimer's than those who only drank this once a week.[152] [153] For those looking to cut calories, eight glasses of water per day may also work. Although it is unclear which of the vitamins and minerals were important in this test, hydration was a strong element.

Staying well hydrated will also make you go to the wash room more regularly. This is good, as a break from the desk will in itself improve your attention, and the added exercise is good for you, too.

ATTENTION HABIT 10:
HAVE A MASSAGE

Book a massage and let your mind drift.

Your pace of life is probably frenetic. You are probably bombarded every day from every angle on every subject. The weekends no longer offer the respite they used to.

Find a refuge from all the noise. A massage is a great way to let go of everything. You are stripped of everything, especially that annoying smart phone. It is switched off and safely put in a locker, far away; it can no longer get under your skin.

Use these precious moments to have your physical muscles pulled and pushed back into something approaching a normal state. Use these precious moments to do the same to your mind.

PROCESSING SPEED

This is not just about being quick, but being accurate as well.

It's about achieving that state of mind where it seems you have that little bit longer to do everything. It's like the batsman at the crease who has all the time in the world to make his next strike; or the show jumper who effortlessly glides over the fences smoothly and serenely; or the leader who walks into a maelstrom and immediately brings about calm.

Processing speed is as much to do with smoothness as with speed; as much to do with finesse as with accuracy. It is the calm amid the storm. It is getting a lot of things done without showing the panic.

To you, processing speed may take practice, but in time you will find that the serene way you manage transfers to everything you do.

PROCESSING SPEED HABIT 1:
BE MORE CREATIVE

Our ability to think of, and deal with, lots of ideas is helped by a healthy processing speed. A 2013 study from Michigan State University[154] found that participation in arts and crafts leads to more creative, innovative ideas and increases your chances of coming up with new ones. It appears that we can improve our processing speed by being more open to the arts and craft world.

The research stated that those who owned businesses had up to eight times more exposure to the arts as children than their peers. You're more likely to be an inventor as measured by the number of patents generated, businesses formed, or articles published if you are also involved in a creative activity.

It has long been an assumption that funding for the arts was not effective because arts and crafts are dispensable extras. However, this research suggests that the arts and crafts have a positive impact to produce innovative scientists and engineers, that creativity increases your ability to come up with and process more ideas, leading to patentable products and the setting up of new companies.

The research looked at Michigan State University Honors College science and technology graduates (1990-1995) and found these interesting results:

- art and craft skills correlate with graduation in science, technology, engineering, and mathematics (STEM) subjects;
- arts and crafts also correlate with producing patents and founding companies;
- most people believe their innovation is stimulated by the arts and crafts;
- continued appreciation of the arts and crafts continues to positively impact innovators and entrepreneurs.

It's never too late to start. Neuroplasticity will kick in whenever given the chance.

Find your creative side and let rip.

PROCESSING SPEED HABIT 2:
REGULAR, NOT OCCASIONAL EXERCISE

Your cognition is the activity of your brain, and your brain is a physical organ. Keeping fit will help your cognition, especially your speed and accuracy.

Regular physical exercise is something you can all incorporate into your daily lives, whether it's standing at your desks when working, or getting off the train a stop earlier and walking the rest of the way. It all helps to make a difference.

Protecting your heart also keeps your mind sharp. New research reveals that a healthy heart protects the brain from age-related decline.

Seniors with exceptional heart health showed considerably faster brain processing speed and experienced significantly less cognitive decline, according to results from a six-year study.[155]

The lead researcher, Hannah Gardener, at the University of Miami's Miller School of Medicine, stated:

"The results of our study highlight the need for patients and physicians to monitor and address heart health factors and strive for ideal levels, as these factors not only influence cardiovascular health but also brain health."

The study followed more than 1,000 individuals (average age 72) for six years. The patients were evaluated to see if they met the goals of "Life's Simple Seven", a template for heart-healthy living created by the American Heart Association.

One of the key goals was to aim for at least 150 minutes of moderate physical activity or 75 minutes of vigorous physical activity – or an equal combination of both – each week.

Initially, participants were tested on their brain-processing speed. Those who stuck to the exercise goal were more likely to maintain healthy brain-processing speed. There is also a positive cross over with executive function, as this also involves organization, and time management, similar to processing speed.

Dr. Gregg Fonarow, professor of cardiology at the University of California, Los Angeles, also stated:

"The benefits of the heart health factors apply to all ages, and it is never too late to begin to make positive changes in lifestyle or make improvements in risk factors."

PROCESSING SPEED HABIT 3:
PRACTISE SPEED ANSWERS

See how quickly and efficiently you can articulate the answer to a difficult question.

Reaction-time tasks are considered to measure information processing skills because they require your mind to undertake continuous information processing, while giving sustained attention to what is being said or presented.

Training processing speed has the primary aim to improve the fluid ability of mental processing speed, such that you can process increasingly more information and increasingly more complex information within a period of time.

Initially, you may require time to think, or to prepare your answers. You may be helped by being given the questions or problems in advance. Over time, you will improve and require less time to develop your answers and you will require less up front knowledge on the questions being posed.

Think of how a brilliant stand-up comedian works with the audience. How they are able to come back to hecklers with hilarious one-line put-downs. The speed of response takes practice. The smoothness of reply requires practice. The pointedness (accuracy) of the retort requires practice.

Practise your speed answers.

PROCESSING SPEED HABIT 4:
RUN SPEED MEETINGS

Try cutting the time of some of your meetings by 10%. If that works then try cutting again by 10%.

To make this work, distribute outlines and agendas prior to all meetings. Appoint a strict timekeeper and schedule task time completion for each item on the agenda. Monitor everyone's reactions to the reduced timing. This may challenge some staff more than others.

Add up the time saved by the number of people in the meeting. This multiple is the number of minutes/hours that can be used in non-meeting productive work.

It's amazing how much time can be saved just by slicing 10% of the time off some of your meetings. Leaders and managers can spend 30 hours or more per week in meetings. A 10% saving gives you at least 6 hours of your life back.

Another form of speed meetings is to have "walking meetings". This is a version of a one-to-one meeting with a colleague, direct report or someone who manages you. The interesting thing is that people find they listen more intently because they don't take notes.

However you view it, you can improve your processing speed and save time at the same time.

PROCESSING SPEED HABIT 5: BEGIN WITH THE END IN MIND

Phillip C. McGraw said that life is a marathon, not a sprint. But some of you run your lives as though you are running a marathon made up of a thousand sprints. That's okay if you are like some of the leaders in the case studies, who are able to manage running from one business thought to another time after time. For example, we have seen some leaders manage several businesses that were very different at the same time in their career, each one successfully. However, most of us are not like Jeff Bezos of Amazon, who can manage life at a sprint every day.

For most of you, if you treat the first kilometre like you treat the last 200-metre-stretch, you would never make it to the last 200 metres. This will inevitably lead to burn out. One day you won't even find time for sleep and when that happens you will soon find that you don't get anything done.

Your mind is meant to be filled with balance. If you want an exceptional processing speed, capable of the fastest and smoothest of sprints, allow your mind to rest sufficiently between those sprints.

Therefore, begin with the end in mind. If necessary, think of the day you die. What do you really want to be remembered for? If there is one achievement that stands out above the rest? Make sure that is where you put most of your energy, that is what you sprint for. When not going for that achievement, make sure you rest.

Covey suggested developing a Personal Mission Statement, a plan for success.[156] This should focus on what you want to be and do, and reaffirm who you are. To put goals into focus and move ideas into the real world. You create your own destiny and secure the future you envision. You need to ensure you have the energy to enjoy the journey, enjoy the hills and the scenery. You will face breezy downhill stretches and daunting uphill sections. Learn from both and enjoy both.

PROCESSING SPEED HABIT 6:
TEA AND COFFEE (IN MODERATION)

Caffeine can help your speed of thought, but only in moderation. Caffeine, found in tea, coffee, and a plethora of energy drinks, will stimulate the mind. Too much can cause shaking of the hands or a tremor in the voice. Over time our bodies may get used to the caffeine in tea and coffee and the receptors will desensitize, but the side effects may endure.

Studies suggest the caffeine in a regular cup of coffee can improve attention and short-term memory, improving your processing speed.[157]

Caffeine probably has multiple targets in the brain, but the main one seems to be adenosine receptors. Adenosine is a brain chemical that dampens brain activity, so by blocking it we can increase our processing speed. In addition, by blocking adenosine's receptors, caffeine enhances the activity of dopamine, which is involved in arousal and pleasure.

Therefore, cut your intake to no more than three reasonable-sized cups of tea or coffee a day and you should see a reasonable improvement in your processing speed.

PROCESSING SPEED HABIT 7:
USE VISUAL AIDS APPROPRIATELY

Some adults have slower processing speed. It makes sense to give them the time to think. Try giving them visual aids along with the verbal description of the problem or issue. Allow them the time to prepare answers to questions by giving them the question in advance of needing an answer, before a meeting or conference. Allow a '10 second rule' to receive a response. If they do not respond, try and simplify the instruction repeatedly.

Remember, you may also find your processing speed slowing as you get older. The same tips you use to help others, could help you in years to come.

The following points should be considered:

- Use visual aids to assist understanding, memory, processing, and sequencing skills. A good visual can convey a thousand words and in using a good visual it can help you get your message across.
- Utilize mind maps or visual representations of what the problem or issue is. Flow charts help to logically walk people through a sequence; it breaks down the processing so you won't get lost.
- Keep background noises and other interruptions to a minimum. Some of you may like complete silence, others prefer some background noise. Find out what works best for you and your team.
- Use clear, unambiguous pictures with keywords or labels. There is a tendency to over-elaborate diagrams because technology allows you too. Don't get caught in this mess.
- Avoid 'busy' worksheets and textbooks with pictures, speech bubbles, and diagrams splattered around.

- Keep things simple and in a logical progression. Try developing a process that even your spouse or children will understand. You can always add to it later, to enhance the sophistication. But undoing complexity is tough.

PROCESSING SPEED HABIT 8: SLEEP AND REST FOR RECOVERY

Elite athletes usually train for up to eight hours a day to reach their optimal physical health. However, they spend most of the other 16 hours of the day sleeping or resting, allowing their body time to recover. The same goes for your cognitive fitness.

New research from Brown University shows that the brain requires sleep to consolidate learning.[158] This helps explain the specifics of how the sleeping brain encodes a new task. The brain may benefit from sleep because energy is available, or because distractions and new inputs are fewer. This will help alleviate the extra encoding required if you are someone with high processing speed activities every day.

Other studies have shown that reduced levels of sleep can decrease cortical grey matter and cause the brain to shrink.[159]

Make sure you get sufficient sleep every night!

PROCESSING SPEED HABIT 9: MAINTAIN SOCIAL HABITS

Man is a "social animal". Maintaining an active social life, especially with different people and in different places, is good for cognitive fitness. A quick chat may do more than just pass the time. Maintaining your strong social networks is a great way to challenge yourself mentally and keep you on your toes. When involved in group activities, the brain performs a range of actions, boosting processing speed which helps to develop problem solving skills.

Pair up with people who enjoy lively discussion and debates. This will necessitate quick thinking on your part; a form of cognitive exercise. Even simple conversations may improve skills like memory and the brain's ability to block out distractions. If you have a big meeting coming up, take a few minutes to talk it out with a colleague before the meeting. This isn't just rehearsing. It's being grilled by a friendly cross-examiner.

Both physical and mental exercises can prove to be more fruitful if they involve social interactions. Therefore, pondering over a problem alone may result in brain exercise, but discussing it with a group could further boost brain activity.

PROCESSING SPEED HABIT 10: LOVED ONES

Tell or, better still, show your loved ones that they mean more to you than any of the other thousands of things you are involved in. A leader with a good processing speed covers a lot of ground. A good leader will control a host of spinning plates, looking sharp, smart, effective and energized.

Don't neglect your loved ones. Don't make them feel that they are just one of the spinning plates in your life. Tell them, show them, that they mean so much more to you than that.

CHAPTER FIVE

CAN YOU USE COMPUTERS TO IMPROVE COGNITIVE FITNESS?

This book draws upon the most recent findings and thinking in the area of cognitive fitness. Recent technical developments now allow you to draw upon more data on the brain and how it functions. This evidence can be used comprehensively to look at brain function primarily with the professional executive in mind.

Not only can you assess your cognitive fitness using computers, but you can train your cognition using computers. This has consequences for leadership. But any training achieved via a computer enables the mind to reach a higher potential that can be linked to real outcomes, such as improvements in leadership, if that ability potential is used in the correct way.

Consider a physical fitness example of training your arm muscles using weights; you will get stronger arms. If you do nothing with that strength, in time it dwindles. However, you can use that strength for a number of purposes. For example, arm strength could be used to throw the javelin, swim faster, or do push ups. If you now do any of these activities on a regular basis, you will retain your arm strength (and you don't necessarily have to do weights again, but it wouldn't hurt if you did).

It's the same with computer training. The extra neurones and connections will dwindle if you don't use them. But you also have a choice how to use them, once you have them.

It would be good to undertake the training alongside a strong leadership habit as they will synergize and together bring about more strength to your cognition than either alone.

PRINCIPLES OF COGNITIVE FITNESS TRAINING

THE SCIENCE BIT

Cognitive-based interventions are commonly classified as either cognitive "training" (or "retraining", "remediation", or "brain training") or cognitive "rehabilitation".[160] These terms are applied somewhat interchangeably and, therefore, the nature of these two related but distinct forms warrants clarification. Table 4 summarizes the main differences between the attributes of cognitive training and cognitive rehabilitation.

Table 4: Main differences between the attributes of cognitive training and cognitive rehabilitation

	Cognitive training	Cognitive rehabilitation
Aims	To enhance a specific cognitive fitness (e.g. memory, attention) through repetition of carefully designed activities and exercises associated with that ability	To improve functioning in personally meaningful day-to-day tasks by identifying individual needs and goals and, by using techniques and strategies, to enable these to be met more easily with the individual's declining abilities

	Cognitive training	Cognitive rehabilitation
Basis/ assumption	Regularly practising tasks related to a given cognitive domain may improve or maintain function in that domain and the benefits may transfer to related functions	Relatively intact cognitive skills and systems can be tapped and strategies that make the most of residual abilities are applied
Theory	Neuroplasticity. Studies using fMRI* have shown changes in patterns of brain activity during memory tasks associated with cognitive training	Evidence-based strategies that have been shown to improve performance on relevant day-to-day tasks
Target	Impairment	Restricted participation
Context	Structured tasks and environments	Real-world setting
Focus of intervention	Isolated cognitive abilities and processes	Groups of cognitive abilities and processes required to perform everyday tasks
Format	Individualized or group	Individualized
Proposed mechanism of action	Mainly restorative, sometimes combined with psychoeducation and strategy training	A combination of restorative and compensatory approaches combined with psychoeducation and strategy training
Goals	Improved or maintained ability in specific cognitive domains	Performance and functioning in relation to collaboratively set goals

*fMRI, functional magnetic resonance imaging

[Adapted from: Bahar-Fuchs et al 2013]

WHY COGNITIVE TRAINING?

Neuroplasticity enables cognitive fitness to be modified in all phases of life – it can be improved, regardless of your age, and cognitive decline can be reversed. Indeed, a growing body of evidence supports the protective effects of cognitive stimulation that promotes dynamic reorganization of higher cerebral functions, thereby helping to maintain function in the elderly[161] [162] [163] and reduce the risk of incident dementia.[164] [165] Additionally, higher education has protective effects on developing dementia.[166] Stimulation of cognitive processes is an important predictor of enhancement and maintenance of cognitive fitness through to old age.

Many cognitive abilities deteriorate during the course of normal ageing, such as speed of processing, working memory, long-term memory, and reasoning.[167] Cognitive training offers retraining in the ability to think, use judgment, and make decisions. Training focuses on correcting deficits in memory, concentration, attention, perception, learning, planning, sequencing, and judgment. Multiple cognitive abilities are involved in everyday tasks and, therefore, cognitive training across abilities may be most beneficial.

GOALS OF COGNITIVE TRAINING

Cognitive training aims to enhance a person's capacity to process and interpret information and to improve their ability to function and integrate in all aspects of their family and community life. Preserving or restoring physical and cognitive fitness enables individuals to maintain an active and engaging life, and to retain autonomy and independence.

The goals of cognitive training may be considered to be:

- to enhance "normal" levels of cognition, thus enhancing leadership, management, and performance;

- to avoid or delay cognitive decline due to ageing or neurological disease (maintaining current level of functioning appears to be the major goal of many older adults), thus to keep going stronger for longer;
- to remediate current cognitive deficits due to ageing or neurological disease, thus to stay fit and healthy.

APPROACHES TO COGNITIVE TRAINING
Cognitive training can be:

- restorative – focusing on improving a specific cognitive domain;
- compensatory – focusing on adapting to the presence of a cognitive deficit.

Specific neuropsychological processes, particularly memory, have shown improvement using cognitive exercises, including those that are computer-assisted. A systematic review found that cognitive exercises can produce moderate-to-large beneficial effects on memory performance and global cognitive measures in a majority of studies.[168] However, some gains resulting from intervention may not be captured adequately by available standardized outcome measures.[169]

Cognitive training can be distinguished to include:[170]

- Applied memory strategies: the instruction and practice of techniques to minimize memory impairment and enhance performance. The strategy involves learning and practising strategies, such as the method of loci, mnemonics, and visual imagery.[171]
- Repetitive cognitive exercises: the repeated practice of targeted cognitive abilities in a repetitions-sessions format. These exercises typically involve repetition of one cognitive task in one session, then continue to new tasks in the next session, and

eventually return to further training on the original task at a harder level. Several software applications have been developed that implement cognitive exercises on computers.[172]

Notably, computer-based cognitive exercise studies have shown an increased frequency of stronger effect sizes and an enhanced generalization of benefits, compared to memory strategy training.[173]

Three approaches may be considered for maintaining or improving cognitive fitness, particularly in relation to older adults:[174]

- Direct instruction strategy: focuses on direct instruction of potentially useful strategies;
- Cognitive stimulation therapy: engages the individual in everyday cognitively stimulating activities;
- Improving central sensory system function: based on the fact that performance of sensory systems in the cerebral cortex can be significantly improved by intensive learning and practice.

To these strategies, interventions that enhance cognitive fitness may be added:

- lifestyle (e.g. physical exercise, a healthy diet, smoking cessation);
- pharmacotherapy (e.g. neural-stimulants, drugs, biopharmaceutical interventions);
- non-pharmaceutical therapies (e.g. meditation, self-hypnosis [autohypnosis] and acupuncture).

The commonly used direct instruction strategy that includes lessons and repetitive practice is highly teacher directed.[175] This strategy is effective for providing information, developing step-by-step skills and knowledge construction. In general, improvements on cognitive tests are seen after direct strategy instruction.[176] However, so far the evidence would suggest gains do not transfer to tasks other than those corresponding directly to the strategies taught and it is not known whether such learned strategies continue to be used. Overall, strategy training programs have not been widely adopted.[177] Moreover, these approaches may be considered relatively uninteresting for the user, thus leaving a window of opportunity for new and interesting approaches to address cognitive dysfunction.

Cognitive stimulation therapy targets cognitive and social function and has a social element. The strategy involves sessions of themed activities that aim to stimulate and engage people in everyday activities, particularly those with mild to moderate dementia. Sessions impart positive benefits from being in a group and some cognitive changes. However, while nonspecific cognitive stimulation can reduce the risk of cognitive decline, the direction of causation between the two is unclear.[178] Critics suggest that time spent on exercise would be at least as beneficial to memory. A moderate amount of aerobic exercise on a regular basis leads to chemical changes in the brain that promote growth of new neurones in the hippocampus.[179]

The importance of sensory system function to cognitive fitness has led to the idea of improving central sensory system function to treat age-related cognitive decline. For example, people who use a computerized "brain workout" program designed to boost the speed at which players process visual stimuli can have positive effects on mental agility.[180] The theory is that neuroplasticity changes across neural networks as a result of intensive learning and practice mediates improvements in the performance of sensory systems.[181] However, critics of brain training believe that enhanced performance could be due to familiarity with the game rather than because cognitive skills have improved, particularly when the training is over a period of time considered too short to allow for plasticity changes.[182]

PREREQUISITES OF COGNITIVE TRAINING

Cognitive training improves cognitive abilities in healthy older people, in people with neurodegenerative diseases, learning difficulties, and traumatic brain injury. However, training requires certain prerequisites to ensure its effectiveness.[183]

Training interventions are heterogeneous. However, they share certain characteristics in that they are structured, systematic, goal-directed, and individualized, and they involve learning, practice, social contact, and a relevant context.

A cognitive training program that incorporates the following principles is likely to be most effective in:

- provision of progressively challenging tasks;
- integration of cognitive skills related to learning and memory;
- integration of visual, auditory, and other sensory stimuli;
- cognitive loading to drive skills to become automatic (i.e. participants should be encouraged to use their limited working memory optimally);
- adequate frequency, intensity, and duration;
- incorporating fun to elicit engagement and motivation.

A key factor in the success of the training technique for improving brain function or reversing functional decline is the seriousness of purpose with which the individual engages with the task. The task must be important, meaningful, or interesting to the person. This underlies the concept of "flow" (Box 1), a term that is used with particular reference to games and gamers. Flow may be considered to represent an individual's focus or immersion in the task, which is delivering high levels of excitement, pleasure, and fulfilment.

Box 1: Flow theory

Flow was originally defined as, "the state in which people are so intensely involved in an activity that nothing else seems to matter; the experience itself is so enjoyable that people will do it even at great cost, for the sheer sake of doing it."[184]

The subjective experience is a function of two variables – perceived challenges and perceived skills. Anxiety is experienced when perceived challenges are greater than skills; boredom is experienced when perceived skills are greater than challenges. Flow is experienced when perceived skills and perceived challenges are both high.

While skills and challenges are the most important variables in flow theory, Csikszentmihalyi (1990) constructs flow into nine dimensions:

- Feeling of balance between personal skills and the challenges
- Merging actions and awareness (i.e. actions feel automatic with deep involvement)
- Having clear goals
- Unambiguous feedback that things are going according to plan
- Concentrating on the task at hand
- Feeling in control
- Loss of self-consciousness
- Time transforms (i.e. passes more rapidly or more slowly or without awareness)
- Having an autotelic experience (i.e. taking on the challenge for its own sake, without expectation of future benefit)

[Reviewed by Liao 2006; Tenenbaum et al 1999]

According to Csikszentmihalyi (1990),[185] there are four requirements for flow. In the context of games, these are:

- Clear Tasks: The gamer understands what has to be done. Own
  goals may have to be formulated.
- Feedback: The game continually gives feedback about progress towards goals and whether the gamer is choosing the
  right options. Choice elicits immediate feedback.
- Balanced, attainable goal: The tasks should be challenging,
  achievable, and not too long.
- Concentration: The gamer must be able to concentrate on the
  game, and the game should not distract from the tasks at hand.

Games that balance challenges and the abilities of the player are
most likely to evoke flow. This feeling may best be elicited by a
game that offers:

- intrinsic reward, so that the player wants to play the game;
- sufficient challenges to match the player's ability, so that the
  player can get deeply involved in the game;
- a sense of personal control over the game activity.

As a matter of course, and to assess the effectiveness of the training, a neuropsychologist and other healthcare professionals, such
as occupational, speech, and language therapists, should evaluate the level and kind of cognitive dysfunction before the start
of the training, and then re-assess the individual over time to
measure cognitive improvement. Specification of the contextual
conditions under which the cognitive changes (neuroplasticity)
are studied is important since the range of plasticity manifested
will vary according to such factors as the duration, intensity, and
procedures used in the intervention.[186]

LIMITATIONS TO COGNITIVE TRAINING

Limitations to cognitive training include:

- limited evidence of effectiveness due to the variability of subjects (e.g. healthy older people, adults with Alzheimer's disease, children with attention deficit hyperactivity disorder), interventions, and outcomes measures (e.g. improved memory, return to work);
- repetitive practice on a single skill usually does not transfer to other cognitive domains or to general functionality in daily life;
- unknown effects (and failure to control for) of confounding factors, such as spontaneous and normal recovery processes, social contact, and concomitant diseases;
- training takes time and should be over many hours and weeks, i.e. over enough time to rebuild neural pathways and to improve skills;
- long-term usage without motivational encouragement and social contact could be a significant barrier to some training programs.

COGNITIVE TRAINING PROGRAMS

Cognitive training that provides structured practice of complex mental activity to enhance cognitive fitness,[187] has attracted intense public, commercial, and scientific interest. The number of cognitive training programs, particularly designed for older adults, has been steadily increasing in recent years, and there is evidence to suggest that such cognitive training interventions can improve cognitive performance in healthy older adults,[188 189 190 191] as well as those with mild cognitive impairment.[192] Improvement may last from months[193] to up to five years after training,[194] and is reported in specific cognitive domains relative to control conditions.[195]

Cognitive training programs have traditionally been delivered one-to-one or in a group by a professional trainer.[196] This is contrary to evidence that greater improvements may be gained from teaching self-testing techniques.[197] Differences in these programs have mainly been with regard to the individuals' ability, such as attention or memory, training frequency, duration, and the method of training. Personal tuition and specific meetings may incur additional costs over the necessary equipment and expensive tuition fees, as well as additional time over that spent training (e.g. travel time).

Computer-based interventions such as computer and video games are rapidly becoming popular, and have been successfully used by individuals of all ages. Indeed, it is suggested that older adults are the fastest growing users of computers and the internet user group in both personal and workplace contexts.[198]

Such computer-based interventions may provide an effective alternative to traditional training programs.[199] Computerized interventions offer the advantages of a cost effective training program that can be widely disseminated for home use by people of all ages. They also have potential to offer a more flexible and personalized approach compared with traditional cognitive training programs. The technology enables real-time performance feedback and can adapt the activity to the user's level of ability. Moreover, it offers an individualized pace of training, allowing the user to focus only on areas that need improvement. Computerized training programs have the means to ensure the activities are engaging and motivational, and computer and video games are specifically designed to be exciting and fun. These qualities have the potential to minimize poor adherence which can be a challenge with traditional cognitive training programs.[200]

Alongside the increasing number of brain training interventions for cognitive improvement, there is an extensive body of evidence regarding the benefit of cognitive training interventions for older adults. A recent systematic review suggested that computerized training, including classic cognitive training tasks, neuropsychological software, and video games, is a means by which the increasing number of individuals, including older adults, who use computers could improve their cognitive fitness and delay cognitive decline in later life. Importantly, computerized training is not limited to older adults that are familiar with computer technology, as even those with no prior computer experience were found to benefit from this form of training.[201]

COMMERCIALLY AVAILABLE COGNITIVE TRAINING

There is a plethora of commercially available cognitive training systems to help maintain or even improve cognitive skills, with varying degrees of scientific evidence and evaluation of clinical effect in terms of gains in cognition over time.

The field of computer-based interventions is changing rapidly, and cognitive training programs designed to motivate individuals to improve cognition are in development. Computer-based interventions could be relatively low cost and easily disseminated, reaching individuals that require such interventions, as well as those who would not otherwise be offered them. Moreover, they have the opportunity to take advantage of the increasing older population and the increasing number of older adults using personal computers to not only delay cognitive decline, but improve cognitive fitness in later life.

EFFICACY OF COGNITIVE TRAINING

Determining the outcome of cognitive training is largely dependent on the study design and variables employed to measure the efficacy of the intervention. To determine whether cognitive training has been successful, it is necessary to show positive transfer, i.e. to show that what is learned in one context enhances learning in a different setting. It is, of course, very likely that practice, rehearsal, and repeated use of a task will lead to improvement. In terms of the training, this would clearly be unremarkable. The challenge is, therefore, to show that practice on the training regime positively transfers to performance on other similar measures. This has proven difficult. While some studies provide no evidence to support improvement in general cognitive fitness beyond the tasks that are actually being trained,[202] a number of study authors have claimed positive results.[203]

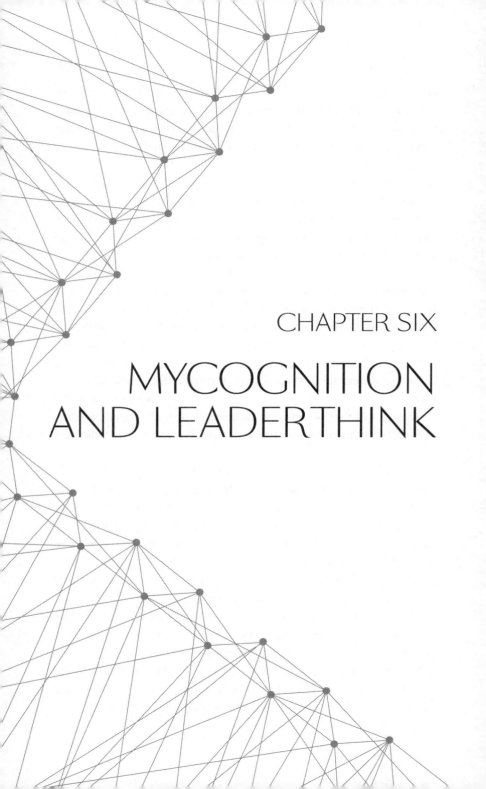

CHAPTER SIX

MYCOGNITION AND LEADERTHINK

LeaderThink is a program developed by Dr. Stephen G. Payne. Through this program you can obtain a broad understanding of the cognitive power of your leadership and management.

LeaderThink assesses the individual function of the five key domains and gives a score for each domain. It then integrates these five scores to provide an overall score of your overall cognitive function. You can undertake the LeaderThink online when you have access to the internet. To claim your one year free subscription to MyCognition Pro, please visit www.mycognition. com/booksub and enter your details. You will then be issued with a personal discount code. It takes less than 15 minutes. It's based on the work of the scientists and technologists at MyCognition, one of the world's leading authorities on measuring and training cognition. Dr Payne has added his years of experience in consulting and coaching at the highest levels to take it to new levels.

The LeaderThink cognition assessment system is designed to provide a relatively brief but broad assessment of the principal cognitive functions and domains recognized by psychologists. The legitimacy of these cognitive domains as constructs is reliant on an understanding of cognition based on more than 200 years of neuropsychological and experimental psychological research.

The tests involved in the LeaderThink system are based on well-known and extensively validated models used in patients with cognitive deficits like HM (who we discussed earlier in this book), or in experimental psychology and psychopharmacological studies undertaken with other subjects.

The tests have also been designed to comply with best practice guidance for objective cognitive test development.[204] These authors stressed the importance of employing tests designed with the following technical and psychometric characteristics:

- Reliability and especially with respect to temporal (also known as 'Test-Retest') reliability, internal consistency, and intra- and inter-rater reliability:
  o Meaning that the tests produced similar results in the same people when repeated in similar circumstances.
- Validity, i.e. does the test measure the cognitive concepts of interest?
  o This means that the tests measure the five core domains in question.
- Sensitivity:
  o Meaning that the tests are able to pick up changes in a subject's cognitive function or differences between subjects.
- Relative immunity to practice or, when this is an issue, the provision of parallel forms:
  o Many cognitive tests have practice effects, whereby, on repeated use the subject gradually improves, as when playing a game;
  o The LeaderThink program has been developed to reduce practice effects, for example, the photos used in memory tests are changed at random.
- Concern for successful cross-cultural use:
  o The test can be used regardless of age, gender, race, or culture.

The tests that LeaderThink is comprised of are best considered to be revised versions of the paradigms that have been commonly used in the assessment of human cognition. There are even measured timed tasks that have an extensive validation history. Simple reaction time, choice reaction time and the go/no go tasks all date back to the work of the physiologist, Franciscus Donders, who worked throughout the 1800s in the Netherlands and published his work on reaction time in 1869. Thus, the research history of LeaderThink goes back almost 200 years.

We have developed several versions of LeaderThink, from a single test version which takes less than 2 minutes, up to a more intense, deep, and broad version that takes 30 minutes. The most extensively used is a 15-minute version. We can thus say, "We have 200 years of neuropsychological and experimental psychological research in 15 minutes!"

In the not too distant past, the tests would have been administered manually by a specialist, using paper and pencil versions of the tests and timed with a stopwatch. It would take all day to test a few subjects and days before they received their results. MyCognition has brought about an amazing transition of cognitive testing. These tests are self-administered. Every key stroke is measured and the computer program knows when you have started and when you have completed a test. The computer knows the accuracy of your behaviour and the speed at which you complete each test. Immediately after you have completed the tests your results are compared to normative data (data obtained from a broad population) so that you can see where you sit in relation to results expected for your age group.

The transition brought about by MyCognition means that you can test entire schools, businesses, and cohorts of subjects in next to no time. You are shining a clear light in an area previously full of shadows. This light is illuminating our knowledge of cognitive function and we are making this knowledge available to as many people as possible. This is the dawn of a new age of cognitive science and you are part of it. Through reading this book you will add to the knowledge and see the power of your cognitive thinking in a whole new light.

LEADERTHINK AND IQ

We often get asked if IQ is the same as LeaderThink. They are related, but in the same way that physical strength is related to overall physical fitness, then IQ is but a segment of Leader-Think. IQ is only a small part of a more detailed and comprehensive picture.

It is like using physical strength as a measure of physical fitness. A person who is physically strong can pick up heavy weights and push heavy objects. But if that is their only physical fitness attribute then they will be lacking in physical speed, stamina, and agility.

We all know people who have a high IQ, but still have difficulty with leadership and management. The analytical skills which are assessed by the traditional IQ scales may not be able to determine skills as planning and organising, which are supposed to be the core of an intelligent behaviour, as these skills also require good cognitive fitness. The most recent trends in studying intelligence are more directed to investigate the elementary cognitive processes (as our five domains) which underlie the high level cognitive skills which characterize intelligence (as planning and organising).

Thus people with a strong IQ may not be able to make simple, everyday decisions, because they have poor working memory. They may not be able to switch quickly across tasks because they have poor processing speeds. They may not be able to focus because they have poor attention, and they may not be able to recall events relevant to the current context because they have poor episodic memory.

It is, therefore, possible for someone to be "extremely" intelligent, but have poor cognitive fitness. There are world leaders who exhibit supreme IQs; they are very clever. But you also see in them faults that would be highlighted through deficits in their cognitive function. Many people reach high office through the manipulation and bullying of their people. The best people use manipulation to bring out the best in their people, for them and their country's sake, whereas the bullying leader will bring about manipulation for their own sake. Often the manipulation takes the form of fear and, ultimately, this will fail.

LeaderThink should, and will, become the universal measure of cognitive fitness to understand the cognitive power of leadership and management. To date, LeaderThink has built a strong picture of cognitive function globally. The tools and programs made available by LeaderThink will help to bring about the greatest global understanding of the power of the human cognitive function there has ever been.

Using the code provided in this book you will be able to obtain free access to the LeaderThink assessment. You can go online and immediately get a LeaderThink assessment. This book will complement and help you further interpret the score attained on LeaderThink. It will give you a deeper and broader meaning to your cognitive fitness and in doing so help you to make greater use of cognition and bring about a better version of yourself.

With this book you will have an even greater understanding of what cognition means, with or without the online assessment obtained from LeaderThink.

Once you begin the processes discussed here, you will accumulate new habits that should be put to "good" use. Thereafter, it is up to you. There have been many people throughout history who have used their cognitive power poorly. You have the choice to use cognitive function to produce a better you, a better organization where you work, a better community where you live, and of course to the betterment of your family and loved ones.

Let's delve a little deeper into the workings and development of the most important organ in your body. The following section looks specifically at the science of cognition.

THE MYCOGNITION APPROACH

MyCognition is one of the leading providers of cognitive wellness technologies, dedicated to improving cognitive fitness and, thereby, health. It allows you to measure and enhance cognitive fitness through a range of interactive products and is a leading provider anchored in evidence-based, sound scientific foundations.

MyCognition promotes scientific advances in healthcare and awareness through the OurCognition Foundation. You can aim to assess and enhance your cognitive fitness and, in doing so, develop your wellbeing, reduce stress, improve work performance, and productivity.

The approach by MyCognition has focused on creating training regimes that are engaging, causing compliance, which results in the positive side-effect of enhancing and/or rescuing cognition.

1. Assessing your cognitive fitness:
   - 200 years of neuropsychiatric research in a 15-minute assessment.
   - In 15 minutes you can assess your total cognition and the cognitive fitness of each of the major five domains.

2. Cognitive training – the personalized approach from MyCognition:
   - Personalized training that targets where you need the training most.
   - Adaptive and constantly challenges you to ensure you get the most out of every training session.
   - Extending it to your kids and their grand-parents.
   - Life-long – never too late to start.

The new and practical approach. Giving people relevant and practical advice to improve their lives, particularly targeting the workplace in which they operate and spend most of their time.

Furthermore, you will be given access to MyCognition's proven Cognitive Fitness Assessment services, so you can measure your baseline function and monitor your progress as you try different interventions to improve your cognition.

Benefits of regularly monitoring cognitive fitness include the following:

- It provides long-term quantitative data for you to regularly check your cognitive fitness.
- It measures the efficacy of intervention programs implemented by your company and allows you or that organization to monitor progress.
- It allows a means to detect the impact of life events (e.g. birth/ death in a family), change in environment, or change in diet and exercise program on your cognitive fitness.
- It allows a quantitative means to assess your cognitive fitness if you are predisposed to potential psychiatric disorders (first level screening for risk).

We are sure that by regular training of just a few minutes a day (minimum recommendation is 90 minutes per week) your cognitive fitness processes will improve. Your training adapts to your individual needs. A personalized MyCognition training program can be created to dovetail with your existing wellbeing provision.

REFERENCES

Ackermann S, Hartmann F, Papassotiropoulos A, et al. "Associations between basal cortisol levels and memory retrieval in healthy young individuals," *Journal of Cognitive Neuroscience*, June 28 (2013). [Epub ahead of print].

Alley D, Suthers K, Crimmins E. "Education and cognitive decline in older Americans: results from the AHEAD sample," *Research on Aging*, 29 (2007): 73–94. Available at http://www.ncbi.nlm.nih.gov/pmc/articles/PMC2760835/ [Accessed July 2013].

Alvarez JA, Emory, E. "Executive function and the frontal lobes: A meta-analytic review," *Neuropsychology Review*, 16 (2006):17–42.

Alzheimer's Association, *Alzheimer's Disease Facts and Figures* (2010). Alzheimer's Association, *Alzheimer's & Dementia* (Chicago, 2010: 6).

Alzheimer's Association, *Alzheimer's Disease Facts and Figures* (2013). Alzheimer's Association, *Alzheimer's & Dementia* (Chicago, 2013: 9).

Alzheimer's Disease International, *Dementia statistics*. Available at http://www.alz.co.uk/research/statistics [Accessed August 2013].

Alzoubi KH, Khabour OF, Alhaidar IA, et al. "Diabetes impairs synaptic plasticity in the superior cervical ganglion: possible role for BDNF and oxidative stress," *Journal of Molecular Neuroscience*, July 6 (2013). [Epub ahead of print].

American Psychiatric Association. *Diagnostic and Statistical Manual of Mental Disorders*, Fourth Edition. Text Revision (DSM-IV-TR). (Washington, D.C, American Psychiatric Association, 2000).

Anon (1). Psychomotor skills. Available at: http://vincesaliba.com/yahoo_site_admin/assets/docs/Psychomotor_Skills.223235325.pdf [Accessed August 2013].

Anon (2). Psychomotor development and learning. Available at http://www.essortment.com/psychomotor-development-learning-25871.html [Accessed August 2013].

Appelman AP, van der Graaf Y, Vincken KL, et al. "Combined effect of cerebral hypoperfusion and white matter lesions on executive functioning–The SMART-MR study," *Dementia and Geriatric Cognitive Disorders*, 29 (2010): 240–247.

Archibald CJ, Fisk JD. "Information processing efficiency in patients with multiple sclerosis," *Journal of Clinical and Experimental Neuropsychology*, 22 (2000): 686–701.

Baddeley A. "Working memory," *Science*, 255 (5044) (1992): 556–559.

Baddeley A. "The fractionation of Working Memory," *Proceedings of the National Academy of Sciences of the USA*, (1996; 93): 13468–13472.

Baddeley A. "The episodic buffer: a new component of Working Memory?" *Trends in Cognitive Sciences*, 4 (2000): 417–423.

Baddeley A, Della Sala S. "Working memory and executive control," *Philosophical Transactions of the Royal Society of London. Series B, Biological Sciences*, 351(1346) (1996): 1397–1403.

Bahar-Fuchs A, Clare L, Woods B. "Cognitive training and cognitive rehabilitation for mild to moderate Alzheimer's disease and vascular dementia," *The Cochrane Database of Systematic Reviews*, 6 (2013): CD003260.

Bailey CH, Kandel ER. "Synaptic remodeling, synaptic growth and the storage of long-term memory in Aplysia," *Progress in Brain Research*, 169 (2008): 179–198.

Ball KK, Berch DB, Helmers KF, et al. "Effects of cognitive training interventions with older adults: A randomized controlled trial," *The Journal of the American Medical Association*, 288 (2002): 2271–2281.

Baltes PB. "The aging mind: potential and limits," *The Gerontologist*, 33 (1993): 580–594.

Baltes P, Baltes M. "Psychological perspectives on successful aging: The model of selective optimization with compensation," In: Baltes P, Baltes M. *Successful Aging: Perspectives from the Behavioral Sciences* (Cambridge, UK: Press Syndicate of the University of Cambridge, (1990): 1–35) Reviewed by Park & Bishop (2013).

Baune BT, Miller R, McAfoose J, et al. "The role of cognitive impairment in general functioning in major depression," *Psychiatry Research* 176 (2-3) (2010): 183–189.

Beason-Held LL, Kraut MA, Resnick SM. "Longitudinal changes in aging brain function," *Neurobiology of Aging*, 29 (2008): 483–496.

Billeke P, Aboitiz F. "Social cognition in schizophrenia: from social stimuli processing to social engagement," *Frontiers in Psychiatry*, 4 (2013): 1–12.

Bisiach E, Luzzatti C. "Unilateral neglect of representational space," *Cortex*, 14 (1978): 129–133.

Bloom B, Englehart M, Furst E, et al. *Taxonomy of educational objectives: The classification of educational goals. Handbook I: Cognitive domain* (New York, Toronto: Longmans, Green, 1956).

Bloor CM. "Angiogenesis during exercise and training," *Angiogenesis*, 8 (2005): 263–271.

Boyke J, Driemeyer J, Gaser C, et al. "Training-induced brain structure changes in the elderly," *Journal of Neuroscience*, 28 (2008): 7031–7035.

Braak H, Braak E. "Neuropathological stageing of Alzheimer-related changes," *Acta Neuropathologica*, 82 (1991): 239–259.

Braak H, Braak E. "Diagnostic criteria for neuropathologic assessment of Alzheimer's disease," *Neurobiology of Aging*, 18 (4 Suppl) (1997): S85–88.

Brehmer Y, Rieckmann A, Bellander M, et al. "Neural correlates of training-related working-memory gains in old age," *NeuroImage*, 58 (2011): 1110–1120.

Brookmeyer R, Johnson E, Ziegler-Graham K, et al. "Forecasting the global burden of Alzheimer's disease," *Alzheimers and Dementia*, 3 (2007): 186–191.

Brunet-Gouet E, Decety J. "Social brain dysfunctions in schizophrenia: A review of neuroimaging studies," *Psychiatry Research*, 148 (2006): 75–92.

Buée L, Troquier L, Burnouf S, et al. "From tau phosphorylation to tau aggregation: what about neuronal death?" *Biochemical Society Transactions*, 38 (2010) 967–972.

Buitenweg JI, Murre JMJ, Ridderinkhof KR. "Brain training in progress: a review of trainability in healthy seniors," *Frontiers in Human Neuroscience*, 6 (article 183) (2012): 1–11. Available at: http://www.frontiersin.org/Human_Neuroscience/10.3389/fnhum.2012.00183/full [Accessed August 2013].

Bullitt E, Rahman FN, Smith JK, et al. "The effect of exercise on the cerebral vasculature of healthy aged subjects as visualized by MR angiography," *American Journal of Neuroradiology*, 30 (2009): 1857–1863.

Burdick DJ, Rosenblatt A, Samus QM, et al. "Predictors of functional impairment in residents of assisted-living facilities: The Maryland Assisted Living Study," *The Journals of Gerontology. Series A, Biological Sciences and Medical Sciences*, 60A (2005): 258–264.

Calabrese M, Favaretto A, Martini V, et al. "Grey matter lesions in MS: from histology to clinical implications," *Prion*, 7 (2013): 20–27.

Callicott JH, Mattay VS, Bertolino A, et al. "Physiological characteristics of capacity constraints in Working Memory as revealed by functional MRI," *Cerebral Cortex*, 9 (1999): 20–26.

Carter J, Lippa CF. "Beta-amyloid, neuronal death and Alzheimer's disease," *Current Molecular Medicine*, 1 (2001): 733–737.

Castrén E, Elgersma Y, Maffei L et al. "Treatment of neurodevelopmental disorders in adulthood," *Journal of Neuroscience*, 32 (2012): 14074–14079.

Centers for Disease Control and Prevention and the Alzheimer's Association. The Healthy Brain Initiative: A National Public Health Road Map to Maintaining Cognitive Health (Chicago, IL: Alzheimer's Association, 2007)

The Healthy Brain Initiative: A National Public Health Road Map to Maintaining Cognitive Health. [Accessed: May 2013].

Centers for Disease Control and Prevention. Healthy aging. Available at: http://www.cdc.gov/aging/pdf/perceptions_of_cog_hlth_factsheet.pdf [Accessed: June 2013].

Chakrabarti S, Sinha M, Thakurta IG, et al. "Oxidative stress and amyloid beta toxicity in Alzheimer's disease: Intervention in a complex relationship by antioxidants," *Current Medicinal Chemistry*, Jun 25 (2013). [Epub ahead of print].

Chan RCK, Shum D, Toulopoulou T, et al. "Assessment of executive functions: Review of instruments and identification of critical issues," *Archives of Clinical Neuropsychology*, 23 (2008): 201–216.

Chapman SB. Neurocognitive stall: a paradox in long term recovery from pediatric brain injury, *Brain Injury Professional*, 3 (2007): 10–13.

Chun MM, Turk-Browne NB. "Interactions between attention and memory," *Current Opinion in Neurobiology*, 17 (2007): 177–184. Accessed: June 2013].

Cohen J. *Statistical Power Analysis for Behavioral Sciences* (New York: Academic Press,1977).

Colcombe SJ, Kramer AF. "Fitness effects on the cognitive function of older adults: a metaanalytic study," *Psychological Science*, 14 (2002): 125–130.

Colcombe SJ, Kramer AF, Erickson KI, et al. "Cardiovascular fitness, cortical plasticity, and aging," *Proceedings of the National Academy of the Sciences of the USA*, 101 (2004): 3316–3321.

Collie A, Darby D, Maruff P. "Computerised cognitive assessment of athletes with sports related head injury," *British Journal of Sports Medicine*, 35 (2001): 297–302.

Corvin A, Donohoe G, Hargreaves A, et al. "The cognitive genetics of neuropsychiatric disorders," *Current Topics in Behavioral Neurosciences*, 12 (2012): 579–613.

Cotter D, Mackay D, Chana G, et al. "Reduced neuronal size and glial cell density in area 9 of the dorsolateral prefrontal cortex in subjects with major depressive disorder," *Cerebral Cortex*, 12 (2002): 386–394. Available at: http://cercor.oxfordjournals.org/content/12/4/386.long#ref-18 [Accessed July 2013].

Cramer SC, Sur M, Dobkin BH, et al. "Harnessing neuroplasticity for clinical applications," *Brain*, 134 (2011): 1591–1609.

Csikszentmihalyi M. *Flow: The psychology of optimal experience* (New York: Harper & Row, 1990).

Czéh B, Simon M, Schmelting B, et al. "Astroglial plasticity in the hippocampus is affected by chronic psychosocial stress and concomitant fluoxetine treatment," *Neuropsychopharmacology*, 31 (2006): 1616–1626.

Dave RH. *Developing and writing behavioral objectives*, RJ Armstrong, ed. (Educational Innovators Press, Tucson, Arizona: 1975).

Davidson PSR, Glisky EL. "Neuropsychological correlates of recollection and familiarity in normal aging," *Cognitive, Affective, and Behavioral Neuroscience*, 2 (2002): 174–186.

Davidson PSR, Cook AP, Glisky EL. "Flashbulb memories for September 11th are preserved in older adults," *Neuropsychology, development, and cognition. Section B, Aging, Neuropsychology and Cognition*, 13 (2006): 196–206.

Deary IJ, Corley J, Gow AJ, et al. "Age-associated cognitive decline," *British Medical Bulletin*, 92 (2009): 135–152.

De La Fuente A, Xia S, Branch C, et al. "A review of attention-deficit/hyperactivity disorder from the perspective of brain networks," *Frontiers in Human Neuroscience*, 7 (2013): 192.

Demars M, Hu YS, Gadadhar A, et al. "Impaired neurogenesis is an early event in the etiology of familial Alzheimer's disease in transgenic mice," *Journal of Neuroscience Research*, 88 (2010): 2103–2117.

Dennis M. "Margaret Kennard (1899–1975): Not a 'Principle' of Neuroplasticity But a Founding Mother of Developmental Neuropsychology," *Cortex*, 46 (2010): 1043–1059.

Derakhshan F, Toth C. "Insulin and the brain," *Current Diabetes Reviews*, 9 (2013): 102–116.

Diaz Heijtz R, Kolb B, Forssberg H. "Can a therapeutic dose of amphetamine during preadolescence modify the pattern of synaptic organization in the brain?" *European Journal of Neuroscience*, 18 (2003): 3394–3399.

Diaz Heijtz R, Wang S, Anuar F, et al. "Normal gut microbiota modulates brain development and behaviour," *Proceedings of the National Academy of Sciences of the USA*, 108 (2011): 3047–3052.

Donders FC (1869). "On the speed of mental processes," In: W. G. Koster (Ed.), *Attention and Performance II. Acta Psychologica*, 30, 412–431.

Dunlosky J, Kubat-Silman AK, Hertzog C. "Training monitoring skills improves older adults' self-paced associative learning," *Psychology and Aging*, 18 (2003): 340–345.

Edwards JD, Jacova C, Sepehry AA, et al. "A quantitative systematic review of domain-specific cognitive impairment in lacunar stroke," *Neurology*, 80 (2013): 315–322.

Eggermont LH, de Boer K, Muller M, et al. "Cardiac disease and cognitive impairment: a systematic review," *Heart*, 98 (2012): 1334–1340.

Ehninger D, Li W, Fox K, et al. "Reversing neurodevelopmental disorders in adults," *Neuron*, 60 (2008): 950–960.

Engstad RT, Engstad TT, Davanger S, et al. "[Executive function deficits following stroke]," *Tidsskr Nor Laegeforen*, 133 (2013): 524–527.

Erickson KI, Gildengers AG, Butters MA. "Physical activity and neuroplasticity in late adulthood," *Dialogues in Clinical Neuroscience*, 15 (2013): 99–108.

Erickson KI, Voss MW, Prakash RS, et al. "Exercise training increases size of hippocampus and improves memory," *Proceedings of the National Academy of the Science of the USA*, 108 (2011): 3017–3022.

Fan F, Zhu C, Chen H, et al. "Dynamic brain structural changes after left hemisphere subcortical stroke," *Human Brain Mapping*, 34 (2013): 1872–1881.

Federal Interagency Forum on Aging Related Statistics. Available at: http://www.agingstats.gov/Main_Site/Data/2012_Documents/Health_Status.aspx [Accessed: June 2013].

Fenoglio KA, Brunson KL, Baram TZ. "Hippocampal neuroplasticity induced by early-life stress: Functional and molecular aspects," *Frontiers in Neuroendocrinology*, 27 (2006): 180–192.

Ferris SH, Lucca U, Mohs R, Dubois B, Wesnes K, Erzigkeit H, Geldmacher D, Bodick N. "Objective psychometric tests in clinical trials of dementia drugs. Position paper from the International Working Group on Harmonization of Dementia Drug Guidelines," *Alzheimer Disease and Associated Disorders*, 11 (Suppl 3) (1997): 34-8.

Fjell AM, Walhovd KB, Fennema-Notestine C, et al. "One-Year Brain Atrophy Evident in Healthy Aging," *Journal of Neuroscience*, 29 (2009): 15223–15231.

Flöel A, Ruscheweyh R, Krüger,K, et al. "Physical activity and memory functions: are neurotrophins and cerebral gray matter volume the missing link?" *Neuroimage*, 49 (2010): 2756–2763.

Fossati P, Ergis AM, Allilaire JF. "[Executive functioning in unipolar depression: a review]," *Encephale*, 28 (2002): 97–107.

Fox SH. "Non-dopaminergic treatments for motor control in Parkinson's disease," *Drugs*, Aug 6 (2013). [Epub ahead of print].

Freitas C, Farzan F, Pascual-Leone A. "Assessing neuroplasticity across the lifespan with transcranial magnetic stimulation: why, how, and what is the ultimate goal?" *Frontiers in Neuroscience*. 7 (2013): 42. doi: 10.3389/fnins.2013.00042. Available at: http://www.ncbi.nlm.nih.gov/pmc/articles/PMC3613699/ [Accessed July 2013].

Friedland RP, Fritsch T, Smyth KA, et al. "Patients with Alzheimer's disease have reduced activities in midlife compared with healthy control-group members," *Proceedings of the National Academy of the Sciences of the USA*, 98 (2001): 3440–3445.

Gasquoine PG. "Cognitive impairment in common, noncentral nervous system medical conditions of adults and the elderly," *Journal of Clinical and Experimental Neuropsychology*, 33 (2011): 486–496.

Gates NJ, Sachdev PS, Fiatarone Singh MA, et al. "Cognitive and memory training in adults at risk of dementia: a Systematic Review," *BMC Geriatrics*, 11 (55) (2011). Available at http://www.biomedcentral.com/1471-2318/11/55 [Accessed August 2013].

Gemma C, Vila J, Bachstetter A, et al. "Chapter 15: Oxidative stress and the aging brain: from theory to prevention," In: Riddle DR (Ed). *Brain aging: models, methods, and mechanisms* (CRC Press: Boca Raton (FL), 2007). Available at: http://www.ncbi.nlm.nih.gov/books/NBK3869/ [Accessed: June 2013].

Glanz BI, Healy BC, Hviid LE, et al. "Cognitive deterioration in patients with early multiple sclerosis: a 5-year study," *Journal of Neurology, Neurosurgery, and Psychiatry*, 83 (2012): 38–43.

Glisky EL. "Chapter 1: Changes in cognitive function in human aging," In: Riddle DR (Ed). *Brain aging: models, methods, and mechanisms* (CRC Press: Boca Raton (FL), 2007). Available at: http://www.ncbi.nlm.nih.gov/books/ NBK3885/ [Accessed: June 2013].

Godbout JP, Chen J, Abraham J, et al. "Exaggerated neuroinflammation and sickness behavior in aged mice following activation of the peripheral innate immune system," *FASEB Journal*, 19 (2005): 1329–1331.

Goldstein JM, Seidman LJ, Horton NJ, et al. "Normal sexual dimorphism of the adult human brain assessed by in vivo magnetic resonance imaging," *Cerebral Cortex*, 11 (2001): 490–497. Available at: http://cercor.oxfordjournals.org/ content/11/6/490.long [Accessed: July 2013].

Gómez-Pinilla F. "Brain foods: the effects of nutrients on brain function," *National Reviews. Neuroscience*, 9 (2008): 568–578. Available at: http://www. ncbi.nlm.nih.gov/pmc/articles/PMC2805706/ [Accessed: July 2013].

Gómez-Pinilla F, Hillman C. "The influence of exercise on cognitive abilities," *Comprehensive Physiology*, 3 (2013): 403–428.

González MF, Díaz U, Buiza C, et al. *HERMES – Cognitive Care and Guidance for Active Aging. D.2.1 Report about the elderly's needs* (2008).

González MF, Facal D, Buiza C, et al. *HERMES – Cognitive Care and Guidance for Active Aging. D.6.1 Cognitive Training Exercises* (2009).

Goodman LJ, Valverde J, Lim F, et al. "Regulated release and polarized localization of brain-derived neurotrophic factor in hippocampal neurons," *Molecular and Cellular Neurosciences*, 7 (1996): 222–238.

Goosens KA, Sapolsky RM. "Chapter 13: Stress and glucocorticoid contributions to normal and pathological aging." In: Riddle DR (Ed). *Brain aging: models, methods, and mechanisms* (CRC Press: Boca Raton (FL): 2007). Available at: http://www.ncbi.nlm.nih.gov/books/NBK3870/ [Accessed: June 2013].

Green MF, Horan WP. "Social cognition in schizophrenia," *Current Directions in Psychological Science*, 19 (2010): 243–248.

Gregory MA, Gill DP, Petrella RJ. "Brain health and exercise in older adults," *Current Sports Medicine Reports*, 12 (2013): 256–271.

Grundman M, Petersen RC, Ferris SH, et al. "Mild cognitive impairment can be distinguished from Alzheimer disease and normal aging for clinical trials," *Archives of Neurology*, 61 (2004): 59–66.

Guidi S, Ciani E, Bonasoni P, et al. "Widespread proliferation impairment and hypocellularity in the cerebellum of fetuses with down syndrome," *Brain Pathology*, 21 (2011): 361–373.

Guimarães J, Sá MJ. "Cognitive dysfunction in multiple sclerosis," *Frontiers in Neurology*, 2012;3:74. Available at http://www.ncbi.nlm.nih.gov/pmc/articles/PMC3359427/#!po=86.0000 [Accessed August 2013].

Harrison J, Henderson L, Kennard C. "Abnormal refractoriness in patients with Parkinson's disease after brief withdrawal of levodopa treatment," *Journal of Neurology, Neurosurgery, and Psychiatry*, 59 (1995): 499–506.

Harrow AJ. *A taxonomy of psychomotor domain: A guide for developing behavioral objectives* (New York: David McKay, 1972).

Hassabis D, Kumaran D, Maguire EA. "Using imagination to understand the neural basis of Episodic Memory," *The Journal of Neuroscience*, 27 (2007): 14356–14374.

Heckman GA, Patterson CJ, Demers C, et al. "Heart failure and cognitive impairment: challenges and opportunities," *Clinical Interventions in Aging*, 2 (2007): 209–218.

Hedden T. "Chapter 11: Imaging Cognition in the Aging Human Brain," In: *Brain Aging: Models, Methods, and Mechanisms*. Riddle DR, editor (Boca Raton (FL): CRC Press, 2007).

Hendrie H, Albert MS, Butters MA, et al. *Critical Evaluation Study Committee of the Cognitive and Emotional Health Project. The NIH Cognitive and Emotional Health Project Report of the Critical Evaluation Study Committee* (2005). Available at: http://trans.nih.gov/cehp/CriticalEvaluationStudyReport.pdf [Accessed June 2013].

Hensch TK, Bilimoria PM. *Re-opening windows manipulating critical periods for brain development* (2012). Available at: http://www.dana.org/news/cerebrum/detail.aspx?id=39360 [Accessed: June 2013].

Hertzog C, Kramer AF, Wilson RS, et al. "Enrichment effects on adult cognitive development: Can the functional capacity of older adults be preserved and enhanced?" *Psychological Science in the Public Interest*, 9 (2008): 1–65.

Heulens I, D'Hulst C, Van Dam D, et al. "Pharmacological treatment of fragile X syndrome with GABAergic drugs in a knockout mouse model," *Behavioural Brain Research*, 229 (2012): 244–249.

Hill NL, Kolanowski AM, Gill DJ. "Plasticity in early Alzheimer's disease: An opportunity for intervention," *Topics in Geriatric Rehabilitation*, 27 (2011): 257–267.

Hilsabeck RC, Anstead GM, Webb AL, et al. "Cognitive efficiency is associated with endogenous cytokine levels in patients with chronic hepatitis," *Journal of Neuroimmunology*, 221 (2010): 53–61.

Hosseini SH, Azari P, Abdi R, et al. "Suppression of obsessive-compulsive symptoms after head trauma," *Case Reports in Medicine*, (2012;2012): 909614. Available at http://www.ncbi.nlm.nih.gov/pmc/articles/PMC3432563/ [Accessed August 2013].

Hubka P. "Neural network plasticity, BDNF and behavioral interventions in Alzheimer's disease," *Bratislavské Lekárske Listy*, 107 (2006): 395–401.

Ibarretxe-Bilbao N, Tolosa E, Junque C, et al. "MRI and cognitive impairment in Parkinson's disease," *Movement Disorders*, 24 Suppl 2 (2009): S748–753.

Insel, Thomas, *Director's blog: the global cost of mental illness*, (National Institute of Mental Health, 2011). Available at http://www.nimh.nih.gov/about/director/2011/the-global-cost-of-mental-illness.shtml

Irwin DJ, Lee VM, Trojanowski JQ. "Parkinson's disease dementia: convergence of α-synuclein, tau and amyloid-β pathologies," Nature Reviews Neuroscience, Jul 31 (2003). doi: 10.1038/nrn3549 [Epub ahead of print].

Jankovic J. "Parkinson's disease: clinical features and diagnosis," *Journal of Neurology, Neurosurgery, and Psychiatry*, 79 (2008): 368–376.

Jellinger KA. "Neurobiology of cognitive impairment in Parkinson's disease," *Expert Review of Neurotherapeutics*, 12 (2012): 1451–1466.

Jennings JM, Jacoby LL. "An opposition procedure for detecting age-related deficits in recollection: telling effects of repetition," *Psychology and Aging*, 12 (1997): 352–361.

Jerskey BA, Cohen RA, Jefferson AL, et al. "Sustained attention is associated with left ventricular ejection fraction in older adults with heart disease," *Journal of the International Neuropsychological Society*, 15 (2009): 137–141.

Jiang L, Xu H, Yu C. "Brain connectivity plasticity in the motor network after ischemic stroke," *Neural Plasticity*, Article ID 924192 (2013). Available at http://dx.doi.org/10.1155/2013/924192 [Accessed August 2013].

Jobe JB, Smith DM, Ball KK, et al. "ACTIVE: A cognitive intervention trial to promote independence in older adults," *Controlled Clinical Trials*, 22 (2001): 453–479.

Jones RN, Marsiske M, Ball K, et al. "The ACTIVE cognitive training interventions and trajectories of performance among older adults," *Journal of Aging and Health*, Dec 6 (2013) [Epub ahead of print].

Jongen PJ, Ter Horst AT, Brands AM. "Cognitive impairment in multiple sclerosis," *Minerva Medica*, 103 (2012): 73–96.

Kadowaki H, Nishitoh H, Urano F, et al. "Amyloid beta induces neuronal cell death through ROS-mediated ASK1 activation," *Cell Death and Differentiation*, 12 (2005): 19–24.

Kähönen-Väre M, Brunni-Hakala S, Lindroos M, et al. "Left ventricular hypertrophy and blood pressure as predictors of cognitive decline in old age," *Aging Clinical and Experimental Research*, 16 (2004): 147–152.

Karl A, Birbaumer N, Lutzenberger W, et al. "Reorganization of motor and somatosensory cortex in upper extremity amputees with phantom limb pain," *Journal of Neuroscience*, 21 (2001): 3609–3618.

Katsnelson A. "A little brain training goes a long way," *Nature* (2013b).

Katz Sand IB, Lublin FD. "Diagnosis and differential diagnosis of multiple sclerosis," *Continuum (Minneapolis, Minn.)*, 19 (4 Multiple Sclerosis) (2013): 922-943.

Katzman R. "Education and the prevalence of dementia and Alzheimer's disease," *Neurology*, 43 (1993): 13–20.

Kelly AM, Garavan H. "Human functional neuroimaging of brain changes associated with practice," *Cerebral Cortex*, 15 (2005): 1089–1102.

Kesler S, Hadi Hosseini SM, Heckler C, et al. "Cognitive training for improving executive function in chemotherapy-treated breast cancer survivors," *Clinical Breast Cancer*, 13 (2013): 299–306.

Kheirbek MA, Klemenhagen KC, Sahay A, et al. "Neurogenesis and generalization: a new approach to stratify and treat anxiety disorders," *Nature Neuroscience*, 15 (2012): 1613–1620.

Kirschstein T. "Synaptic plasticity and learning in animal models of tuberous sclerosis complex," *Neural Plasticity* (2012; 2012): 279834. Available at: http://www.hindawi.com/journals/np/2012/279834/ [Accessed: June 2013].

Kolb B, Gibb R. "Neuroplasticity and behaviour in the developing brain," *Journal of the Canadian Academy of Child and Adolescent Psychiatry*, 20 (2011): 265–276.

Kolb B, Teskey GC and Gibb R. "Factors influencing cerebral plasticity in the normal and injured brain," Frontiers in Human Neuroscience 4 (2010): 204. Available at: http://www.frontiersin.org/human_neuroscience/10.3389/fnhum.2010.00204/abstract [Accessed: June 2013].

Kolb B, Whishaw IQ. "Brain plasticity and behaviour," *Annual Review of Psychology*, 49 (1998): 43–64.

Koob GF, Volkow ND. "Neurocircuitry of addiction," *Neuropsychopharmacology*, 35 (2010): 217–238.

Kristián T, Siesjö BK. "Calcium in Ischemic Cell Death," *Stroke*, 29 (1998): 705–718.

Kronenberg G, Reuter K, Steiner B, et al. "Subpopulations of proliferating cells of the adult hippocampus respond differently to physiologic neurogenic stimuli," *The Journal of Comparative Neurology*, 467 (2003): 455–463.

Kueider AM, Parisi JM, Gross AL, et al. "Computerized Cognitive Training with Older Adults: A Systematic Review," *PLoS One*, 7(7) (2012): e40588. Available at: http://www.plosone.org/article/info%3Adoi%2F10.1371%2Fjournal. pone.0040588 [Accessed: June 2013].

La Rue A. "Healthy brain aging: role of cognitive reserve, cognitive stimulation, and cognitive exercises," *Clinics in Geriatric Medicine*, 26 (2010): 99–111.

Lewis DA, Gonzalez-Burgos G. "Neuroplasticity of neocortical circuits in schizophrenia," *Neuropsychopharmacology*, 33 (2008): 141–65.

Liao L-F. "A Flow Theory Perspective on Learner Motivation and Behavior in Distance Education," *Distance Education*, 27 (2006): 45–62. [Accessed August 2013]

LLoret A, Badia MC, Giraldo E, et al. "Amyloid-β toxicity and tau hyperphosphorylation are linked via RCAN1 in Alzheimer's disease," *Journal of Alzheimer's Disease*, 27 (2011): 701–709.

Logan JM, Sanders AL, Snyder AZ, et al. "Under-recruitment and nonselective recruitment: dissociable neural mechanisms associated with aging," *Neuron*, 33 (2002): 827–840.

Lopes JP, Tarozzo G, Reggiani A, et al. "Galantamine potentiates the neuroprotective effect of memantine against NMDA-induced excitotoxicity," *Brain and Behavior*, 3 (2013): 67-67. Available at http://www.ncbi.nlm.nih.gov/ pmc/articles/PMC3607148/ [Accessed August 2013].

Lövden M, Schaefer S, Noack H, et al. "Spatial navigation training protects the hippocampus against age-related changes during early and late adulthood," *Neurobiology of Aging*, 33 (2012): 620.e9-620.e22.

Luengo-Fernandez R, Leal J, GrayA. *Dementia 2010* (Alzheimer's Research Trust, 2010). [Accessed August 2013].

Lu PH, Edland SD, Teng E et al. (on behalf of the Alzheimer's Disease Cooperative Study Group). "Donepezil delays progression to AD in MCI subjects with depressive symptoms," *Neurology*, 72 (2009): 2115–2121.

Ma Y, Zechariah A, Qu Y, et al. "Effects of vascular endothelial growth factor in ischemic stroke," *Journal of Neuroscience Research*, 90 (2012): 1873–1882.

Mahncke HW, Connor BB, Appelman J, et al. "Memory enhancement in healthy older adults using a brain plasticity-based training program: A randomized, controlled study," *Proceedings of the National Academy of the Sciences of the USA*, 103 (2006): 12523–12528.

Martin M, Clare L, Altgassen AM, et al. "Cognition-based interventions for healthy older people and people with mild cognitive impairment," *The Cochrane Database of Systematic Reviews*, (1) (2011): CD006220.

McAllister AK, Katz LC, Lo DC. "Neurotrophins and synaptic plasticity," *Annual Review of Neuroscience*, 22 (1999): 295–318.

McCarney R, Warner J, Iliffe S, et al. "The Hawthorne Effect: a randomised, controlled trial," *BMC Medical Research Methodology*, 7 (2007):30.

McLennan SN, Mathias JL, Brennan LC, et al. "Cognitive impairment predicts functional capacity in dementia-free patients with cardiovascular disease," *The Journal of Cardiovascular Nursing*, 25 (2010): 390–397.

Meng X, D'Arcy C. "Education and dementia in the context of the cognitive reserve hypothesis: a systematic review with meta-analyses and qualitative analyses," *PLOS One*, 7(6) (2012): e38268. doi: 10.1371/journal.pone.0038268.

Millan MJ, Agid Y, Brüne M, et al. "Cognitive dysfunction in psychiatric disorders: characteristics, causes and the quest for improved therapy," *Nature Reviews. Drug Discovery*, 11 (2012): 141–168.

Mitchell AJ, Shiri-Feshki M. "Rate of progression of mild cognitive impairment to dementia--meta-analysis of 41 robust inception cohort studies," *Acta Psychiatrica Scandinavica*, 119 (2009): 252–265.

Mitchell KJ, Johnson MK. "Source monitoring 15 years later: what have we learned from fMRI about the neural mechanisms of source memory?" *Psychological Bulletin*, 135 (2009): 638–677.

Morales I, Farias G, Maccioni RB. "Neuroimmunomodulation in the pathogenesis of Alzheimer's disease," *Neuroimmunomodulation*, 17 (2010): 202–204.

Morris JC, Storandt M, Miller JP, et al. "Mild cognitive impairment represents early-stage Alzheimer disease," *Archives of Neurology*, 58 (2001): 397–405.

Muller M, van der Graaf Y, Visseren FL, et al. (SMART Study Group). "Blood pressure, cerebral blood flow, and brain volumes. The SMART-MR study," *Journal of Hypertension*, 28 (2010): 1498–1505.

Murphy C. *Why games work and the science of learning.* http://www.goodgamesbydesign.com/Files/WhyGamesWork_ TheScienceOfLearning_CMurphy_2011.pdf [Accessed August 2013].

Murray CJL, Vos T, Lozano R, et al. "Disability-adjusted life years (DALYs) for 291 diseases and injuries in 21 regions, 1990–2010: a systematic analysis for the Global Burden of Disease Study 2010," *Lancet*, 380 (2012): 2197–2223.

Myers MM, Brunelli SA, Squire JM, et al. "Maternal behavior of SHR rats and its relationship to offspring blood pressure," *Developmental Psychobiology*, 22 (1989): 29–53.

National Centre for Biotechnology information. *Processing speed* (1983). Available at http://www.ncbi.nlm.nih.gov/mesh?Db=mesh&term =Psychomotor+Performance [Accessed August 2013]

National Institute for Health and Care Excellence, *NICE care pathway: dementia interventions*, April (2013). Available at http://pathways.nice.org. uk/pathways/dementia#path=view%3A/pathways/dementia/dementia-interventions.xml&content=close [Accessed August 2013].

National Institute for Health and Clinical Excellence (NICE), *Donepezil, galantamine, rivastigmine (review) and memantine for the treatment of Alzheimer's disease (review of NICE technology appraisal guidance 111). NICE technology appraisal 217*, March (2011)..

Nebel K, Wiese H, Seyfarth J, et al. "Activity of attention related structures in multiple sclerosis patients," *Brain Research*, 1151 (2007): 150–160.

Norman DA, Shallice T (1980). "Attention to action: Willed and automatic control of behaviour," In: Gazzaniga M (Ed) *Cognitive Neuroscience: A Reader* (Oxford: Blackwell, 2000). Available at

Nudo RJ. "Postinfarct cortical plasticity and behavioral recovery," *Stroke*, 38 (2007): 840–845.

Nyberg L, Sandblom J, Jones S, et al . "Neural correlates of training-related memory improvement in adulthood and aging," *Proceedings of the National Academy of the Sciences of the USA*, 100 (2003): 13728–13733.

O'Connor ML, Hudak EM, Edwards JD. "Cognitive speed of processing training can promote community mobility among older adults: A brief review," *Journal of Aging Research*, (2011; 2011): 430802.

Owen AM, Hampshire A, Grahn JA, et al. "Putting brain training to the test," *Nature*, 465 (7299) (2010): 775–778.

Panza F, Frisardi V, Capurso C, et al. "Effect of donepezil on the continuum of depressive symptoms, mild cognitive impairment, and progression to dementia," *Journal of the American Geriatrics Society*, 58 (2010): 389–390. Available at http://onlinelibrary.wiley.com/doi/10.1111/j.1532-5415.2009.02702.x/full [Accessed August 2013].

Papazacharias A, Nardini M. "The relationship between depression and cognitive deficits," *Psychiatria Danubina*, 24 (Suppl. 1) (2012): 179–182.

Park DC, Bischof GN. "The aging mind: neuroplasticity in response to cognitive training," *Dialogues in Clinical Neuroscience*, 15 (2013): 109–119. Available at: http://www.dialogues-cns.com/publication/the-aging-mind-neuroplasticity-in-response-to-cognitive-training/ [Accessed: June 2013].

Park DC, Gutchess AH, Meade ML, et al. "Improving cognitive function in older adults: nontraditional approaches," *The Journals of Gerontology. Series B, Psychological Sciences and Social Sciences*, 62 (2007): 45–52.

Park DC, Lautenschlager G, Hedden T, et al. "Models of visuospatial and verbal memory across the adult life span," *Psychology and Aging*, 17 (2002): 299–320.

Park DC, Reuter-Lorenz PA. "The adaptive brain: aging and neurocognitive scaffolding," *Annual Review of Psychology*, 2 (2009): 173–196.

Pascual-Leone A, Amedi A, Fregni F, et al. "The plastic human brain cortex," *Annual Review of Neuroscience*, 28 (2005): 377–401.

Pascual-Leone A, Freitas C, Oberman L. "Characterizing brain cortical plasticity and network dynamics across the age-span in health and disease with TMS-EEG and TMS-fMRI," *Brain Topography*, 24 (2011): 302–315.

Peluso MJ, Lewis SW, Barnes TR, et al. "Extrapyramidal motor side-effects of first- and second-generation antipsychotic drugs," *The British Journal of Psychiatry*, 200 (2012): 387–392.

Pendlebury ST, Rothwell PM. "Prevalence, incidence, and factors associated with pre-stroke and post-stroke dementia: a systematic review and meta-analysis," *The Lancet. Neurology*, 8 (2009): 1006–1018.

Peters A. "Chapter 5: The Effects of Normal Aging on Nerve Fibers and Neuroglia in the Central Nervous System," In: *Brain Aging: Models, Methods, and Mechanisms*. Riddle DR, editor. (Boca Raton (FL): CRC Press, 2007). Available at http://www.ncbi.nlm.nih.gov/books/NBK3873/ [Accessed August 2013]

Picconi B, Piccoli G, Calabresi P. "Synaptic dysfunction in Parkinson's disease," *Advances in Experimental Medicine and Biology*, 970 (2012): 553–572.

Piras F, Piras F, Chiapponi C, et al. "Widespread structural brain changes in OCD: A systematic review of voxel-based morphometry studies," *Cortex*, Feb 26 (2013). pii: S0010-9452(13)00046-4. [Epub ahead of print].

Pittenger C, Kandel ER. "In search of general mechanisms for long-lasting plasticity: Aplysia and the hippocampus," *Philosophical Transactions of the Royal Society of London. Series B, Biological Sciences*, 358 (2003): 757–763.

Popescu BF, Pirko I, Lucchinetti CF. "Pathology of multiple sclerosis: where do we stand?" *Continuum (Minneapolis, Minn.)*, 19 (4 Multiple Sclerosis) (2013): 901–921.

Pressler SJ, Subramanian U, Kareken D, *et al.* Cognitive deficits in chronic heart failure. *Nursing Research*, 59 (2010): 127–139.

Price JL, Morris JC. "Tangles and plaques in nondemented aging and "preclinical" Alzheimer's disease," *Annals of Neurology*, 45 (1999): 358–368.

Prince DA, Parada I, Scalise K, et al. "Epilepsy following cortical injury: cellular and molecular mechanisms as targets for potential prophylaxis," *Epilepsia*, 50 (Suppl 2) (2009): 30–40.

Prusky GT, Silver BD, Tschetter WW, et al. "Experience-dependent plasticity from eye opening enables lasting, visual cortex-dependent enhancement of motion vision," *The Journal of Neuroscience*, 28 (2008): 9817–9827.

Ramanathan D, Conner JM, Tuszynski MH. "A form of motor cortical plasticity that correlates with recovery of function after brain injury," *Proceedings of the National Academy of the Sciences of the USA*, 103 (2006): 11370–11375.

Rantamäki T, Kemppainen S, Autio H, et al. "The Impact of Bdnf gene deficiency to the memory impairment and brain pathology of APPswe/PS1de9 mouse model of Alzheimer's disease," *PLoS One*, 8 (2013): e68722.

Rao AA. "Views and opinion on BDNF as a target for diabetic cognitive dysfunction," *Bioinformation*, 9 (2013): 551–554.

Raz N, Rodrigue KM. "Differential aging of the brain: patterns, cognitive correlates and modifiers," *Neuroscience and Biobehavioral Reviews*, 30 (2006): 730–748.

Reagan LP. "Diabetes as a chronic metabolic stressor: causes, consequences and clinical complications," *Experimental Neurology*, 233 (1) (2012): 68–78.

Rebok GW, Carlson MC, Langbaum JB. "Training and maintenance memory abilities in healthy older adults: traditional and novel approaches," *The Journals of Gerontology. Series B, Psychological Sciences and Social Sciences*, 62 (Spec No 1) (2007): 53–61.

Richards M, Deary IJ. "A Life Course Approach to Cognitive Reserve: A Model for Cognitive Aging and Development?" *Annals of Neurology*, 58 (2005): 617–622.

Robinson TE, Kolb B. "Structural plasticity associated with exposure to drugs of abuse," *Neuropharmacology*, 47 (Suppl 1) (2004): 33–46.

Rodgers JM, Robinson AP, Miller SD. "Strategies for protecting oligodendrocytes and enhancing remyelination in multiple sclerosis," *Discovery Medicine*, 16 (2013): 53–63.

Roig M, Nordbrandt S, Geertsen SS, et al. "The effects of cardiovascular exercise on human memory: a review with meta-analysis," *Neuroscience and Biobehavioral Reviews*, 37 (2013):1645–1666.

Rola R, Raber J, Rizk A, et al. "Radiation-induced impairment of hippocampal neurogenesis is associated with cognitive deficits in young mice," *Experimental Neurology*, 188 (2004): 316–330.

Rommelse NN, Altink ME, Oosterlaan J, "Support for an independent familial segregation of executive and intelligence endophenotypes in ADHD families," *Psychological Medicine*, 38 (2008): 1595–1606.

Rothman SM, Griffioen KJ, Wan R, et al. "Brain-derived neurotrophic factor as a regulator of systemic and brain energy metabolism and cardiovascular health," *Annals of the New York Academy of Sciences*, 1264 (2012): 49–63.

Salthouse TA. "When does age-related cognitive decline begin?" *Neurobiology of Aging*, 30 (2009): 507–514.

Salthouse TA. "Consequences of age-related cognitive declines," *Annual Review of Psychology*, 63 (2012): 201–226.

Savage RC. "The developing brain after TBI: predicting long term deficits and services for children, adolescents and young adults," *North American Brain Injury Society*. Available at: http://www.internationalbrain.org/articles/the-developing-brain-after-tbi/ [Accessed June 2013].

Sbardella E, Petsas N, Tona F, et al. "Assessing the correlation between grey and white matter damage with motor and cognitive impairment in multiple sclerosis patients," *PLoS One*, 8 (2013): e63250.

Scarmeas N, Levy G, Tang MX, et al. "Influence of leisure activity on the incidence of Alzheimer's disease," *Neurology*, 57 (2001): 2236–2242.

Schmidt SJ, Mueller DR, Roder V. "Social cognition as a mediator variable between neurocognition and functional outcome in schizophrenia: empirical review and new results by structural equation modelling," *Schizophrenia Bulletin*, 37 (Suppl 2) (2011): S41–54.

Schmiedek F, Lövdén M, Lindenberger U. "Hundred days of cognitive training enhance broad cognitive abilities in adulthood: findings from the COGITO study," *Frontiers in Aging Neuroscience*, 2 (2010): 27. Available at http://www.ncbi.nlm.nih.gov/pmc/articles/PMC2914582/#!po=72.5000 [Accessed August 2013].

Schoenfeld TJ, Gould E. "Differential effects of stress and glucocorticoids on adult neurogenesis," *Current Topics in Behavioral Neurosciences*, 15 (2013): 139–164.

Schuele CM, Justice LM. "The Importance of Effect Sizes in the Interpretation of Research," *The ASHA Leader*, 15 August (2006).

Schug MC, Tarver SG, Western RD. "Direct instruction and the teaching of early reading," *Wisconsin Policy Research Institute Report*, 14 (March 2001): 1-27.

Scoville WB & Milner B. "Loss of recent memory after bilateral hippocampal lesions," *Journal of Neurology, Neurosurgery, and Psychiatry*, 20(1) (1957): 11-21.

Scuteri A, Coluccia R, Castello L, et al. "Left ventricular mass increase is associated with cognitive decline and dementia in the elderly independently of blood pressure," *European Heart Journal*, 30 (2009): 1525–1529.

Sehgal M, Song C, Ehlers VL, et al. "Learning to learn - Intrinsic plasticity as a metaplasticity mechanism for memory formation," *Neurobiology of Learning and Memory*, (2013 Jul 18). pii: S1074-7427(13)00121-4. doi: 10.1016/j.nlm.2013.07.008. [Epub ahead of print].

Sheldon S, Macdonald RL, Cusimano M, et al. "Long-term consequences of subarachnoid hemorrhage: Examining Working Memory," *Journal of the Neurological Sciences*, 332 (2013): 145–147.

Shim YS, Morris JC. "Biomarkers predicting Alzheimer's disease in cognitively normal aging," *Journal of Clinical Neurology*, 7 (2011): 60–68. Available at http://www.ncbi.nlm.nih.gov/pmc/articles/PMC3131540/#!po=59.5238 [Accessed August 2013].

Shin NY, Lee TY, Kim E, et al. "Cognitive functioning in obsessive-compulsive disorder: a meta-analysis," *Psychological Medicine*, 19 (2013): 1–10. [Epub ahead of print].

Shweiki D, Itin A, Soffer D, et al. "Vascular endothelial growth factor induced by hypoxia may mediate hypoxia-initiated angiogenesis," *Nature*, 359 (1992): 843–845.

Simen AA, Bordner KA, Martin MP, et al. "Cognitive dysfunction with aging and the role of inflammation," *Therapeutic Advances in Chronic Disease*, 2 (2011): 175–195.

Simpson E J. *The classification of educational objectives in the psychomotor domain* (Washington, DC: Gryphon House, 1972).

Singh-Manoux A, Marmot MG, Glymour M, et al. "Does cognitive reserve shape cognitive decline?" *Annals of Neurology*, 70 (2011): 296–304.

Small GW. "What you need to know about age related memory loss," *The British Medical Journal*, 324(7352) June 22 (2002): 1502–1505. Available at: http://www.ncbi.nlm.nih.gov/pmc/articles/PMC1123445/ [Accessed July 2013].

Smith GE, Housen P, Yaffe K, et al. A cognitive training program based on principles of neuroplasticity: results from the improvement in Memory with Plasticity-based Adaptive Cognitive Training (IMPACT) study. Journal of the American Geriatrics Society, 57 (2009): 594–603.

Snyder P. "Exercise Produces Super-Agers," *Colorado Community Media* (2013a). Available at: http://www.ourcoloradonews.com/health/fitness/exercise-produces-super-agers/article_8b68ce2e-cd58-11e2-a017-0019bb2963f4.html [Accessed: June 2013].

Sonntag WE, Eckman DE, Ingraham J, et al. "Chapter 12: Regulation of cerebrovascular aging," In: Riddle DR (Ed). *Brain aging: models, methods, and mechanisms* (Boca Raton (FL): CRC Press, 2007). Available at: http://www.ncbi.nlm.nih.gov/books/NBK3879/ [Accessed: June 2013].

Stern PC, Carstensen LL (Eds). Committee on Future Directions for Cognitive Research on Aging, Board on Behavioral, Cognitive, and Sensory Sciences, National Research Council, *The Aging Mind: Opportunities in Cognitive Research* (2000). Available at: http://www.nap.edu/catalog/9783. html [Accessed: May 2013].

Stern Y. "What is cognitive reserve? Theory and research application of the reserve concept," *Journal of the International Neuropsychological Society*, 8 (2002): 448–460.

Stern Y. "The concept of cognitive reserve: a catalyst for research," *Journal of Clinical and Experimental Neuropsychology*, 25 (2003): 589–593.

Stern Y. "Cognitive reserve in ageing and Alzheimer's disease," *The Lancet. Neurology*, 11 (2012): 1006–1012.

Stern Y, Alexander GE, Prohovnik I, et al. "Inverse relationship between education and parietotemporal perfusion deficit in Alzheimer's disease," *Annals of Neurology*, 32 (1992): 371–375.

Stip E. "[Cognition, schizophrenia and the effect of antipsychotics]," *Encephale*, 32 (3 Pt 1) (2006): 341-50.

Stokowski LA. "Cognitive Health for an Aging Population," *Medscape*, (2009). Log in required at: http://www.medscape.com/viewarticle/712095_3

Strauss J, Barr CL, George CJ, et al. "Brain-derived neurotrophic factor variants are associated with childhood-onset mood disorder: confirmation in a Hungarian sample," *Molecular Psychiatry*, 10 (2005): 861–867.

Takeuchi N, Izumi S. "Maladaptive plasticity for motor recovery after stroke: mechanisms and approaches," *Neural Plasticity*, (2012; 2012): 359728. Available at http://www.ncbi.nlm.nih.gov/pmc/articles/PMC3391905/ [Accessed August 2013].

Tan ZS, Seshadri S. "Inflammation in the Alzheimer's disease cascade: Culprit or innocent bystander?" *Alzheimer's Research and Therapy*, 2 (2010): 6.

Tenenbaum G, Fogarty G, Jackson S. "The flow experience: A Rasch analysis of Jackson's Flow State Scale," *Journal of Outcome Measurement*, 3 (1999): 278-294. Available at http://eprints.usq.edu.au/927/1/Fogarty_Tenenbaum-Fogarty-Jackson_Flow_state_scale_1999.pdf [Accessed August 2013]

Thies W, Bleiler L, (Alzheimer's Association), "Alzheimer's disease facts and figures," *Alzheimer's and Dementia*, 9 (2013): 208–245.

The Brain from Top to Bottom. Available at http://thebrain.mcgill.ca/flash/a/a_07/a_07_p/a_07_p_tra/a_07_p_tra.html#3 [Accessed August 2013].

Thomas AG, Dennis A, Bandettini PA, et al. "The effects of aerobic activity on brain structure," *Frontiers in Psychology*, 3 (2012): 86.

Thomas RM, Hotsenpiller G, Peterson DA. "Acute psychosocial stress reduces cell survival in adult hippocampal neurogenesis without altering proliferation," *The Journal of Neuroscience*, 27 (2007): 2734–2743.

Todd S, Barr S, Roberts M, et al. "Survival in dementia and predictors of mortality: a review," *International Journal of Geriatric Psychiatry*, Mar 22 (2013a). [Epub ahead of print].

Toescu EC. "Chapter 14: Altered calcium homeostasis in old neurons," In: Riddle DR (Ed). *Brain aging: models, methods, and mechanisms* (Boca Raton (FL): CRC Press, 2007). Available at: http://www.ncbi.nlm.nih.gov/books/NBK3871/ [Accessed: June 2013].

Trivedi JK. "Cognitive deficits in psychiatric disorders: Current status," *Indian Journal of Psychiatry*, 48 (1) (2006): 10–20. Available at: http://www.ncbi. nlm.nih.gov/pmc/articles/PMC2913637/#CIT1 [Accessed July 2013].

Tröster A. *Cognition and Parkinson's*. Parkinson's Disease Foundation. Available at http://www.pdf.org/en/cognitive_impairment_pd [Accessed August 2013].

Tsang PS, Shaner TL. "Age, attention, expertise, and time-sharing performance," *Psychology and Aging*, 13 (1998): 323–347.

Tulving E, Szpunar KK. "Episodic memory," *Scholarpedia*, 4 (8) (2009): 3332 Available at: http://www.scholarpedia.org/article/Episodic_memory [Accessed 31 May 2013].

Tur C, Penny S, Khaleeli Z, et al. "Grey matter damage and overall cognitive impairment in primary progressive multiple sclerosis," *Multiple Sclerosis*, 17 (2011): 1324–1332.

US National Institute of Health (National Institute on Aging) *2011–2012 Alzheimer's Disease Progress Report: A primer on Alzheimer's disease and the brain*. Available at http://www.nia.nih.gov/alzheimers/publication/2011-2012-alzheimers-disease-progress-report/primer-alzheimers-disease-and [Accessed August 2013].

Van Oijen M, de Jong FJ, Witteman JC, *et al.* "Atherosclerosis and risk for dementia," *Annals of Neurology*, 61 (2007): 403–410.

van Praag H, Christie BR, Sejnowski TJ, et al. "Running enhances neurogenesis, learning, and long-term potentiation in mice," *Proceedings of the National Academy of the Sciences of the USA*, 96 (1999): 13427–13431.

Verhaeghen P, Cerella J. "Aging, executive control, and attention: a review of meta-analyses," *Neuroscience and Biobehavioral Reviews*, 26 (2002): 849–857.

Viikki M, Anttila S, Kampman O, et al. "Vascular endothelial growth factor (VEGF) polymorphism is associated with treatment resistant depression," *Neuroscience Letters*, 477 (2010): 105–108.

Vogels RL, Scheltens P, Schroeder-Tanka JM, et al. "Cognitive impairment in heart failure: a systematic review of the literature," *European Journal of Heart Failure*, 9 (2007): 440–449.

Voineskos D, Rogasch NC, Rajji TK, et al. "A review of evidence linking disrupted neural plasticity to schizophrenia," *Canadian Journal of Psychiatry*, 58 (2013): 86–92.

Wagner N, Hassanein K, Head M. "Computer-use by older adults: a multidisciplinary review," *Computers in Human Behavior*, 26 (2010): 870–882.

Wainwright SR, Galea LA. "The Neural Plasticity Theory of Depression: Assessing the Roles of Adult Neurogenesis and PSA-NCAM within the Hippocampus," *Neural Plasticity*, (2013; 2013): 805497.

Wiesel TN, Hubel DH. "Single-cell responses in striate cortex of kittens deprived of vision in one eye," *Journal of Neurophysiology*, 26 (1963): 1003–1017.

Williams K, Kemper S. "Exploring Interventions to reduce cognitive decline in aging," *Journal of Psychosocial Nursing and Mental Health Services*, 48 (2010): 42–51. Available at http://www.ncbi.nlm.nih.gov/pmc/articles/ PMC2923489/#R7 [Accessed August 2013].

Williams-Gray CH, Mason SL, Evans JR, et al. "The CamPaIGN study of Parkinson's disease: 10-year outlook in an incident population-based cohort," *Journal of Neurology, Neurosurgery, and Psychiatry*, Jun 18 (2013). [Epub ahead of print].

Willis SL, Schaie KW. "Cognitive training in the normal elderly," In: Forette F, Christen Y, Boller F (eds). *Plasticité cérébrale et stimulation Cognitive* (Paris: Fondation National de Gérontologie, 1994

Willis SL, Schaie KW. "Cognitive training and plasticity: Theoretical perspective and methodological consequences," *Restor Neurol Neurosci*, 27 (2009): 375–389. Available at http://www.ncbi.nlm.nih.gov/pmc/articles/ PMC3607292/pdf/nihms333018.pdf

Willis SL, Tennstedt SL, Marsiske M, et al. "Long-term effects of cognitive training on everyday functional outcomes in older adults," *The Journal of the American Medical Association*, 296 (2006): 2805–2814.

Wilson RS, Mendes de Leon CF, Barnes LL, et al. "Participation in cognitively stimulating activities and risk of incident Alzheimer disease," *The Journal of the American Medical Association*, 287 (2002): 742–748.

Wimo A. *Cost of illness and burden of dementia - The base option.* Alzheimer Europe (2013a). Available at http://www.alzheimer-europe.org/Research/ European-Collaboration-on-Dementia/Cost-of-dementia/Cost-of-illness-and-burden-of-dementia [Accessed August 2013].

Wimo A. *Cost of illness and burden of dementia in Europe - Prognosis to 2030,* Alzheimer Europe (2013b). Available at http://www.alzheimer-europe. org/Research/European-Collaboration-on-Dementia/Cost-of-dementia/ Prognosis-to-2030 [Accessed August 2013].

Wimo A, Jönsson L, Bond J, et al. "The worldwide economic impact of dementia 2010," Alzheimer's and Dementia, 9 (2013): 1–11.e3.

Wimo A, Jönsson L, Gustavsson A, et al. "The economic impact of dementia in Europe in 2008-cost estimates from the Eurocode project," *International Journal of Geriatric Psychiatry,* 26 (2011): 825–832.

Wimo A, Winblad B, Jönsson L. "The worldwide societal costs of dementia: Estimates for 2009," *Alzheimer's and Dementia,* 6 (2010): 98–103.

Wolinsky FD, Mahncke HW, Vander Weg MW, et al. "The ACTIVE cognitive training interventions and the onset of and recovery from suspected clinical depression," *The Journals of Gerontology Series B: Psychological Sciences and Social Sciences,* 64B (2009b): 577–585.

Wolinsky FD, Mahncke HW, Vander Weg MW, et al. "Speed of processing training protects self-rated health in older adults: Enduring effects observed in the multi-site ACTIVE randomized control trial," *International Psychogeriatrics,* 22 (2010): 470–478.

Wolinsky FD, Unverzagt FW, Smith DM, et al. The effects of the ACTIVE cognitive training trial on clinically relevant declines in health-related quality of life. *The Journals of Gerontology Series B: Psychological Sciences and Social Sciences,* 61B (2006): S281–S287.

Wolinsky FD, Unverzagt FW, Smith DM, et al. "The ACTIVE cognitive training trial and health-related quality of life: Protection that lasts for five years," *The Journals of Gerontology, Series A: Biomedical Sciences and Medical Sciences,* 61A (2006): 1324–1329.

Wolinsky FD, Vander Weg MW, Howren MB, et al. "A Randomized Controlled Trial of Cognitive Training Using a Visual Speed of Processing Intervention in Middle Aged and Older Adults," *PLoS One*, 8 (2013): e61624. Available at http://www.plosone.org/article/info%3Adoi%2F10.1371%2Fjournal. pone.0061624 [Accessed June 2013].

Wolinsky FD, Vander Weg MW, Martin R, et al. "The effect of speed-of-processing training on depressive symptoms in ACTIVE," *The Journals of Gerontology. Series A: Biomedical Sciences and Medical Sciences*, 64A (2009): 468–472.

Wolinsky FD, Vander Weg MW, Martin R, et al. "Does cognitive training improve internal locus of control among older adults?" *The Journals of Gerontology Series B: Psychological Sciences and Social Sciences*, 65 (2010): 591–598.

World Health Organization. *Tenth Revision of the International Classification of Diseases and Related Health Problems Classification of Mental and Behavioural Disorders (ICD-10)* (World Health Organization, Geneva, 1992).

World Health Organization. *Global health and aging. NIH publication 11-7737.* October 2011. Available at http://www.who.int/ageing/publications/global_ health.pdf [Accessed August 2013].

Yarnall AJ, Rochester L, Burn DJ. "Mild cognitive impairment in Parkinson's disease," *Age and Ageing*, Jul 17 (2013). [Epub ahead of print].

Ylvisaker M, Hanks R, Johnson-Greene D. "American Speech-Language-Hearing Association. Rehabilitation of children and adults with cognitive communication disorders after brain injury [Technical report]," *American Speech-Language-Hearing Association*, (2003).

Zehnder F, Martin M, Algussen M. "Memory training effects in old age as markers of plasticity: a meta-analysis," *Restorative Neurology and Neuroscience*, 27 (2009): 507–520.

1. Baddeley, A. (1996). Exploring the central executive. The Quarterly Journal of Experimental Psychology: Section A, 49(1), 5-28.
2. https://en.wikipedia.org/wiki/Great_Internet_Mersenne_Prime_Search
3. http://oxforddictionaries.com/definition/english/cognition
4. http://www.encyclopedia.com/topic/Cognition.aspx
5. http://www.encyclopedia.com/topic/Social_cognitive_theory.aspx
6. http://www.projectlearnet.org/tutorials/cognition.html
7. Ylvisaker et al (2003)
8. http://www.projectlearnet.org/tutorials/cognition.html
9. Ylvisaker et al (2003)
10. Trivedi (2006)
11. Small (2002)
12. Small (2002)
13. The Brain from Top to Bottom (2013)
14. ibid
15. Freitas et al (2013)
16. Sehgal et al (2013)
17. Pascual-Leone et al (2011)
18. Pascual-Leone et al (2005)
19. Pittenger & Kandel (2003)
20. Dennis (2010)
21. Stern & Carstensen (2000)
22. Freitas et al (2013)
23. Sehgal et al (2013)
24. Freitas et al (2013)
25. Kolb & Gibb (2011)
26. Kolb & Gibb (2011)
27. Thomas et al (2012)
28. Thomas et al (2012)
29. Kolb & Gibb (2011)
30. Kolb & Gibb (2011)
31. Kolb & Gibb (2011)
32. Kolb & Gibb (2011)
33. Kolb & Gibb (2011)
34. Kolb & Gibb (2011)
35. Kolb & Gibb (2011)
36. Rola et al (2004)
37. Demars et al (2010)
38. Kheirbek et al (2012)
39. Guidi et al (2011)
40. Thomas et al (2012)
41. Goodman et al (1996)
42. McAllister et al (1999)
43. Shweiki et al (1992)
44. Bloor (2005)
45. Thomas et al (2012)
46. Rantamäki et al (2013)
47. Rao 2013; Viikki et al (2010)
48. Ma et al (2012)
49. Kolb et al (2010)
50. Kolb & Gibb (2011)
51. Legg, S., & Hutter, M. (2007). A collection of definitions of intelligence. Frontiers in Artificial Intelligence and applications, 157, 17.
52. Thomas Insel, NIH, (2011)
53. A report by the World Economic Forum and the Harvard School of Public Health, September 2011
54. Wimo et al (2011)
55. Wimo (2013a)
56. Wimo et al (2013b)
57. Wimo et al (2013b)
58. Luengo-Fernandez et al (2010)
59. Luengo-Fernandez et al (2010)
60. Luengo-Fernandez et al (2010)
61. Alvarez & Emory (2006)
62. Glisky (2007)
63. Glisky (2007)
64. Norman & Shallice (2000)

65. Available at: https://www.uakron.edu/gage/story.dot
66. Available at: http://mindhacks.com/2007/06/28/the-hardest-cut-penfield-and-the-fight-for-his-sister/]
67. Baddeley (1996)
68. Gliski (2007)
69. Calllicott et al (1999)
70. N-back tests are where subjects are asked to remember a sequence of images, words, or numbers, and to recall if the current vision is identical to that seen one-back, or two-back, or three-back, etc. Versions of this test can be found in the LeaderThink programme.
71. Glisky (2007)
72. Glisky (2007)
73. Gliski (2007)
74. Gliski (2007)
75. Glisky (2007)
76. Hassabis et al (2007)
77. Tulving & Szpunar (2009)
78. Tulving & Szpunar (2009)
79. Tulving & Szpunar (2009)
80. Tulving & Szpunar (2009)
81. Tulving & Szpunar (2009)
82. [Available at: http://en.wikipedia.org/wiki/KC_(patient)]
83. [Available at: http://en.wikipedia.org/wiki/Patient_HM
84. Glisky (2007)
85. Mitchell & Johnson (2009)
86. Glisky (2007)
87. Davidson et al (2006)
88. Glisky (2007)
89. Jennings & Jacoby (1997)
90. The Brain From Top To Bottom (2013)
91. http://startups.co.uk/lord-alan-sugar-i-only-take-risks-in-things-i-understand/
92. http://startups.co.uk/lord-alan-sugar-i-only-take-risks-in-things-i-understand/
93. Glisky (2007)
94. Glisky (2007)
95. Glisky (2007)
96. Chun & Turk-Browne (2007)
97. Glisky (2007)
98. Tsang & Shaner (1998)
99. Glisky (2007)
100. Verhaeghen & Cerella (2002)
101. Glisky (2007)
102. Glisky (2007)
103. Glisky (2007)
104. Bisiach & Luzzatti (1978)
105. http://www.lizannefalsetto.com/
106. https://next.ft.com/content/26495d54-518d-11e5-8642-453585f2cfcd
107. National Centre for Biotechnology information (1983)
108. https://www.washingtonpost.com/national/jeff-bezos-on-post-purchase/2013/08/05/e5b293de-fe0d-11e2-9711-3708310f6f4d_story.html
109. http://www.medscape.org/viewarticle/764365
110. http://www.brainhealth.utdallas.edu/blog_page/study-finds-aerobic-exercise-improves-memory-brain-function-and-physical-fi
111. https://www.psychologytoday.com/blog/the-athletes-way/201404/physical-activity-improves-cognitive-function
112. Kolb et al (2010)
113. Kolb & Gibb (2011)
114. Gregory et al (2013)
115. Ackermann et al (2013)

116. Gómez-Pinilla (2003)
117. Gómez-Pinilla (2003)
118. Williams & Kemper (2010)
119. Gómez-Pinilla (2003)
120. David Perlmutter; Brain maker (2015)
121. Diaz Heijtz et al (2011)
122. Diaz Heijtz et al (2011)
123. Flöel et al (2010)
124. Bullitt et al (2009)
125. Thomas et al (2012)
126. van Praag et al (1999)
127. Kronenberg et al (2003)
128. Gomez-Pinilla & Hillman (2013)
129. Erickson et al (2013)
130. Rothman et al (2012)
131. Reagan (2012)
132. Derakhshan & Toth (2013)
133. Rantamäki et al (2013)
134. Alley et al (2007)
135. Alley et al (2007)
136. Alley et al (2007)
137. Alley et al (2007)
138. Goosens & Sapolsky (2007)
139. Kolb & Gibb (2011)
140. http://www.ucl.ac.uk/news/news-articles/0801/08011705
141. https://www.psychologytoday.com/articles/199607/happily-ever-laughter
142. Covey, Steven; Seven habits of highly effective people (1989)
143. http://healthysleep.med.harvard.edu/healthy/matters/benefits-of-sleep/learning-memory
144. Gómez-Pinilla (2008)
145. http://brainworldmagazine.com/learning-memory-how-do-we-remember-and-why-do-we-often-forget/
146. The Relative Benefits of Green Versus Lean Office Space: Three Field Experiments Marlon Nieuwenhuis, Craig Knight, Tom Postmes, and S. Alexander Haslam Online First Publication, July 28, 2014. http://dx.doi.org/10.1037/xap0000024
147. http://www.hbs.edu/faculty/Pages/profile.aspx?facId=491042
148. Colcombe et al (2004)
149. Simpson, John., Independent newspaper, UK (29 May, 2010)
150. http://today.uconn.edu/2012/02/even-mild-dehydration-can-alter-mood/
151. ibid
152. Am J Med. 2006 Sep;119(9):751-9.
153. http://psychcentral.com/news/2006/08/31/drink-juice-reduce-alzheimers/230.html
154. Economic Development Quarterly August 2013 vol. 27 no. 3 221-229
155. Gardener, et al Journal of the American Heart Association (March 16, 2016)
156. Covey, Steven; Seven habits of highly effective people (1989)
157. http://www.health.harvard.edu/staying-healthy/what-is-it-about-coffee
158. https://news.brown.edu/articles/2013/11/sleep
159. https://www.sciencedaily.com/releases/2010/02/100201091638.htm
160. Bahar-Fuchs et al (2013)
161. Kelly & Garavan (2005)
162. Boyke et al (2008)
163. Erickson et al (2011)
164. Scarmeas et al (2001)
165. Wilson et al (2002)

166. Meng & D'Arcy (2012)
167. Park et al (2002)
168. Gates et al (2011)
169. Bahar-Fuchs et al (2013)
170. Gates et al (2011)
171. Zehnder et al (2009)
172. Mahncke et al (2006)
173. Gates et al (2011)
174. Smith et al (2009)
175. Schug et al (2001)
176. Smith et al (2009)
177. Smith et al (2009)
178. Smith et al (2009)
179. Snyder (2013a)
180. Wolinsky et al (2013)
181. Smith et al (2009)
182. Snyder (2013b)
183. González et al (2008), (2009)
184. Csikszentmihalyi (1990)
185. Murphy (2013)
186. Willis & Schaie (2009)
187. Martin et al (2011)
188. O'Connor et al (2011)
189. Martin et al (2011)
190. Mahnche et al (2006)
191. Smith et al (2009)
192. Gates et al (2011)
193. Gates et al (2011)
194. Willis et al (2006)
195. Martin et al (2011)
196. Kueider et al (2012)
197. Dunlosky et al (2003)
198. Wagner et al (2010)
199. Kueider et al (2012)
200. Rebok et al (2007)
201. Kueider et al (2012)
202. Owen et al (2010)
203. Schmiedek et al (2010)
204. Ferris et al (1997)